Principles of Accounting

SECOND EDITION

Instructor's Handbook

Belverd E. Needles, Jr.
DePaul University

Edward H. Julius
California Lutheran College

Houghton Mifflin Company **Boston**

Dallas   Geneva, Illinois   Hopewell, New Jersey   Palo Alto

Printed in the U.S.A.

ISBN: 0-395-34331-3

CDEFGHIJ-A-898765

PREFACE

This Instructor's Handbook has been prepared expressly for use with <u>Principles of Accounting</u>, Second Edition, by Needles/Anderson/Caldwell. We hope it will assist you in your preparations for class sessions.

For each chapter in the text, the Instructor's Handbook provides the following:

<u>Chapter Outline</u>

<u>Resource Materials and Lecture Outlines</u>. This section is organized by learning objectives. For each objective the Instructor's Handbook provides:

- A verbatim statement of the objective.
- A summary statement of the material.
- A list of new words and terms, each with the page where it is introduced in the text.
- A list of related text illustrations, each with the page where it appears in the text. An asterisk beside the figure or table number indicates that the figure or table is also available as a teaching transparency.
- A lecture outline, triple-spaced to allow room for the instructor's own notes.

<u>Learning Objectives Chart</u>. This chart indicates which chapter assignments (exercises, problems, etc.) test which learning objectives. The same chart also appears in the Instructor's Solutions Manual.

<u>Difficulty and Time Chart</u>. This chart indicates the approximate difficulty and time required for each problem and case in the text. It also appears in the Instructor's Solutions Manual.

<u>Ten-Minute Quiz</u>. This brief quiz, consisting of ten true-false and ten multiple-choice questions, may be photocopied for use in class sessions. None of the questions appears in the same form in any other part of the package.

<u>Answers to Ten-Minute Quiz</u>

If you have any suggestions for enhancing this Handbook in future editions, we would be very happy to hear from you.

B.E.N.
E.H.J.

CONTENTS

ACCOUNTING IN BUSINESS AND SOCIETY

CHAPTER OUTLINE

Accounting and Decision Making
Accounting Defined
    Bookkeeping: An Accounting Process
    The Computer: An Accounting Tool
    Accounting and Management Information Systems
Decision Makers: The Users of Accounting Information
    Management
    Users with a Direct Financial Interest
        Present or Potential Investors
        Present or Potential Creditors
    Users with an Indirect Financial Interest
        Taxing Authorities
        Regulatory Agencies
        Economic Planners
        Other Groups
The Accounting Profession
    Management Accounting
        General Accounting
        Cost Accounting
        Budgeting
        Tax Accounting
        Information Systems Design
        Internal Auditing
    Public Accounting
        Auditing
        Tax Services
        Management Advisory Services
        Small Business Services
    Government and Other Nonprofit Accounting
    Accounting Education
Forms of Business Organization
    Sole Proprietorships
    Partnerships
    Corporations
Accounting Theory and Practice
    Generally Accepted Accounting Principles
    Organizations Concerned with Accounting Practice
        American Institute of Certified Public Accountants
        Financial Accounting Standards Board

LEARNING OBJECTIVES:

RESOURCE MATERIALS AND LECTURE OUTLINES

OBJECTIVE 1: Describe the role of accounting in making informed business
and economic decisions (pp. 2-4)

Summary Statement

Making a decision involves (a) setting a goal, (b) examining alternatives,
(c) making the actual decision, (d) taking action, and (e) evaluating the results. Accounting assists in the planning, control, and evaluation stages by
providing useful financial information to the decision maker. <u>Planning</u> involves formulating a course of action. <u>Control</u> involves comparing actual operations with planned operations. <u>Evaluation</u> involves using feedback to appraise
the decision system and improve it.

New Words and Terms

planning (p. 3)
control (p. 3)
evaluation (p. 4)

Related Text Illustrations

*Figure 1-1 A Decision System (p. 3)
*Figure 1-2 A Decision System and Accounting Information (p. 4)

Lecture Outline

A. To make a wise decision, one should follow five steps:

   1. Set a goal.

   2. Examine alternatives.

   3. Make the decision.

4. Take action.

5. Evaluate the results.

B. Accounting provides useful information in three stages to the decision maker:

1. The planning stage

2. The control stage

3. The evaluation stage

OBJECTIVE 2: Define accounting (pp. 4-7)

Summary Statement

Accounting is an information system that measures, processes, and communicates economic information. Bookkeeping, a small but important aspect of accounting, deals with the mechanical and repetitive record-keeping process. A distinction is usually made between management accounting, which focuses on internal users, and financial accounting, which involves the preparation, reporting, analysis, and interpretation of accounting information for external users.

The computer is an electronic tool that rapidly collects, organizes, and communicates vast amounts of information. The computer does not take the place of the accountant, but the accountant must understand how it operates since it is an integral part of the accounting information system.

A management information system (MIS) is an information network encompassing all major functions of a business, called subsystems. The accounting information system is an integral part of the management information system.

New Words and Terms

accounting (p. 5)
management accounting (pp. 5-6)
financial accounting (p. 6)
bookkeeping (p. 6)
computer (p. 6)
management information system (MIS) (p. 7)

<u>Related Text Illustrations</u>

*Figure 1-3 Accounting as an Information System for Business Decisions (p. 5)

<u>Lecture Outline</u>

A. Accounting measures, processes, and communicates economic information.

B. Bookkeeping is merely the record-keeping aspect of accounting.

C. Distinguish between management accounting and financial accounting.

D. The computer is an integral part of the accounting information system.

E. A management information system is an information network encompassing <u>all</u> functions of a business.

OBJECTIVE 3: Recognize the many users of accounting information in society (pp. 7-11)

<u>Summary Statement</u>

There are basically three groups that use accounting information: management, financially interested outsiders, and government and citizen groups.

a. For a business to survive, <u>management</u> must achieve a satisfactory profit in order to hold investor capital (called <u>profitability</u>) and must maintain sufficient funds to pay debts as they fall due (called <u>liquidity</u>). The company will have other goals, such as improving its products and expanding operations. It is management that directs the company toward these goals by making decisions.

b. Most businesses publish financial statements that report the profitability and financial position of the company. Potential investors use these financial statements to assess the strength or weakness of the company. Financial statements are also examined by potential creditors to determine the company's ability to repay a loan.

c. Society as a whole, through its government and citizen groups, also makes use of financial information. Society's interest is represented by taxing authorities, regulatory agencies, economic planners, and citizen groups.

<u>New Words and Terms</u>

management (p. 7)
profitability (p. 9)
liquidity (p. 9)

<u>Related Text Illustrations</u>

*Figure 1-4   The Users of Accounting Information   (p. 8)

<u>Lecture Outline</u>

A. Financial statements communicate financial information to the decision
   maker.

B. Three major groups use accounting information:

   1. Management (internal users)

   2. Outsiders with a direct financial interest

   3. Government and citizen groups (society as a whole) with an indirect
      financial interest

C. Businesses (through management) must achieve profitability and liquidity
   to survive.

   1. Profitability--Achievement of a satisfactory profit

   2. Liquidity--Maintain sufficient funds to pay debts

OBJECTIVE 4:   Recognize accounting as a profession with a wide career choice
               (pp. 11-15)

<u>Summary Statement</u>

The accounting profession can be divided into four broad fields: management
accounting, public accounting, nonprofit accounting, and accounting instruction.

An accountant employed by a business is said to be in <u>management accounting</u>.
Although decision making is the function of management, the management account-

ant must first provide relevant data and then help management make the best
decision. The specific activities of management accountants include general
accounting, cost accounting, budgeting, decision making, tax accounting, information systems design, and internal auditing.

Public accounting is a profession that has achieved the same stature as law and
medicine. Certified public accountants (CPAs) are accountants licensed by the
state. To become a licensed CPA, one must pass the uniform CPA exam and meet
educational and experience requirements. The CPA must be called upon to perform a number of services, most of which are classified as auditing, tax services, or management advisory services.

a. An auditor is a public accountant engaged to express his or her independent
   professional opinion as to whether a company's financial statements present
   fairly its financial position and results of operations. Auditing, or the
   attest function, enables users to rely on the statements as a basis for their
   decisions. The auditor must, of course, gather together sufficient evidence
   before he or she can express an opinion.

b. Public accountants perform tax services by preparing tax returns and by
   bringing tax considerations into the decision-making process.

c. Management advisory services consist of any recommendations that the public
   accountant can make to improve a company's operations. Many CPA firms have
   established small business practice units, which perform such services as
   setting up an accounting system and preparing financial statements.

Nonprofit accounting is practiced by thousands of accountants in various capaci-
ties. Here, accountants are concerned, not with profitability, but with the
proper and efficient use of public resources. For example, government accountants prepare financial reports and audit tax returns for many agencies, such as
the FBI, the IRS, the GAO, the SEC, the ICC, and the FCC. When accountants are
hired to evaluate the impact of government and other human service programs,
they are engaged in social accounting. These programs deal with such concerns
as welfare, housing, education, and pollution, and are an added challenge to
the accountant because they cannot easily be measured in dollars and cents.
Hospitals, colleges, foundations, and other nonprofit organizations also employ
accountants.

Accounting instructors are needed in both secondary schools and colleges. In
either setting they need to meet certain educational qualifications.

New Words and Terms

management accounting (p. 11)
public accounting (p. 13)
certified public accountants (CPAs) (p. 13)
auditing (p. 13)
tax services (p. 14)
management advisory services (p. 14)
social accounting (p. 15)

<u>Lecture Outline</u>

A. The accounting profession is divided into four broad fields:

  1. Management accounting -- Provides accounting information for internal use

  2. Public accounting -- Provides auditing, tax, and management advisory services

  3. Nonprofit accounting -- Accounting for government agencies, hospitals, etc.

  4. Accounting instruction

B. A CPA (may be any of the above) is an accountant licensed by the state after fulfilling certain requirements.

OBJECTIVE 5:   Describe the three basic forms of business organization
               (pp. 15-17)

<u>Summary Statement</u>

The three basic forms of business organization are sole proprietorships, partnerships, and corporations. Accountants recognize each form as an economic unit separate from its owners.

a. A <u>sole proprietorship</u> is a business owned and managed by one person. The owner receives all profits, absorbs all losses, and is personally liable for all debts of the business.

b. A <u>partnership</u> is a business owned and managed by two or more persons. The owners divide profits and losses according to a predetermined ratio, and each is personally liable for all debts of the business.

c. A <u>corporation</u> is a business owned by stockholders but managed by a board of directors. Each stockholder is liable only to the extent of his or her investment, and ownership can be transferred without affecting operations.

<u>New Words and Terms</u>

sole proprietorship (p. 16)
partnership (p. 16)
corporation (p. 17)

<u>Related Text Illustrations</u>

Table 1-1 Comparative Features of the Forms of Business Organization (p. 16)

<u>Lecture Outline</u>

A. There are three basic forms of business organization:

   1. Sole proprietorship -- One owner

   2. Partnership -- Two or more owners

   3. Corporation -- Owned by many stockholders, but managed by a board of
      directors

OBJECTIVE 6: Relate accounting theory and practice to generally accepted
              accounting principles (GAAP) (pp. 17-18)

<u>Summary Statement</u>

<u>Accounting theory</u> provides the reasoning behind and framework for accounting
practice. <u>Generally accepted accounting principles (GAAP)</u> are the set of
guidelines and procedures that constitute acceptable accounting practice at a
given point in time. The set of GAAP changes continually as business conditions change and practices improve.

<u>New Words and Terms</u>

accounting practice (p. 17)
accounting theory (p. 17)
generally accepted accounting principles (GAAP) (p. 18)

<u>Lecture Outline</u>

A. GAAP **are** guidelines for acceptable accounting practice at a given point in
   time.

CHAPTER ONE

OBJECTIVE 7: Recognize the organizations that influence generally accepted
              accounting principles (pp. 19-20)

<u>Summary Statement</u>

The <u>American Institute of Certified Public Accountants (AICPA)</u>, the professional association of CPAs, was instrumental in developing GAAP, principally
through the Accounting Principles Board (APB), from 1959 to 1973.

In 1973, the <u>Financial Accounting Standards Board (FASB)</u>, an independent body,
succeeded the Accounting Principles Board as the authoritative body in the
development of GAAP. The FASB issues Statements of Financial Accounting
Standards.

The <u>Securities and Exchange Commission (SEC)</u> is an agency of the federal government that has the legal power to set and enforce accounting practice for
companies whose securities are traded by the general public.

The <u>Internal Revenue Service (IRS)</u> has its own set of rules, which govern the
assessment and collection of taxes.

The <u>Government Accounting Standards Board (GASB)</u> was established in 1983, and
is responsible for issuing accounting standards for state and local government.

There are other organizations of accountants besides the AICPA. The National
Association of Accountants (NAA) was organized to deal with cost and managerial
accounting, the Financial Executives Institute (FEI) is interested primarily in
financial accounting, and the American Accounting Association (AAA) is concerned chiefly with accounting education and accounting theory.

<u>New Words and Terms</u>

American Institute of Certified Public Accountants (AICPA) (p. 19)
Financial Accounting Standards Board (FASB) (p. 19)
Securities and Exchange Commission (SEC) (p. 19)
Internal Revenue Service (IRS) (p. 20)
Government Accounting Standards Board (GASB) (p. 20)

<u>Lecture Outline</u>

A. The AICPA helped develop GAAP (1959-1973) through its Accounting Principles
   Board (APB).

B. The FASB is now responsible for developing GAAP.

C. The SEC has set its own standards for companies whose securities are listed
   on the stock exchanges.

D. The IRS's guidelines were established to collect taxes.

E. GASB was established to issue standards for state and local governments.

F. Other accounting organizations are the NAA, FEI, AAA, IASC, and IFAC.

Chapter One   Accounting in Business and Society

Learning Objectives	Questions	Exercises	A & B Problems	Case
1. Describe the role of accounting in making informed business and economic decisions.	1, 2	7		1
2. Define accounting.	4, 5	1		
3. Recognize the many users of accounting information in society.	3, 6, 7, 8, 9	2		
4. Recognize accounting as a profession with a wide career choice.	10, 11, 12, 13, 14, 19	3, 4, 6		
5. Describe the three basic forms of business organization.	15	5		
6. Relate accounting theory and practice to generally accepted accounting principles (GAAP).	16, 17			
7. Recognize the organizations that influence generally accepted accounting principles.	18			

TEN-MINUTE QUIZ

T F   1. To become a proficient bookkeeper requires about the same amount of study and experience as it does to become a proficient accountant.

T F   2. The primary purpose of an audit is to keep management honest.

T F   3. Profitability means having enough funds on hand to pay debts when they fall due.

T F   4. The principal and most distinctive function of a CPA is to perform tax services.

T F   5. Management accounting focuses mainly on external users of financial information.

T F   6. Taking action is the last step in making a decision.

T F   7. Accounting is an example of an information system.

T F   8. Internal auditing is an area of specialization within public accounting.

T F   9. One of the services provided by a CPA is advice on the operations of a business.

T F   10. Corporate stockholders have direct control over the operations of the business.

_____ 11. Generally accepted accounting principles
        a. constitute accepted accounting theory and practice at a point in time.
        b. are laws of science and thus do not change.
        c. are unwritten but generally understood.
        d. may be found in their entirety in the Internal Revenue Code.
        e. apply only to the corporate form of business.

_____ 12. Companies whose securities are sold to the public must file financial statements with the
        a. GASB   b. SEC   c. FASB   d. AICPA   e. AAA

_____ 13. Which of the following forms of business organization is considered an entity separate from its owner(s) for accounting purposes?
a. Sole proprietorship only
b. Partnership only
c. Corporation only
d. All of the above
e. Sole proprietorship and partnership only

_____ 14. Which of the following is not a broad subdivision within the accounting profession?
a. Public accounting
b. Accounting education
c. Management accounting
d. Nonprofit accounting
e. Auditing

_____ 15. Reporting accounting information to users outside the business is the focus of
a. general accounting
b. government accounting
c. management accounting
d. public accounting
e. financial accounting

_____ 16. Under which of the following forms of business organization are the personal assets of the owner(s) at stake?
a. Sole proprietorship only
b. Partnership only
c. Corporation only
d. All of the above
e. Sole proprietorship and partnership only

_____ 17. Currently, the primary determinant of generally accepted accounting principles is the
a. FASB
b. AICPA
c. IRS
d. FEI
e. CMA

_____ 18. Accounting for hospitals, colleges, and government is part of which broad subdivision within the accounting profession?
a. Nonprofit accounting
b. Management accounting
c. Public accounting
d. Social accounting
e. Cost accounting

_____ 19. Management advisory services might include assisting the client in
a. budgeting.
b. marketing.
c. systems design.
d. cost accounting.
e. All of the above

_____ 20. Which of the following forms of business organization is (are)
dissolved upon the death of an owner?
a. Corporation only
b. Partnership only
c. Sole proprietorship only
d. All of the above
e. Sole proprietorship and partnership only

ANSWERS TO TEN-MINUTE QUIZ

True-False		Multiple-Choice Questions	
1.	F	11.	a
2.	F	12.	b
3.	F	13.	d
4.	F	14.	e
5.	F	15.	e
6.	F	16.	e
7.	T	17.	a
8.	F	18.	a
9.	T	19.	e
10.	F	20.	e

CHAPTER TWO

ACCOUNTING AS AN INFORMATION SYSTEM

CHAPTER OUTLINE

Accounting Measurement
     What Is to Be Measured?
     The Concept of Separate Entity
     Business Transactions as the Object of Measurement
     Money Measure
The Effects of Transactions on Financial Position
     Financial Position and the Accounting Equation
     Assets
     Liabilities
     Owner's Equity
     Some Illustrations
          Investment by Owner
          Purchase of an Asset for Cash
          Purchase of an Asset on Credit
          Payment of a Liability
          Sale of an Asset for Cash
          Sale of an Asset on Credit
          Collection of Accounts Receivable
          Revenues
          Expenses
          Withdrawal by Owner
Accounting Communication Through Financial Statements
     The Accounting View of Business Activities
     The Income Statement
     The Statement of Owner's Equity
     The Balance Sheet
     The Statement of Changes in Financial Position
     Relationship of the Four Statements
Chapter Review
     Review of Learning Objectives
     Self-Test
     Review Problem: Effect of Transactions on the Accounting Equation
     Answer to Review Problem
Chapter Assignments
     Questions
     Classroom Exercises
     Interpreting Accounting Information: Foote, Cone, & Belding Communications

LEARNING OBJECTIVES:

RESOURCE MATERIALS AND LECTURE OUTLINES

OBJECTIVE 1: Discuss the concept of accounting measurement (pp. 26-27)

Summary Statement

In order to make an accounting measurement, the accountant must answer the following basic questions:

a. What is to be measured?

b. When should the measurement occur?

c. What value should be placed on the measurement?

d. How is the measurement to be classified?

Lecture Outline

A. Four questions must be answered to make an accounting measurement:

   1. _What_ is to be measured?

   2. _When_ should the measurement occur?

   3. What _value_ should be placed on the measurement?

   4. How is the measurement to be _classified_?

OBJECTIVE 2: Recognize the importance of separate entity, business transactions, and the unit of measure in accounting measurement
              (pp. 27-28)

Summary Statement

Accounting is concerned with measuring specific transactions of specific business entities in terms of money.

a. For accounting purposes, a business is treated as a <u>separate entity</u> distinct from its owners, creditors, and customers.

b. <u>Business transactions</u> are economic events that relate directly to a business and that therefore affect the financial position of the business. Business transactions may involve an exchange of value (for example, sales, borrowings, and purchases) or a nonexchange (for example, the physical wear and tear on machinery, and losses due to fire or theft). The <u>money measure</u> concept states that business transactions should be measured in terms of money.

New Words and Terms

separate entity (p. 27)
business transactions (p. 27)
money measure (p. 28)

Lecture Outline

A. In accounting, a business is treated as a separate entity from its owners.

B. A business transaction is an economic event that affects the financial position of a business.

   1. It may involve an exchange of value (purchase, sale, etc.)

   2. It may not involve an exchange of value (losses, etc.)

C. The money measure concept states that a transaction should be measured in money.

OBJECTIVE 3: Demonstrate the effects of simple transactions on financial position (pp. 28–34)

Summary Statement

The balance sheet presents two ways of viewing the same business: the left side shows the assets (resources) of the business, and the right side shows who provided the assets. Providers consist of owners (listed under "owner's equity") and creditors (evidenced by the existence of "liabilities").

Therefore, it is logical that the total dollar amount of assets must equal the total dollar amount of liabilities and owner's equity. This is the <u>balance sheet equation</u>. It is formally stated as

    assets = liabilities + owner's equity

Other correct forms are

    assets - liabilities = owner's equity
    assets - owner's equity = liabilities

<u>Assets</u> are the economic resources of a business. Examples of assets are cash, accounts receivable, inventory, buildings, equipment, patents, and copyrights.

<u>Liabilities</u> are debts of the business. Examples of liabilities are money borrowed from banks, amounts owed to creditors for goods bought on credit, and taxes owed to the government.

<u>Owner's equity</u> represents resources invested by the owner.

Every transaction changes the balance sheet in some way. In practice, companies do not prepare a new balance sheet after each transaction. However, it is important for the accounting student to understand the exact effect of each transaction on the components of the balance sheet.

Although every transaction changes the balance sheet, the balance sheet equation always remains in balance. In other words, dollar amounts may change, but assets must always equal liabilities plus owner's equity.

<u>New Words and Terms</u>

financial position (p. 28)
balance sheet equation (p. 29)
assets (p. 29)
liabilities (p. 29)
equity (p. 29)
owner's equity (p. 29)

<u>Related Text Illustrations</u>

Figure 2-1 Summary of the Effects of Typical Transactions on the Balance Sheet
            Equation (p. 34)

<u>Lecture Outline</u>

A. A balance sheet discloses a business's assets, liabilities, and owner's
   equity.

B. The balance sheet equation is: Assets = Liabilities + Owner's Equity

C. Provide some examples of assets and liabilities.

D. Owner's equity represents resources invested by the owner.

E. Illustrate how transactions affect the balance sheet.

   1. Investment by the owner

   2. Purchase of an asset for cash

   3. Purchase of an asset on credit

   4. Payment of a liability

   5. Sale of an asset for cash

   6. Sale of an asset on credit

   7. Collection on an account receivable

   8. The earning of revenue

   9. The incurrence of an expense

   10. Withdrawal of cash by the owner

OBJECTIVE 4: Briefly describe the role of financial statements in accounting
              (pp. 34-36)

Summary Statement

Financial statements are the primary means by which accountants communicate the
financial position and activities of a business to those who have an interest
in the business. Although financial statements have their limitations, they
can be very useful to the user if he or she understands these limitations.

CHAPTER TWO

<u>New Words and Terms</u>

financial statements (p. 34)

<u>Related Text Illustrations</u>

Figure 2-2 Earnings During the Life of a Business (p. 35)
Figure 2-3 Realistic Growth of Owner's Investment During the Life of a
            Business (p. 36)

<u>Lecture Outline</u>

A. Financial statements are the primary means of communication to interested
   users.

B. Financial statements have their limitations but are still useful.

OBJECTIVE 5: Identify the four basic financial statements (pp. 36-39)

<u>Summary Statement</u>

Accountants communicate their information through <u>financial statements</u>. The
four principal statements are the income statement, balance sheet, statement of
owner's equity, and statement of changes in financial position.

The balance sheet shows the <u>financial position</u> of a business at a particular
point in time. The resources used in the business are called assets, debts of
the business are called liabilities, and the owner's financial interest in the
business is called owner's equity. <u>Equity</u> is sometimes described as the residual interest in assets after deducting the liabilities.

The <u>income statement</u>, whose components are revenues and expenses, is perhaps
the most important financial statement. Its purpose is to measure the business's success or failure in earning a profit over a given period of time.

The <u>statement of owner's equity</u> relates the income statement to the balance
sheet by showing how the owner's capital changed during the period. The
owner's capital at the beginning of the period is the first item on the statement. Because net income accrues to the owner, it is added to beginning capital, as are any additional investments made by the owner during the period.
Finally, any withdrawals by the owner during the period are subtracted, as is a
net loss, to arrive at the owner's capital at the end of the period. This ending figure is then transferred to the owner's capital account in the balance
sheet.

The <u>statement of changes in financial position</u> provides much information that
is not present in the balance sheet or income statement. The statement

discloses all of the business's important financing and investing activities
during the accounting period. Financing activities might include obtaining cash
through an owner's investment or through the sale of equipment. Investing
activities might include the purchase of a building or land.

Every financial statement has a three-line heading. The first line gives the
name of the company, the second line gives the name of the statement, and the
third line gives the relevant dates (the date of the balance sheet or the period
of time covered by the other three statements).

New Words and Terms

income statement (p. 36)
statement of owner's equity (p. 37)
balance sheet (p. 38)
statement of changes in financial position (p. 38)

Related Text Illustrations

*Figure 2-4 Income Statement, Statement of Owner's Equity, and Balance Sheet
             for Shannon Realty (p. 37)
*Figure 2-5 Statement of Changes in Financial Position for Shannon Realty
             (p. 39)

Lecture Outline

A. There are four principal financial statements:

   1. Balance sheet -- Presents a business's financial position at the end of
      the period

   2. Income statement -- Calculates the profit or loss for the period

   3. Statement of owner's equity -- Computes the change in owner's capital
      during the period

   4. Statement of changes in financial position -- Shows significant financing
      and investment activities during the period

B. Assets are resources used in a business.

C. Liabilities are debts of the business.

D. Owner's equity represents the owner's financial interest in the business.

E. A financial statement's heading should include the company name, type of statement, and date (or time period covered).

Chapter Two   Accounting as an Information System

Learning Objectives	Questions	Exercises	A & B Problems	Case
1. Discuss the concept of accounting measurement.	1			
2. Recognize the importance of separate entity, business transactions, and the unit of measure in accounting measurement.	2, 3, 4, 5			
3. Demonstrate the effects of simple transactions on financial position.	6, 7, 8, 9	1, 2, 3	1, 2, 3, 5	
4. Briefly describe the role of financial statements in accounting.	10			1
5. Identify the four basic financial statements.	11, 12, 13, 14	4, 5, 6, IAI	4	1

DIFFICULTY AND TIME CHART

A & B Problems	Difficulty	Time (in minutes)
1	easy	15
2	easy	20
3	medium	20
4	medium	25
5	medium	30
Case 2-1	difficult	40

TEN-MINUTE QUIZ

T F   1. The statement of owner's equity relates the income statement to the balance sheet.

T F   2. The purchase of an asset on credit will increase owner's equity.

T F   3. The account Commissions Earned may be found on the asset side of the balance sheet.

T F   4. The income statement shows the financial position of a business as of a certain date.

T F   5. Payment of a liability will decrease both assets and liabilities.

T F   6. Significant investing and financing activities are disclosed in the statement of changes in financial position.

T F   7. Withdrawals by the owner are disclosed in the statement of owner's equity.

T F   8. An expense has the effect of decreasing owner's equity.

T F   9. Collection of an account receivable will increase owner's equity.

T F   10. Net income is a component of the statement of owner's equity.

_____   11. Which of the following is classified as a liability?
        a. Patents
        b. John Doe, Withdrawals
        c. Notes Payable
        d. Wages Expense
        e. Both Notes Payable and Wages Expense

_____   12. The heading, "For the year ended June 30, 19xx," would not be appropriate for
        a. the balance sheet.
        b. the income statement.
        c. the statement of owner's equity.
        d. the statement of changes in financial position.
        e. It would be appropriate for all the above statements.

_____ 13. Which of the following, if any, is not a satisfactory statement of
the balance sheet equation?
a. Assets = liabilities - owner's equity
b. Assets - liabilities = owner's equity
c. Assets = liabilities + owner's equity
d. Assets - owner's equity = liabilities
e. All are acceptable.

_____ 14. An investment by the owner in a business
a. increases assets and owner's equity.
b. increases assets and liabilities.
c. increases liabilities and owner's equity.
d. increases assets only.
e. increases owner's equity only.

_____ 15. A revenue has the effect of
a. increasing assets and liabilities.
b. increasing assets and owner's equity.
c. increasing assets and decreasing owner's equity.
d. decreasing net income.
e. leaving the entire balance sheet unchanged.

_____ 16. A withdrawal by an owner has the effect of
a. increasing assets and owner's equity.
b. increasing assets and decreasing owner's equity.
c. decreasing assets and owner's equity.
d. decreasing assets and increasing owner's equity.
e. leaving the entire balance sheet unchanged.

_____ 17. One could find which of the following accounts listed in the
statement of owner's equity?
a. Interest Income
b. Interest Payable
c. Interest Receivable
d. Interest Expense
e. None of the above

_____ 18. A company's owner's equity is one-third of its total assets. Its
liabilities total $100,000. What is the amount of its total
assets?
a. $50,000   b. $100,000   c. $150,000   d. $200,000   e. $300,000

_____ 19. The assumption of stability of the dollar relates to the concept of
a. separate entity.
b. financial position.
c. money measure.
d. residual interest.

_____ 20. Inventory is classified as a(n)
a. asset.
b. liability.
c. revenue.
d. expense.
e. asset _and_ an expense.

ANSWERS TO TEN-MINUTE QUIZ

<u>True-False</u>

1.   T
2.   F
3.   F
4.   F
5.   T
6.   T
7.   T
8.   T
9.   F
10. T

<u>Multiple-Choice</u>

11. c
12. a
13. a
14. a
15. b
16. c
17. e
18. c
19. c
20. a

CHAPTER THREE

THE DOUBLE-ENTRY SYSTEM

CHAPTER OUTLINE

Measurement Problems
    The Recognition Problem
    The Valuation Problem
    The Classification Problem
Accounts
    Management's Use of Accounts
    The Ledger
    Types of Commonly Used Accounts
        Assets
            Cash
            Notes Receivable
            Prepaid Expenses
            Land
            Buildings
            Equipment
        Liabilities
            Notes Payable
            Accounts Payable
            Other Short-term Liabilities
            Long-term Liabilities
        Owner's Equity Accounts
            Capital Account
            Withdrawals Account
            Revenue and Expense Accounts
        Titles of Accounts
The Double-Entry System: The Basic Method of Accounting
    The T-Account
    The Account Illustrated
    Analysis of Transactions
    Transaction Analysis Illustrated
    Summary of Transactions
Recording Transactions
    Steps in the Recording Process
    The Journal
    The General Journal
    The Ledger Account Form
    Relationship Between the Journal and the Ledger
The Trial Balance
Some Notes on Bookkeeping Techniques

Chapter Review
    Review of Learning Objectives
    Self-Test
    Review Problem: Journal Entries, T Accounts, and Trial Balance
    Answer to Review Problem
Chapter Assignments
    Questions
    Classroom Exercises
    Interpreting Accounting Information: Zenith Radio Corporation
    Problem Set A
    Problem Set B
    Financial Decision Case 3-1: Gonzalez Repair Service Company

LEARNING OBJECTIVES:

RESOURCE MATERIALS AND LECTURE OUTLINES

OBJECTIVE 1:   Explain in simple terms the generally accepted ways of solving the measurement problems of recognition, valuation, and classification (pp. 54-57)

Summary Statement

Before recording a business transaction, the accountant must determine three things:

a. When the transaction occurred (recognition problem)

b. What value should be placed on the transaction (valuation problem)

c. How the components of the transaction should be categorized (classification problem)

A sale is recognized (entered in the accounting records) when the title to merchandise passes from the supplier to the purchaser, regardless of when payment is made or received.

The dollar value of any item involved in a business transaction is its original cost (also called historical cost). Generally, any change in value subsequent to the transaction is not reflected in the accounting records.

New Words and Terms

recognition problem (p. 55)
valuation problem (p. 55)
cost (p. 55)
classification problem (p. 56)

Lecture Outline

A. Three measurement problems must be solved before recording a business transaction:

1. Recognition problem -- When did the transaction occur?

2. Valuation problem -- What dollar amount should be recorded?

3. Classification problem -- Which accounts are affected?

B. A sale is recognized when title passes to the buyer.

C. Transactions should be recorded at their original cost (historical cost).

OBJECTIVE 2: Define and use the terms account and ledger (pp. 57-58)

Summary Statement

Every business transaction is classified by means of records called accounts. Each asset, liability, owner's equity, revenue, and expense has a separate account.

An account in its simplest form, a T account, has three parts:

a. A title that expresses the name of the asset, liability, owner's equity, revenue, or expense.

b. A left side, which is called the debit side

c. A right side, which is called the credit side

At the end of an accounting period, account balances must be determined for use in preparing the financial statements. There are three steps to follow in determining these account balances:

a. Foot (add up) the debit entries. The footing (total) should be made in small numbers beneath the last entry.

b. Foot the credit entries.

c. Subtract the smaller total from the larger. A debit balance exists when total debits exceed total credits; a credit balance exists when the opposite is the case.

All of a company's accounts are contained in a book called the ledger. Each account appears on a separate page, and the accounts generally are in the fol-lowing order: assets, liabilities, owner's equity, revenues and expenses. A listing of the accounts with their respective account numbers, called a chart of accounts, is presented at the beginning of the ledger for easy reference.

CHAPTER THREE

<u>New Words and Terms</u>

account (p. 57)
ledger (p. 57)
chart of accounts (p. 57)

<u>Lecture Outline</u>

A. An account is the basic storage unit for accounting data.

B. A T account (simplest form of an account) has three parts:

   1. A title expressing the name of the asset, liability, etc.

   2. A debit (left) side

   3. A credit (right) side

C. An account occupies its own page in the ledger.

D. Determining an account balance consists of footing the debits and credits,
   and taking the difference.

E. A chart of accounts is presented at the beginning of the ledger.

OBJECTIVE 3: Recognize commonly used assets, liabilities, and owner's equity
              accounts (pp. 58-62)

<u>Summary Statement</u>

Although the accounts used by companies will vary, there are some that are common to most businesses. Some typical assets are Cash, Accounts Receivable,
Notes Receivable, Prepaid Expenses, Land, Buildings, and Equipment. Some typical liabilities are Accounts Payable, Notes Payable, and Bonds Payable.

The owner's capital account (an owner's equity account) represents the owner's
investment in the company at any point in time. If William Marshall were an
owner, the name of the account would be William Marshall, Capital. If there is
more than one owner, a separate capital account must be kept for each.

The owner's withdrawals account (also an owner's equity account) records
amounts withdrawn from the business for personal living expenses, in

anticipation of earning a profit. If Paula Post were an owner, her withdrawals account would be called "Paula Post, Withdrawals," or "Paula Post, Drawing." Like the capital account, there must be a separate withdrawals account for each owner.

A separate account is also kept for each type of revenue and expense. The exact revenue and expense accounts used will vary depending on the type of business and nature of its operations. Revenues cause an increase in owner's equity, whereas expenses cause a decrease.

<u>Related Text Illustrations</u>

*Figure 3-1 Relationships of Owner's Equity Accounts (p. 61)

<u>Lecture Outline</u>

A. Discuss typical assets, such as Cash, Accounts Receivable, Notes Receivable, Prepaid Expenses, Land, Buildings, and Equipment.

B. Discuss typical liabilities, such as Accounts Payable, Notes Payable, Wages Payable, Taxes Payable, Rent Payable, Interest Payable, Bonds Payable, and Unearned Revenue.

C. A capital account is maintained for each owner.

D. A withdrawals account is maintained for each owner.

E. Discuss typical revenue accounts, such as Sales and Commissions Earned, and illustrate their positive effect on owner's equity.

F. Discuss typical expense accounts, such as Rent Expense and Supplies Expense, and illustrate their negative effect on owner's equity.

OBJECTIVE 4: State the rules for debit and credit (pp. 62-65)

<u>Summary Statement</u>

The <u>double-entry system</u> of accounting requires that for each transaction there must be one or more accounts debited and one or more accounts credited, and that total debits must equal total credits.

CHAPTER THREE

To determine which accounts are debited and which are credited in a given transaction, one uses the following rules:

a. Increases in assets are debited.

b. Decreases in assets are credited.

c. Increases in liabilities and owner's equity are credited.

d. Decreases in liabilities and owner's equity are debited.

e. Revenues increase owner's equity, and are therefore credited.

f. Expenses decrease owner's equity and are therefore debited.

New Words and Terms

double-entry system (p. 63)
debit (p. 63)
credit (p. 63)
T account (p. 63)
footings (p. 64)
balance (p. 64)
account balance (p. 64)

Lecture Outline

A. Increases in assets are debited.

B. Decreases in assets are credited.

C. Increases in liabilities and owner's equity are credited.

D. Decreases in liabilities and owner's equity are debited.

E. Increases in revenues are credited.

F. Increases in expenses are debited.

OBJECTIVE 5: Apply the procedure for transaction analysis to simple
               transactions (pp. 65-72)

Summary Statement

To record a transaction, one must (a) obtain a description of the transaction, (b) determine which accounts are involved and what type each is (for example, asset or revenue), (c) determine which accounts are increased and which are decreased, and (d) apply the rules previously stated.

Related Text Illustrations

*Figure 3-2   Summary of Illustrative Accounts and Transactions for Joan Miller Advertising Agency   (p. 72)

Lecture Outline

A. Four steps are involved in recording a transaction:

1. Obtain a description of the transaction.

2. Determine the accounts and account classifications.

3. Determine which accounts are increased or decreased.

4. Apply the rules of debit and credit.

OBJECTIVE 6:   Record transactions in the general journal   (pp. 71-74)

Summary Statement

As transactions occur, they are recorded initially and chronologically in a book called the journal. The general journal is the simplest and most flexible type of journal. Each transaction journalized (recorded) in the general journal contains (a) the date, (b) the account names, (c) the dollar amounts debited and credited, (d) an explanation, and (e) the account numbers, if posted. A space should be skipped between each journal entry, and more than one debit or credit may be entered for a single transaction (called a compound entry).

New Words and Terms

journal (p. 73)
journal entry (p. 73)
journalizing (p. 73)
general journal (p. 73)
compound entry (p. 73)

CHAPTER THREE

<u>Related Text Illustrations</u>

Figure 3-3 The General Journal (p. 74)

<u>Lecture Outline</u>

A. Transactions are initially recorded in the journal (book of original entry).

B. Every journal entry contains five components:

  1. The date

  2. Account names

  3. Dollar amounts debited and credited

  4. Explanation

  5. Account number, if posted

C. A space should be skipped between journal entries.

D. A compound entry is an entry with more than one debit or credit.

OBJECTIVE 7: Explain the relationship of the journal to the ledger (pp. 74-76)

<u>Summary Statement</u>

Each day's journal entries must be posted to the ledger accounts. <u>Posting</u> is a
transferring process which results in an updated balance for each account. Not
only must the dates and amounts be transferred and new account balances computed, but also the Post. Ref. columns must be used for cross-referencing
between the journal and ledger. When more increases than decreases have been
recorded for an account (the usual case), then its balance (debit or credit) is
referred to as its <u>normal balance</u>. For example, assets have a normal debit
balance.

<u>New Words and Terms</u>

ledger account form (p. 74)
posting (p. 75)

<u>Related Text Illustrations</u>

Figure 3-4   Accounts Payable in the General Ledger
Figure 3-5   Posting from the General Journal to the Ledger (p. 76)

<u>Lecture Outline</u>

A. Journal entries are posted (transferred) to the ledger when convenient
   (usually daily).

   1. The date and amounts are posted.

   2. A new account balance is computed.

   3. Place the journal page number in the Post. Ref. column of the ledger
      account.

   4. Place the account number in the Post. Ref. column of the journal.

B. Explain the concept of normal balance.

OBJECTIVE 8:   Prepare a trial balance and recognize its value and limitations
               (pp. 76-78)

<u>Summary Statement</u>

Before the financial statements are prepared, the accountant must double-check
the equality of the debits and credits in the accounts. This is formally done
by means of a <u>trial balance</u>. If the trial balance does not balance, one or
more of several possible errors have been made in the journal, ledger, or trial
balance. Once the errors have been located, and the trial balance is in balance, the financial statements may be prepared. It is important to know, however, that it is possible to make errors which would not cause the trial
balance to be out of balance (i.e., would not be detected through the trial
balance).

To summarize, proper accounting procedure requires that certain steps be followed (additional steps will be introduced in subsequent chapters):

a. Journalize transactions as they occur

b. Post the journal entries to the ledger accounts when convenient

c. Prepare a trial balance at the end of each accounting period

d. Use the trial balance to prepare the financial statements

New Words and Terms

trial balance (p. 76)
normal balance (p. 77)

Related Text Illustrations

Figure 3-6 Trial Balance (p. 77)

Lecture Outline

A. A trial balance tests the equality of debits and credits in the ledger
   before the financial statements are prepared.

   1. If the trial balance does not balance, the error or errors may have
      occurred in the journal, ledger, or trial balance.

   2. It is possible to make an error in the records (such as omission of an
      entry) which would not cause the trial balance to be out of balance.

B. Review the order of accounting procedures covered thus far.

Chapter Three   The Double-Entry System

Learning Objectives	Questions	Exercises	A & B Problems	Case
1. Explain in simple terms the generally accepted ways of solving the measurement problems of recognition, valuation, and classification.	1, 2, 3, 4, 5	4		1
2. Define and use the terms account and ledger.	6, 20			
3. Recognize commonly used assets, liabilities, and owner's equity accounts.	14	IAI		1
4. State the rules for debit and credit.	7, 8, 9, 10, 11, 13, 15, 23	2, IAI		
5. Apply the procedure for transaction analysis to simple transactions.	12, 13	1, 2	2, 3, 4	1
6. Record transactions in the general journal.	15, 18, 20	8, IAI	3, 4, 5, 6	
7. Explain the relationship of the journal to the ledger.	15, 19, 20, 21, 22	7	5, 6	
8. Prepare a trial balance and recognize its value and limitations.	12, 16, 17	3, 5, 6, 9	1, 2, 3, 4, 5, 6	1

DIFFICULTY AND TIME CHART

A & B Problems	Difficulty	Time (in minutes)
1	easy	15
2	easy	35
3	easy	45
4	medium	50
5	medium	50
6	medium	65
Case 3-1	difficult	60

TEN-MINUTE QUIZ

T F   1. In a journal entry, assets are always recorded as debits, and liabilities are always recorded as credits.

T F   2. The account Revenue from Services is increased with a credit.

T F   3. In the trial balance, all the accounts with debit balances are usually listed before the accounts with credit balances.

T F   4. The dollar amounts on the basic set of financial statements should not be adjusted for general price level changes.

T F   5. A compound entry is an entry with more than one debit or credit.

T F   6. The recognition problem is the difficulty of deciding when a business transaction has occurred.

T F   7. Prepaid Rent is an asset.

T F   8. When we issue a promissory note to a creditor, we would record Notes Receivable.

T F   9. All transactions are initially recorded in T accounts.

T F   10. The withdrawal account is increased with a debit.

_____ 11. The account Unearned Revenue is classified as a(n)
        a. asset.
        b. liability.
        c. revenue.
        d. expense.
        e. owner's equity account.

_____ 12. Which of the following errors could cause the trial balance to be out of balance?
        a. A debit entry was entered in the wrong debit account.
        b. An entire transaction was entered in the general journal as $96 instead of $69.
        c. The balance of an account was incorrectly computed.
        d. An entire transaction was not recorded in the general journal.
        e. An entire journal entry was not posted to the ledger.

_____ 13. The Post. Ref. column in the general journal is used to show that an item has been posted to the ledger when which of the following is placed in it?
a. The journal number
b. The account number
c. The journal page number
d. A check mark
e. An X

_____ 14. Which of the following would _not_ result in the recording of an expense?
a. Receipt of a bill from the telephone company
b. Recording of wages
c. Withdrawals by the owner for personal expenses
d. Purchase of gasoline for fill-up of the company car
e. The expiration of insurance

_____ 15. Which of the following is the correct sequence of accounting procedures?
a. Ledger, trial balance, journal, financial statements
b. Journal, ledger, trial balance, financial statements
c. Financial statements, trial balance, ledger, journal
d. Financial statements, journal, ledger, trial balance
e. Ledger, journal, trial balance, financial statements

_____ 16. Which of the following accounts is increased by crediting it?
a. Office Equipment
b. Copyrights
c. Telephone Expense
d. Notes Payable
e. Inventory

_____ 17. If Accounts Receivable has debit postings of $26,000, credit postings of $28,000, and an ending normal balance of $24,000, which of of the following was its beginning balance?
a. $2,000
b. $22,000
c. $24,000
d. $26,000
e. $50,000

_____ 18. When we receive cash in advance of painting a house, we
a. debit Cash and credit Painting Revenue.
b. debit Unearned Painting Revenue and credit Painting Revenue.
c. debit Cash and credit Unearned Painting Revenue.
d. debit Unearned Painting Revenue and credit Cash.
e. make no journal entry because we have not started painting the house.

_____ 19. The journal entry to record the completion of a service for which
payment has not been received would be
a. a debit to Accounts Receivable and a credit to Revenue from
Services.
b. a debit to Revenue from Services and a credit to Accounts
Payable.
c. a debit to Revenue from Services and a credit to Accounts
Receivable.
d. a debit to Cash and a credit to Revenue from Services.
e. No entry is made until the cash is received.

_____ 20. Which of the following is not necessarily true about a proper
journal entry?
a. All debits must be recorded before any credits.
b. An explanation must always follow the journal entry.
c. Liabilities are indented.
d. The Post. Ref. column is left blank until after the entry has
been posted.
e. Decreases in assets are indented.

ANSWERS TO TEN-MINUTE QUIZ

<u>True-False</u>

1. F
2. T
3. F
4. T
5. T
6. T
7. T
8. F
9. F
10. T

<u>Multiple-Choice</u>

11. b
12. c
13. b
14. c
15. b
16. d
17. d
18. c
19. a
20. c

BUSINESS INCOME AND ADJUSTING ENTRIES

CHAPTER OUTLINE

The Measurement of Business Income
    Net Income
        Revenues
        Expenses
        Real and Nominal Accounts
    The Accounting Period Problem
    The Continuity Problem
    The Matching Problem
    Accrual Accounting
        Recognizing Revenues When Earned and Expenses When Incurred
        Adjusting the Accounts
The Adjustment Process
    Apportioning Recorded Costs Between Two or More Accounting Periods
        (Deferrals)
        Prepaid Expenses
        Depreciation of Plant and Equipment
        Accumulated Depreciation--A Contra Account
    Apportioning Recorded Revenues Between Two or More Accounting
        Periods (Deferrals)
    Unrecorded or Accrued Revenues
    Unrecorded or Accrued Expenses
    The Adjusted Trial Balance
    Using the Adjusted Trial Balance to Prepare Financial Statements
The Importance of Adjustments in Accounting
Correcting Errors
A Note About Journal Entries
Chapter Review
    Review of Learning Objectives
    Self-Test
    Review Problem: Adjusting Entries, T Accounts, and Adjusted Trial Balance
    Answer to Review Problem
Chapter Assignments
    Questions
    Classroom Exercises
    Interpreting Accounting Information: City of Chicago
    Problem Set A
    Problem Set B
    Financial Decision Case 4-1: Lockyer Systems Company

LEARNING OBJECTIVES:

RESOURCE MATERIALS AND LECTURE OUTLINES

OBJECTIVE 1: Define net income and its components, revenues and expenses
(pp. 99-101)

Summary Statement

Earning a <u>profit</u> is an important goal of most businesses, and it is a major function of accounting to measure and report the success or failure of a company in achieving this goal. This is done by means of an income statement.

<u>Net income</u> results when revenues exceed expenses, and a net loss results when expenses exceed revenues.

<u>Revenue</u> is the price of goods sold and services rendered during a specific period of time. Examples of revenue are Sales (the account used when merchandise is sold), Commissions Earned, and Earned Services.

<u>Expenses</u> are the costs of goods and services used in the process of obtaining revenue. Examples of expenses are Telephone Expense, Wages Expense, and Advertising Expense.

Revenue and expense accounts are sometimes referred to as <u>nominal accounts</u> because they are temporary in nature. Their purpose is to record revenues and expenses during a particular accounting period. At the end of that period, their totals are transferred to the owner's capital account, leaving zero balances to begin the next accounting period.

Balance sheet accounts are sometimes referred to as <u>real accounts</u> because their balances extend past the end of an accounting period and are *not* set back to zero.

New Words and Terms

profit (p. 99)
net income (p. 100)
revenues (p. 100)
expenses (p. 100)
nominal accounts (p. 101)
real accounts (p. 101)

<u>Lecture Outline</u>

A. Net income is the excess of revenue over expenses.

B. Revenue is the price of goods sold and services rendered.

C. Expenses are the cost of goods and services used in the process of obtaining revenue.

D. Revenue and expense accounts are referred to as nominal (temporary) accounts because they begin each period with zero balances.

E. Assets, liabilities, and owners' equity accounts are referred to as real (permanent) accounts because their balances carry over to the following period.

OBJECTIVE 2a: Recognize the difficulties of income measurement caused by the accounting period problem (pp. 101-102)

<u>Summary Statement</u>

The <u>periodicity</u> assumption (the solution to the <u>accounting period problem</u>) states that although measurements of net income for short periods of time are approximate, they are nevertheless useful to users. Income statement comparison is made possible through accounting periods of equal length. A <u>fiscal year</u> covers any twelve-month period. Many companies' fiscal year corresponds to the calendar year, which is a twelve-month period that ends on December 31.

<u>New Words and Terms</u>

accounting period problem (p. 101)
periodicity (p. 102)
fiscal year (p. 102)

<u>Lecture Outline</u>

A. The accounting period problem recognizes that the measurement of net income for a given period is at best an estimate.

B. A fiscal year is any 12-month period, and may or may not correspond to the calendar year.

          50

OBJECTIVE 2b: Recognize the difficulties of income measurement caused by the
continuity problem   (p. 102)

Summary Statement

Under the going-concern assumption (the solution to the continuity problem), the
accountant assumes that the business will continue to operate indefinitely, unless there is evidence to the contrary.

New Words and Terms

continuity problem   (p. 102)
going concern   (p. 102)

Lecture Outline

A. The going-concern assumption states that (without evidence to the contrary)
the accountant, when measuring income, should assume that a business will
continue indefinitely.

OBJECTIVE 2c: Recognize the difficulties of income measurement caused by the
matching problem   (p. 103)

Summary Statement

When the cash basis of accounting is used, revenues are recorded when cash is
received, and expenses are recorded when cash is paid. This method, however,
can lead to distortion of net income for the period.

According to the matching rule, revenues should be recorded in the period(s)
when they are actually earned, and expenses should be recorded in the period(s)
when the expenses are incurred; the timing of cash payments or receipts is irrelevant. Accrual accounting consists of all techniques used to apply the
matching rule.

New Words and Terms

cash basis of accounting   (p. 103)
matching rule   (p. 103)

Lecture Outline

A. Under the cash basis of accounting, revenues and expenses are recognized (recorded) when cash is received or paid.

B. According to the matching rule, revenues are recorded when earned, and expenses are recorded in the same period as the revenue generated by that particular expense; the timing of cash receipts and payments is irrelevant.

OBJECTIVE 3: Define accrual accounting and explain two broad ways of accomplishing it (pp. 103-105)

Summary Statement

Accrual accounting consists of all techniques used to apply the matching rule. Specifically, it involves (1) recognizing revenues when earned and expenses when incurred, and (2) adjusting the accounts at year-end.

New Words and Terms

accrual accounting (p. 103)

Related Text Illustrations

Figure 4-1 Trial Balance for the Joan Miller Advertising Agency (p. 104)

Lecture Outline

A. Accrual accounting consists of all techniques used to apply the matching rule.

1. When revenue is recorded before cash is received, a receivable is also recorded.

2. When an expense is recorded before cash is paid, a payable is also recorded.

CHAPTER FOUR

OBJECTIVE 4: State the four principal situations that require adjusting
              entries (p. 105)

<u>Summary Statement</u>

A problem arises when revenues or expenses apply to more than one accounting
period. The problem is solved by making <u>adjusting entries</u> at the end of the
accounting period. Adjusting entries allocate to the current period the revenues and expenses that apply to the current period, deferring the remainder to
future periods. A <u>deferral</u> is the postponement of the recognition of an expense
already paid or of a revenue already received (see "a" and "b" below). An <u>accru-
al</u> is the recognition of an expense or revenue that has arisen but has not yet
been recorded (see "c" and "d" below).

Adjusting entries are required to accomplish several things:

a. Apportion recorded costs (such as the cost of machinery or prepaid rent)
   among two or more accounting periods.

b. Apportion recorded revenue (such as commissions collected in advance) among
   two or more accounting periods.

c. Record unrecorded expenses (such as wages earned by employees after the last
   payday in an accounting period).

d. Record unrecorded revenue (such as commissions earned but not yet billed to
   customers).

<u>New Words and Terms</u>

adjusting entries (p. 105)
deferral (p. 105)
accrual (p. 105)

<u>Lecture Outline</u>

A. Adjusting entries (made at the end of the period) accomplish four things:

   1. Apportion recorded costs among two or more accounting periods.

   2. Apportion recorded revenue among two or more accounting periods.

   3. Record unrecorded expenses.

   4. Record unrecorded revenue.

B. A deferral is the postponement of the recognition of a revenue or an expense
   (cash has already changed hands).

                    53

C. An accrual is the recognition of a revenue earned or an expense incurred (but cash has not yet changed hands).

OBJECTIVE 5: Prepare typical adjusting entries (pp. 105-112)

Summary Statement

When an expenditure is made that will benefit more than just the current period, the initial debit is usually made to an asset account instead of to an expense account. Then, at the end of the accounting period, the amount that has been used up or that has expired is transferred from the asset account to an expense account by means of an adjusting entry.

a. Prepaid Rent and Prepaid Insurance are debited when rent and insurance are paid for in advance.

b. An account called Office Supplies is debited when supplies are purchased. At the end of the accounting period, an inventory of office supplies is taken. The difference between office supplies available for use during the period and ending inventory represents the amount consumed during the period.

c. Long-lived assets such as machinery, building, equipment, or company vehicles are debited to an asset account when purchased. At the end of each accounting period, an adjusting entry must be made to transfer a portion of the original cost of each long-lived asset to an expense account. The amount transferred or allocated is called depreciation. The Accumulated Depreciation account is called a contra account because it appears on the balance sheet as a deduction from its associated asset. Proper balance sheet presentation will therefore disclose the original cost, the accumulated depreciation as of the balance sheet date, and the undepreciated balance.

In making the adjusting entry to record depreciation, Depreciation Expense is debited and Accumulated Depreciation is credited.

When payment is received for goods before they are delivered or for services before they are rendered, a liability account such as Unearned Revenue would appear on the balance sheet, representing revenue that still must be earned.

When expenses have been incurred but cash has not yet been paid by the end of the accounting period, an adjusting entry must nevertheless be made to record these accrued (accumulated) expenses. For example, interest may have accrued on a loan that does not require payment until the next period. A debit to Interest Expense and a credit to Interest Payable will record the current period's interest for the income statement as well as recording the liability for the balance sheet.

When revenues have been earned for which no payment has been received, adjusting entries must be made to record these accrued revenues. For example, if interest that has been earned will not be received until the next period, a debit must be made to Interest Receivable and a credit to Interest Earned.

<u>New Words and Terms</u>

prepaid expenses (p. 106)
depreciation (p. 108)
depreciation expense (p. 108)
accumulated depreciation (p. 109)
contra accounts (p. 109)
unearned revenues (p. 110)
unrecorded or accrued revenues (p. 110)
accrued expenses (p. 111)

<u>Related Text Illustrations</u>

Figure 4-2 Plant and Equipment Section of Balance Sheet (p. 109)

<u>Lecture Outline</u>

A. Prepaid rent, prepaid insurance, and prepaid advertising are transformed (at
   least in part) into expense accounts.

B. Office supplies used are recorded as Office Supplies Expense. Usually an
   inventory of office supplies is taken to infer the costs of supplies used.

C. Depreciation must be recorded on buildings and equipment.

   1. Define depreciation as the logical allocation of asset cost to the
      accounting periods benefited.

   2. Distinguish between Depreciation Expense and Accumulated Depreciation.

   3. Show balance sheet presentation of accumulated depreciation.

D. Unearned revenue (a liability) is transformed (at least in part) into earned
   revenue.

E. Accrued expenses (incurred but not paid) are recorded. Examples are accrued
   interest, wages, and taxes.

F. Accrued revenue (revenue earned but not received) is recorded.

OBJECTIVE 6: Prepare an adjusted trial balance (pp. 112-114)

Summary Statement

After all the adjusting entries have been posted to the ledger accounts and new account balances have been computed, an _adjusted trial balance_ can be prepared. If it is in balance, the adjusted trial balance is then used to prepare the financial statements.

New Words and Terms

adjusted trial balance (p. 112)

Related Text Illustrations

Figure 4-3 Determination of the Adjusted Trial Balance (p. 113)

Lecture Outline

A. An adjusted trial balance is prepared after all the adjusting entries have been posted to the ledger.

B. If the adjusted trial balance is in balance, the financial statements can now be prepared.

OBJECTIVE 7: Relate the need for adjusting entries to the usefulness of accounting information (pp. 114-117)

Summary Statement

Adjusting entries are made primarily in order to enable financial statements to conform to accounting standards. They provide a means of implementing accrual accounting so that financial statements may be comparable between periods and relevant to users. Adjusting entries often involve estimates, but the estimates should be supported by objective evidence.

Related Text Illustrations

*Figure 4-4 Relationship of Adjusted Trial Balance to Income Statement (p. 115)
*Figure 4-5 Relationship of Adjusted Trial Balance to Balance Sheet (p. 116)

CHAPTER FOUR

<u>Lecture Outline</u>

A. Adjusting entries are a means of implementing accrual accounting so that all
   revenue and expenses that relate to a particular period are reflected in that
   period's financial statements.

OBJECTIVE 8: Prepare correcting entries (p. 117)

<u>Summary Statement</u>

Errors that are discovered in the journal or ledger must always be corrected by
drawing a line through the incorrect data or by preparing a correcting entry,
depending on the type of error. In no case should the errors be erased.

<u>Lecture Outline</u>

A. Errors made in the journal or ledger should never be erased.

B. Sometimes errors are corrected by drawing a line through the incorrect items
   and entering the correct items.

   1. An incorrect journal entry not yet posted.

   2. An incorrect amount posted to the wrong ledger account.

C. Sometimes errors are corrected by preparing a new journal entry.

   1. A journal entry was either prepared or posted incorrectly.

   2. Other errors whereby it would be inappropriate to draw a line through the
      incorrect items (i.e., a new entry is needed).

Chapter Four Business Income and Adjusting Entries

Learning Objectives	Questions	Exercises	A & B Problems	Case
1. Define net income and its components, revenues and expenses.	1, 2, 3			
2. Recognize the difficulties of income measurement caused by (a) the accounting period problem, (b) the continuity problem, and (c) the matching problem.	4, 5, 6, 18	IAI		
3. Define accrual accounting and explain two broad ways of accomplishing it.	7, 8, 19	IAI		
4. State the four principal situations that require adjusting entries.	9, 10, 11, 12, 13, 14, 15, 16, 17, 20			
5. Prepare typical adjusting entries.	22, 23	1, 2, 3, 4, 5, 6	1, 2, 3, 4, 5, 6	1
6. Prepare an adjusted trial balance.	21		3, 4, 5, 6	
7. Relate the need for adjusting entries to the usefulness of accounting information.	22	6	6	1
8. Prepare correcting entries.	23	7	6	

DIFFICULTY AND TIME CHART

A & B Problems	Difficulty	Time (in minutes)
1	easy	15
2	medium	20
3	easy	40
4	medium	50
5	medium	55
6	difficult	60
Case 4-1	difficult	60

TEN-MINUTE QUIZ

T F   1. The balance of a nominal account may extend past the end of an accounting period.

T F   2. Assets become expenses when they expire.

T F   3. Under accrual accounting, revenue is equal to the cash received by a company during the accounting period.

T F   4. An accrual is the postponement of the recognition of a revenue or an expense.

T F   5. The account Office Equipment is a real account.

T F   6. A contra account is an account whose balance is subtracted from an associated account in the financial statements.

T F   7. The normal balance of Accumulated Depreciation is a debit.

T F   8. An adjusted trial balance proves the balance of the ledger accounts after the adjusting entries have been posted.

T F   9. A contra account will have the same balance as the account it is contra to.

T F   10. A company's fiscal year must correspond to the calendar year.

_____ 11. The going concern assumption recognizes that
        a. net income is at best an estimate.
        b. all financial statements should cover a fiscal year.
        c. the value of an asset may vary from month to month.
        d. the company may continue indefinitely.
        e. a company's major objective is to earn a profit.

_____ 12. Which of the following is not an application of accrual accounting?
        a. Adjusting the accounts at the end of the year
        b. Recognizing revenue when earned
        c. Recognizing expenses when incurred
        d. Recording depreciation
        e. Recording all expenses when paid for

_____ 13. A company recorded purchases of office supplies in Office Supplies Expense when purchased. If that company failed to take an inventory and make an adjusting entry, the result would probably be
a. an understatement of assets.
b. an overstatement of owners' equity.
c. an understatement of liabilities.
d. an overstatement of assets.
e. an overstatement of net income.

_____ 14. A company's weekly payroll is $150, paid on Fridays. Assuming that the last day of the month falls on a Wednesday, the adjusting entry would be
a. a debit to Salaries Expense for $90 and a credit to Salaries Payable for $90.
b. a debit to Salaries Expense for $60 and a credit to Cash for $60.
c. a debit to Unpaid Salaries for $90 and a credit to Salaries Payable for $90.
d. a debit to Salaries Payable for $90 and a credit to Salaries Expense for $90.
e. a debit to Salaries Expense for $90 and a credit to Cash for $90.

_____ 15. Which of the following pairs of accounts could not be included in the same adjusting entry?
a. Wages Expense and Wages Payable
b. Unearned Revenue and Revenue from Services
c. Depreciation Expense and Accumulated Depreciation
d. Rent Expense and Rent Payable
e. Interest Expense and Interest Receivable

_____ 16. In November, cash is received in advance of rendering a service. Assuming that much of the service has been earned by December 31, the adjusting entry would be
a. a debit to Unearned Services and a credit to Cash.
b. a debit to Revenue from Services and a credit to Prepaid Services.
c. a debit to Unearned Services and a credit to Revenue from Services.
d. a debit to Cash and a credit to Revenue from Services.
e. a debit to Prepaid Services and a credit to Revenue from Services.

_____ 17. On December 10, A issues a 90-day promissory note to B. The December 31 adjusting entry to A is
a. a debit to Interest Expense and a credit to Cash.
b. a debit to Interest Receivable and a credit to Interest Earned.
c. a debit to Interest Payable and a credit to Cash.
d. a debit to Interest Expense and a credit to Interest Payable.
e. a debit to Cash and a credit to Interest Earned.

_____ 18. Which of the following is (are) correct accounting procedure(s)
when an error has been made?
a. Erasing the item in error
b. Lining out the incorrect item and writing in the correct one
c. Ignoring the error if a very small amount is involved
d. Preparing a new entry to correct the error
e. Both b and d

_____ 19. The entry to record depreciation on a building is
a. a debit to Depreciation Expense and a credit to Buildings.
b. a debit to Accumulated Depreciation and a credit to Buildings.
c. a debit to Depreciation Expense and a credit to Cash.
d. a debit to Depreciation Expense and a credit to Accumulated
Depreciation.
e. a debit to Buildings and a credit to Accumulated Depreciation.

_____ 20. In July, a company pays two years' insurance in advance. The
December 31 adjusting entry is
a. a debit to Insurance Expense and a credit to Prepaid Insurance.
b. a debit to Insurance Expense and a credit to Cash.
c. a debit to Prepaid Insurance and a credit to Cash.
d. a debit to Prepaid Insurance and a credit to Insurance Expense.
e. a debit to Insurance Expense and a credit to Insurance Payable.

ANSWERS TO TEN-MINUTE QUIZ

<u>True-False</u>

1. F
2. T
3. F
4. F
5. T
6. T
7. F
8. T
9. F
10. F

<u>Multiple-Choice</u>

11. d
12. e
13. a
14. a
15. e
16. c
17. d
18. e
19. d
20. a

CHAPTER FIVE

COMPLETING THE ACCOUNTING CYCLE

CHAPTER OUTLINE

Overview of the Accounting System
The Work Sheet: A Tool of Accountants
Steps in Preparing the Work Sheet
Uses of the Work Sheet
    Preparing the Financial Statements
    Recording the Adjusting Entries
    Recording the Closing Entries
Required Closing Entries
    Closing the Revenue Accounts to the Income Summary
    Closing the Expense Accounts to the Income Summary
    Closing the Income Summary to the Capital Account
    Closing the Withdrawals Account to the Capital Account
    The Accounts After Closing
The Post-Closing Trial Balance
Reversing Entries: Optional First Step of the Next Accounting Period
Chapter Review
    Review of Learning Objectives
    Self-Test
    Review Problem: Completion of Work Sheet, Preparation of Financial
                     Statements, Adjusting Entries, and Closing Entries
Chapter Assignments
    Questions
    Classroom Exercises
    Interpreting Accounting Information: Sperry & Hutchinson
    Problem Set A
    Problem Set B
    Financial Decision Case 5-1: Judy's Quik-Type

LEARNING OBJECTIVES:

RESOURCE MATERIALS AND LECTURE OUTLINES

OBJECTIVE 1: State all the steps in the accounting cycle (pp. 140-141)

<u>Summary Statement</u>

The steps in the <u>accounting system</u> (also called the <u>accounting cycle</u>) are as follows:

a. The transactions are analyzed from the source documents.

b. The transactions are recorded in the journal.

c. The journal entries are posted to the ledger.

d. The accounts are adjusted at the end of the period, usually with the aid of a work sheet.

e. Financial statements are prepared from the work sheet.

f. The nominal accounts are closed to conclude the current accounting period and to prepare for the new accounting period.

<u>New Words and Terms</u>

accounting system (p. 140)
accounting cycle (p. 140)

<u>Related Text Illustrations</u>

*Figure 5-1 An Overview of the Accounting System (p. 141)

<u>Lecture Outline</u>

A. Transactions are analyzed from source documents.

B. Transactions are journalized.

C. Entries are posted to the ledger.

D. End-of-period adjustments are made, usually with the aid of the work sheet.

E. Formal financial statements are prepared.

F. Nominal accounts are closed.

OBJECTIVE 2: Prepare a work sheet (pp. 141-148)

<u>Summary Statement</u>

Accountants use <u>working papers</u> to help organize their work and to provide evidence in support of the financial statements. The <u>work sheet</u> is one such working paper. It reduces the chance of overlooking an adjustment, provides a check on the arithmetical accuracy of the accounts, and facilitates the preparation of financial statements. The work sheet is never published but is a useful tool to the accountant.

The five steps in the preparation of the work sheet are as follows:

a. Enter the account balances (debit or credit) into the Trial Balance columns, and total the columns.

b. Enter the adjustments into the Adjustments columns, key each adjustment to a brief explanation at the bottom of the work sheet, and total the columns.

c. Enter into the Adjusted Trial Balance columns (by means of <u>crossfooting</u>) the account balances as adjusted, and total the columns.

d. Extend (transfer) the account balances from the Adjusted Trial Balance to either the Income Statement column or the Balance Sheet column, depending on which type of account is involved.

e. Total the Income Statement and Balance Sheet columns. Then enter the net income or loss in the Income Statement and Balance Sheet columns (one will be a debit, the other a credit) as a balancing figure, and recompute the column totals.

<u>New Words and Terms</u>

working papers (p. 142)
work sheet (p. 142)

<u>Related Text Illustrations</u>

Figure 5-2   Entering the Account Balances in the Trial Balance Columns (p. 143)
Figure 5-3   Entries in the Adjustments Columns (p. 144)
Figure 5-4   Entries in the Adjusted Trial Balance Columns (p. 145)
Figure 5-5   Entries in the Income Statement and Balance Sheet Columns (p. 146)
*Figure 5-6   Entries in the Balance Sheet Columns and Totals (p. 147)

<u>Lecture Outline</u>

A. A work sheet is an accountant's working paper which facilitates the preparation of financial statements.

B. There are five steps in the preparation of a work sheet:

1. Enter ledger account balances into the trial balance columns.

2. Enter and key adjustments into the adjustments columns.

3. Crossfoot the first two columns to produce the adjusted trial balance columns.

4. Extend account balances to either the income statement or balance sheet columns.

5. Enter net income as a balancing figure for the income statement and balance sheet columns.

OBJECTIVE 3:   Identify the three principal uses of a work sheet   (p. 148)

<u>Summary Statement</u>

Once the work sheet is completed, it can be used to (a) prepare the formal financial statements, (b) record the formal adjusting entries in the journal, and (c) record the formal closing entries in the journal, thus preparing the records for the new period.

CHAPTER FIVE

<u>Lecture Outline</u>

A. A work sheet facilitates preparation of:

   1. The formal financial statements.

   2. Formal adjusting entries.

   3. Formal closing entries.

OBJECTIVE 4: Prepare financial statements from a work sheet (pp. 148-150)

<u>Summary Statement</u>

The income statement may be prepared from the information found in the work
sheet's income statement columns. Calculations of the change in owner's equity
for the period may be shown in the balance sheet or in a separate statement of
owner's equity. Information for this calculation may be found in the balance
sheet columns of the work sheet (beginning capital, net income, and withdrawals).
The balance sheet may be prepared from information found in the work sheet's
balance sheet columns, and in the statement of owner's equity (if prepared).

<u>Related Text Illustrations</u>

Figure 5-7   Income Statement for the Joan Miller Advertising Agency (p. 149)
Figure 5-8   Statement of Owner's Equity for the Joan Miller Advertising Agency
             (p. 149)
Figure 5-9   Balance Sheet for the Joan Miller Advertising Agency (p. 150)

<u>Lecture Outline</u>

A. Prepare an income statement for the work sheet's income statement columns.

B. Calculate the change in owner's equity either in a statement of owner's
   equity or directly in the balance sheet.

C. Prepare a balance sheet from the work sheet's balance sheet columns and from
   the statement of owner's equity (if prepared).

OBJECTIVE 5: Record the adjusting entries from a work sheet (pp. 148-151)

Summary Statement

Formal adjusting entries must be recorded in the journal and posted to the ledger so that the account balances on the books will agree with those on the financial statements. This is easily accomplished by referring to the adjustments columns (and footnoted explanations) of the work sheet.

Related Text Illustrations

Figure 5-10 Adjustments on Work Sheet Entered in the General Journal (p. 151)

Lecture Outline

A. Formal adjusting entries may easily be prepared by referring to the work sheet's adjustments columns and keyed explanations.

OBJECTIVE 6: Explain the purposes of closing entries (pp. 149-152)

Summary Statement

Closing entries (also called clearing entries) serve two purposes. First, they transfer net income or loss to the owner's capital account. Second, they reduce revenue and expense accounts to zero so that these accounts may begin accumulating net income for the next accounting period.

New Words and Terms

closing entries (p. 149)
Income Summary (p. 150)
clearing entries (p. 152)

Lecture Outline

A. Closing entries serve two purposes:

1. They transfer net income or loss into the owner's capital account.

2. They "zero-out" all nominal accounts.

OBJECTIVE 7: Prepare the required closing entries (pp. 152-162)

Summary Statement

There are four closing entries, as follows:

a. Revenue accounts are closed. This is accomplished by a compound entry that debits each revenue for the amount required to give it a zero balance, and that credits Income Summary for the revenue total. The Income Summary account exists only during closing entries and does not appear in the work sheet or in the financial statements.

b. Expense accounts are closed. This is accomplished by a compound entry that credits each expense for the amount required to give it a zero balance, and that debits Income Summary for the expense total.

c. The Income Summary account is closed. After revenues and expenses have been closed, the Income Summary account will have either a debit balance or a credit balance. If a credit balance exists, then Income Summary must be debited for the amount required to give it a zero balance, and the owner's capital account is credited for the same amount. The reverse is done when Income Summary has a debit balance.

d. The withdrawals account is closed. This is accomplished by crediting the owner's withdrawals account by the amount required to give it a zero balance, and by debiting the owner's capital account by the same amount.

Related Text Illustrations

*Figure 5-11 Posting the Closing Entry of the Revenue Accounts to the Income Summary (p. 153)
*Figure 5-12 Posting the Closing Entry of the Expense Accounts to the Income Summary (p. 154)
*Figure 5-13 Posting the Closing Entry of the Income Summary to the Capital Account (p. 155)
*Figure 5-14 Posting the Closing Entry of the Withdrawals Account to the Capital Account (p. 156)
 Figure 5-15 The Accounts After Closing Entries Are Posted (pp. 156-162)

Lecture Outline

A. There are four closing entries:

1. Close revenue accounts.

2. Close expense accounts.

3. Close Income Summary.

4. Close the withdrawals account.

OBJECTIVE 8: Prepare the post-closing trial balance (pp. 162-163)

Summary Statement

After posting the closing entries to the ledger, it is necessary to prepare a post-closing trial balance to verify again the equality of the debits and credits in the accounts. Only balance sheet accounts are included because all income statement accounts have zero balances at this point.

New Words and Terms

post-clearing trial balance (p. 162)

Related Text Illustrations

Figure 5-16 Post-Closing Trial Balance (p. 163)

Lecture Outline

A. Prepare a post-closing trial balance as a final check of the equality of debits and credits in the ledger.

B. Only real accounts are included in the post-closing trial balance.

OBJECTIVE 9: Prepare reversing entries as appropriate (pp. 162-165)

Summary Statement

At the end of each accounting period, the accountant makes adjusting entries to record accrued revenues and expenses. Many of the adjusting entries are followed in the next period by the receipt or payment of cash. Thus it would become necessary in the next period to make a special entry apportioning amounts between the two periods. To avoid this inconvenience, the accountant can make reversing entries (dated the beginning of the new period), and can now make the routine bookkeeping entry when cash eventually changes hands.

CHAPTER FIVE

<u>New Words and Terms</u>

reversing entry (p. 162)

<u>Lecture Outline</u>

A. A reversing entry is the opposite of an adjusting entry.

B. Reversing entries are never required.

C. Reversing entries are dated the beginning of the new period.

D. Reversing entries enable the bookkeeper to continue making routine journal
   entries at the beginning of the new period (show how).

E. Discuss when a reversing entry <u>may</u> be made.

Chapter Five   Completing the Accounting Cycle

Learning Objectives	Questions	Exercises	A & B Problems	Case
1. State all the steps in the accounting cycle.	1	IAI		
2. Prepare a work sheet.	6, 7, 8, 9, 10, 11	1, 5	3, 4, 5	
3. Identify the three principal uses of a work sheet.	2, 3, 4			
4. Prepare financial statements from a work sheet.		4	1, 2, 3, 4, 5	1
5. Prepare the adjusting entries from a work sheet.	5, 13, 14	2, 6 IAI	1, 2, 3, 4, 5	
6. Explain the purposes of closing entries.	12, 14, 15			
7. Prepare the required closing entries.	16	3, IAI	1, 2, 3, 4	
8. Prepare the post-closing trial balance.	17, 18		4	
9. Prepare reversing entries as appropriate.	19, 20	2, 7	1, 2	

DIFFICULTY AND TIME CHART

A & B Problems	Difficulty	Time (in minutes)
1	easy	40
2	easy	45
3	medium	65
4	medium	100
5	difficult	40
Case 5-1	difficult	45

TEN-MINUTE QUIZ

T F   1. After <u>all</u> closing entries have been posted, the balance in the Income Summary account will equal the amount of the net income or net loss.

T F   2. An expense is closed with a credit to the expense and a debit to Income Summary.

T F   3. The account Income Summary will not be found in any financial statement.

T F   4. Closing entries may be prepared by referring exclusively to the Balance Sheet columns of the work sheet.

T F   5. The Adjusted Trial Balance columns of the work sheet are prepared by crossfooting the Trial Balance and Adjustments columns of the work sheet.

T F   6. Preparation of reversing entries helps make the bookkeeper's job easier.

T F   7. An important use of the work sheet is as an aid in the preparation of the financial statements.

T F   8. The post-closing trial balance will include the account Accumulated Depreciation, but will not include the account Depreciation Expense.

T F   9. When the income statement columns of the work sheet are initially totaled, they should be in balance.

T F   10. The work sheet is published in a company's annual report with the company's financial statements.

_____ 11. A major purpose of closing entries is to
           a. make all real accounts zero.
           b. update all the revenue and expense accounts.
           c. enable the nominal accounts to begin the new period with zero balances.
           d. transfer net income into the Income Summary account.
           e. allocate revenues and expenses to the proper accounting periods.

_____ 12. Which of the following accounts would not be closed out?
    a. Jane Doe, Capital
    b. Income Summary
    c. Interest Income
    d. Jane Doe, Withdrawals
    e. Depreciation Expense

_____ 13. Which of the following sequences of documents or records describes the proper sequence in the accounting cycle?
    a. Source documents, ledger, journal, work sheet, financial statements
    b. Work sheet, source documents, journal, ledger, financial statements
    c. Source documents, journal, ledger, work sheet, financial statements
    d. Source documents, work sheet, journal, ledger, financial statements
    e. Source documents, journal, ledger, financial statements, work sheet

_____ 14. Which of the following adjusting entries could be reversed in a company that uses the reversing procedure?
    a. Adjustment for prepaid rent
    b. Adjustment for depreciation expense
    c. Adjustment for accrued interest earned
    d. Adjustment for supplies expense
    e. None of the above

_____ 15. When there is a net loss, the entry to close out Income Summary is
    a. a debit to Net Loss and a credit to Income Summary.
    b. a debit to John Doe, Capital and a credit to Income Summary.
    c. a debit to Income Summary and a credit to Net Loss.
    d. a debit to Income Summary and a credit to John Doe, Capital.
    e. a debit to John Doe, Withdrawals and a credit to Income Summary.

_____ 16. The entry to close out John Doe's Withdrawals account is
    a. a debit to Income Summary and a credit to John Doe, Withdrawals.
    b. a debit to John Doe, Withdrawals and a credit to Income Summary.
    c. a debit to John Doe, Capital and a credit to John Doe, Withdrawals.
    d. a debit to John Doe, Withdrawals and a credit to John Doe, Capital.
    e. a debit to Cash and a credit to John Doe, Withdrawals.

_____ 17. In the work sheet, when there is a net loss
    a. the net loss will be placed in the debit side of the Income Statement column.
    b. the net loss will be placed in the credit side of the Income Statement column.
    c. the net loss will be placed in the debit side of the Balance Sheet column.
    d. both b and c are correct.
    e. both a and c are correct.

_____ 18. In the completed work sheet, which set of columns would usually be
out of balance after the initial footing?
a. The Adjustments columns
b. The Adjusted Trial Balance columns
c. The Income Statement columns
d. The Balance Sheet columns
e. Both c and d

_____ 19. In preparing adjustments in the work sheet, which of the following
accounts could not be added to the account column?
a. Insurance Expense
b. Cash
c. Rent Payable
d. Revenue from Services
e. Accumulated Depreciation

_____ 20. Which of the following is the most useful aid to the accountant in
preparing closing entries?
a. Journal
b. Ledger
c. Financial statements
d. Work sheet
e. Trial balance

ANSWERS TO TEN-MINUTE QUIZ

<u>True-False</u>

1. F
2. T
3. T
4. F
5. T
6. T
7. T
8. T
9. F
10. F

<u>Multiple-Choice</u>

11. c
12. a
13. c
14. c
15. b
16. c
17. d
18. e
19. b
20. d

CHAPTER SIX

ACCOUNTING FOR MERCHANDISING OPERATIONS

CHAPTER OUTLINE

Chapter Assignments
    Questions
    Classroom Exercises
    Interpreting Accounting Information: Sears and K mart
    Problem Set A
    Problem Set B
    Financial Decision Case 6-1: Jefferson Jeans Company

LEARNING OBJECTIVES:

RESOURCE MATERIALS AND LECTURE OUTLINES

OBJECTIVE 1:   Identify the components of income statements for merchandising concerns (pp. 188-189)

Summary Statement

The income of a merchandising firm is computed as follows:

Revenues from sales (net sales)
- <u>Cost of goods sold</u>
= Gross margin from sales
- <u>Operating expenses</u>
= Net income

a. Revenues from sales (net sales) consists of gross proceeds from the sale of merchandise (<u>gross sales</u>) less sales returns and allowances and sales discounts.

b. <u>Cost of goods sold</u> is the amount that the merchandising company originally paid for the goods that it sold during a given period. If, for example, a merchandising firm sells for $100 a radio that cost the company $70, then revenue from sales is $100, cost of goods sold is $70, and gross margin from sales is $30. This $30 gross margin helps pay for <u>operating expenses</u> (all expenses other than cost of goods sold), and the remainder or deficiency represents net income or net loss, respectively. Preparing an income statement in this fashion provides useful information to management, which is continually striving to improve net income.

New Words and Terms

revenues from sales (p. 188)
cost of goods sold (p. 188)
gross margin from sales (p. 189)
gross margin (p. 189)
operating expenses (p. 189)
net income (p. 189)

<u>Related Text Illustrations</u>

Figure 6-1   The Parts of an Income Statement for a Merchandising Concern
             (p. 189)

<u>Lecture Outline</u>

A. Explain a merchandiser's condensed income statement (see Fig. 6-1 of the
   text).

   1. Revenues from Sales (net sales) = Gross sales less sales discounts and
      sales returns and allowances.

   2. Cost of goods sold is the amount paid (for goods) by the merchandiser to
      the supplier.

   3. Gross margin from sales = Revenues from sales less cost of goods sold.

   4. Operating expenses are all expenses other than cost of goods sold.

   5. Net income = Gross margin from sales less operating expenses.

OBJECTIVE 2:   Journalize transactions involving revenues for merchandising con-
               cerns   (pp. 190-192)

<u>Summary Statement</u>

When a cash sale is made, Cash is debited and Sales is credited for the amount
of the sale. When a credit sale is made, Accounts Receivable is debited and
Sales is credited (at the point of sale, it is not known whether the customer
will pay within the discount period or will return some goods). Generally, a
sale is recorded when the goods are delivered and title passes to the customer,
regardless of when payment is made.

When a cash customer returns goods for a refund, <u>Sales Returns and Allowances</u>
is debited and Cash is credited. For a credit customer, Sales Returns and Allowances is debited and Accounts Receivable is credited. The Sales Returns and
Allowances account is debited instead of the Sales account to provide management with data about dissatisfied customers. In the income statement it is a
contra account to Gross Sales.

When goods are sold on credit, terms will vary as to when payment must be made
and the discount that is available. For instance, n/30 means that full payment

is due within 30 days after the invoice date, and n/10 eom means that full payment is due 10 days after the end of the month.

Often a customer is given a discount for early payment, and the merchandiser records a sales discount. Terms of 2/10, n/30, for example, mean that a 2 percent discount will be given if payment is made within 10 days of the invoice date. Otherwise, the net amount is due within 30 days.

Sales Discounts is recorded when payment is received within the discount period. Cash and Sales Discounts are debited; Accounts Receivable is credited. Sales Discounts is a contra account to Gross Sales in the income statement.

New Words and Terms

gross sales (p. 190)
Sales Returns and Allowances (p. 191)
sales discounts (p. 191)
2/10, n/30 (p. 191)

Related Text Illustrations

Figure 6-2 Partial Income Statement--Revenues from Sales (p. 190)

Lecture Outline

A. A sale is recorded when title passes to the customer.

B. Journalize a cash sale.

C. Journalize a credit sale.

D. Journalize a sales return (for cash and for credit).

E. Explain discount terms (e.g., 2/10, n/30).

F. Journalize the receipt of cash within the discount period.

OBJECTIVE 3: Calculate cost of goods sold (pp. 192-193)

<u>Summary Statement</u>

The accountant calculates the cost of goods sold as follows:

      Beginning inventory (at cost)
    + <u>Net purchases</u>
    = Cost of goods available for sale
    - <u>Ending inventory (at cost)</u>
    = Cost of goods sold

Net purchases is calculated as follows:

      (Gross) purchases
    - Purchases discounts
    - <u>Purchases returns and allowances</u>
    = Subtotal
    + <u>Freight in</u>
    = Net purchases

<u>New Words and Terms</u>

merchandise inventory (p. 192)
beginning inventory (p. 193)
ending inventory (p. 193)

<u>Related Text Illustrations</u>

Figure 6-3 Partial Income Statement--Cost of Goods Sold (p. 193)

<u>Lecture Outline</u>

A. Explain Fig. 6-3 of the text, line by line.

OBJECTIVE 4: Differentiate the perpetual inventory method from the periodic
             inventory method (pp. 194-195)

<u>Summary Statement</u>

There are two ways of determining inventory.

a. The <u>perpetual inventory method</u> is used when it is necessary to keep a record
   of the cost of each inventory item when it is purchased and when it is sold.

b. The <u>periodic inventory method</u> is used where it is unnecessary or impractical
   to keep track of the cost of each item. Under this method, the company instead waits until the end of the accounting period to <u>take a physical inven-
   tory</u>. This physical count figure is then multiplied by a derived cost-per-

unit figure (explained in Chapter Eleven) to arrive at the cost of ending
inventory.

The ending inventory of one period automatically becomes the beginning inventory
of the next period. The beginning inventory is removed from the inventory account, and the ending inventory is entered into the inventory account by means
of closing entries.

Merchandise inventory appears as an asset in the balance sheet, and includes all
salable goods owned by the company regardless of where the goods are located.
Goods in transit to which a company has acquired title are included in ending
inventory, whereas goods that the company has formally sold are not included,
even if the company has not yet delivered them. In order to simplify inventory
taking, many companies end their fiscal year during the slow season.

New Words and Terms

perpetual inventory method (p. 194)
periodic inventory method (p. 194)
taking a physical inventory (p. 195)

Lecture Outline

A. The perpetual inventory method updates the records with every purchase and
   every sale.

B. The periodic inventory method updates records only at the end of the period,
   when a physical count is taken.

C. Ending inventory of one period automatically becomes the beginning inventory
   of the next period (under either method).

OBJECTIVE 5: Journalize transactions involving purchases of merchandise
              (pp. 195-199)

Summary Statement

Under the periodic inventory method, all purchases of merchandise are debited
to the Purchases account and credited to Cash or Accounts Payable. The purpose
of the Purchases account is to accumulate the cost of merchandise purchased
during the period.

Upon returning goods to the supplier, the merchandiser debits Cash or Accounts
Payable and credits Purchases Returns and Allowances. Purchases Returns and
Allowances is a contra account to Purchases in the income statement.

When a merchandising concern is offered a discount if it pays within a given number of days, it may select either the gross method or the net method of recording the transaction.

a. Under the gross method, the purchase is initially recorded at the gross purchase price. If the company makes payment within the discount period, it would debit Accounts Payable, credit Purchases Discounts, and credit Cash.

b. Under the net method, the purchase is initially recorded at the net purchase price (that is, the gross purchase price less purchase discount available). If the company does *not* make payment within the discount period, it would debit Accounts Payable, debit Discounts Lost, and credit Cash. However, if payment *is* made within the discount period, no discount account is recorded.

When a merchandising firm pays for transportation costs on goods purchased, it debits Freight In (or Transportation In) and credits Cash. A merchandiser in Chicago, for instance, must pay the freight in from Boston if the terms specify FOB Boston or FOB shipping point. However, the supplier in Boston pays if the terms are FOB Chicago or FOB destination. Freight out is a cost of selling (not buying) merchandise, and should not be confused with freight in.

Inventory loss results from theft and spoilage, and is automatically included in the cost of goods sold under the periodic inventory method.

New Words and Terms

Purchases (p. 195)
purchases returns and allowances (p. 196)
purchases discounts (p. 196)
freight in (p. 197)
transportation in (p. 197)
FOB shipping point (p. 197)
FOB destination (p. 197)

Lecture Outline

A. Journalize the purchase of merchandise (cash and credit) under the periodic inventory method.

B. Journalize the return of merchandise to the supplier.

C. When a purchase discount is offered, the gross method or net method may be used by the buyer.

   1. Journalize a purchase under the gross method.

   2. Journalize payment within the discount period, under the gross method.

3. Journalize payment outside the discount period, under the gross method.

D. Illustrate the net method of recording merchandise purchases.

1. Upon purchase

2. When payment is made within the discount period

3. When payment is not made within the discount period

E. Journalize freight-in, and explain FOB shipping point and destination.

OBJECTIVE 6: Explain the objectives of handling merchandise inventory at the end of the accounting period and how they are achieved (pp. 200-201)

Summary Statement

Under a periodic inventory system, the objectives in dealing with inventory at the end of the period are to (a) remove the beginning balance from the Merchandise Inventory account, (b) enter the ending balance into the Merchandise Inventory account, and (c) enter these two amounts into the Income Summary account. These objectives are met by applying either the adjusting entry method or the closing entry method. Though different in form, both methods credit Merchandise Inventory and debit Income Summary for the beginning balance and debit Merchandise Inventory and credit Income Summary for the ending balance.

Lecture Outline

A. There are three objectives in dealing with ending inventory.

1. Remove the beginning balance from the Merchandise Inventory account.

2. Enter the ending balance into the Merchandise Inventory account.

3. Enter the above two amounts into Income Summary.

B. The above objectives may be achieved through the adjusting entry or closing
   entry method.

   1. Illustrate the adjusting entry method, and/or

   2. Illustrate the closing entry method.

OBJECTIVE 7: Prepare a work sheet for a merchandising concern under one of two
              alternative methods (pp. 202-204)

Summary Statement

Preparation of a merchandiser's work sheet depends upon whether the adjusting
entry method or closing entry method is being used. Under either method, the
Adjusted Trial Balance column may be eliminated if only a few adjustments are
necessary. In addition, many income statement accounts appear in the merchandiser's work sheet that do not appear in the service company's work sheet.
Merchandise Inventory, however, must receive special treatment.

a. Under the adjusting entry method, Merchandise Inventory is debited and
   credited for ending and beginning inventory, respectively, in the adjustments column; the corresponding credit and debit are to Income Summary.

b. Under the closing entry method, Merchandise Inventory bypasses the adjust-
   ments column. Instead, beginning inventory appears as a debit in the Income
   Statement column, and ending inventory appears as a credit in the Income
   Statement column and as a debit in the Balance Sheet column.

Related Text Illustrations

*Figure 6-4 Work Sheet for Fenwick Fashions Company--Adjusting Entry Method
             (p. 203)
*Figure 6-6 Work Sheet for Fenwick Fashions Company--Closing Entry Method
             (p. 206)

Lecture Outline

A. Refer to Chapter 4, objective #2, for the basic format of the work sheet for
   a service company.

B. The merchandiser's work sheet differs from that of a service company in two
   ways.

1. Several additional income statement accounts appear in the work sheet.

2. Beginning and ending inventory must receive special treatment.

C. Illustrate the treatment of inventory in the work sheet, under the adjusting entry method, and/or

D. Illustrate the treatment of inventory in the work sheet, under the closing entry method.

OBJECTIVE 8: Prepare adjusting and closing entries for a merchandising concern (pp. 202-209)

Summary Statement

The formal adjusting and closing entries for a merchandiser are similar to those for a service company, with the following exceptions.

a. Under the adjusting entry method, merchandise inventory is handled through adjusting entries, and all nominal accounts are closed in the normal manner.

b. Under the closing entry method, beginning inventory, Sales Returns and Allowances, Sales Discounts, Purchases, Freight In, and Freight Out are closed in the same entry that closes expenses. Purchases Returns and Allowances and Purchases Discounts are closed, and ending inventory is debited (to record the new balance), in the same entry that closes revenues.

Related Text Illustrations

*Figure 6-4 Work Sheet for Fenwick Fashions Company--Adjusting Entry Method
         (p. 203)
*Figure 6-5 Closing Entries for a Merchandising Concern--Adjusting Entry Method
         (p. 205)
*Figure 6-6 Work Sheet for Fenwick Fashions Company--Closing Entry Method
         (p. 206)
 Figure 6-7 Closing Entries for a Merchandising Concern--Closing Entry Method
         (p. 208)

Lecture Outline

A. Illustrate adjusting and closing entries, under the adjusting entry method.

1. Inventory is handled through adjusting entries.

    a. Close beginning inventory with a credit (debit Income Summary).

    b. Establish ending inventory with a debit (credit Income Summary).

2. All nominal accounts are closed in the normal manner.

B. Illustrate adjusting and closing entries, under the closing entry method.

1. Inventory is handled through closing entries.

    a. Close nominal accounts with debit balances and remove beginning inventory.

    b. Close nominal accounts with credit balances and establish ending inventory.

    c. Close Income Summary into the owner's capital account.

    d. Close Withdrawals into the owner's capital account.

OBJECTIVE 9:   Prepare an income statement for a merchandising concern
               (pp. 209-210)

Summary Statement

The income statement of a merchandising company consists of a revenues from sales section, a cost of goods sold section, a gross margin from sales figure, and an operating expenses section consisting of selling expenses and general and administrative expenses. In general, each section will provide detailed listings or computations for the benefit of the reader.

Related Text Illustrations

*Figure 6-8 Income Statement for Fenwick Fashions Company (p. 210)

Lecture Outline

A. Discuss the income statement presented in Fig. 6-8 of the text, emphasizing the major sections of the statement

Learning Objectives	Questions	Exercises	A & B Problems	Case
1. Identify the components of income statements for merchandising concerns.	1, 2	IAI		
2. Journalize transactions involving revenues for merchandising concerns.	5, 6, 7, 8, 9	1, 3	1, 3	
3. Calculate cost of goods sold.	3, 4, 10, 11, 12	4, 5		1
4. Differentiate the perpetual inventory method from the periodic inventory method.	17, 18, 19			
5. Journalize transactions involving purchases of merchandise.	13, 14, 15, 16	1, 2	1, 3	
6. Explain the objectives of handling merchandise inventory at the end of the accounting period and how they are achieved.	20			
7. Prepare a work sheet for a merchandising concern under one of two alternative methods.		8	2, 4, 5	
8. Prepare adjusting and closing entries for a merchandising concern.		7	2, 4, 5	
9. Prepare an income statement for a merchandising concern.		4, 6	2, 4, 5	

DIFFICULTY AND TIME CHART

A & B Problems	Difficulty	Time (in minutes)
1	easy	20
2	easy	45
3	easy	30
4	easy	45
5	medium	45
Case 6-1	difficult	30

TEN-MINUTE QUIZ

T F 1. Sales Returns and Allowances and Sales Discounts can be described as contra-revenue accounts.

T F 2. FOB shipping point means that the seller incurs the shipping costs.

T F 3. The primary difference between the work sheet for a merchandising company and that for a service company can be found in the Income Statement columns.

T F 4. Advertising is classified as an operating expense in a merchandiser's income statement.

T F 5. Under the periodic method, the Purchases account is used to accumulate all purchases of merchandise for resale.

T F 6. A company would be more likely to know the amount of inventory on hand at any time using the perpetual method rather than the periodic method.

T F 7. Ending inventory is included in the calculation of cost of goods available for sale.

T F 8. The terms 2/10, n/30 mean that a 2% discount is allowed on payments made more than 10 days but less than 30 days after the invoice date.

T F 9. Under the net method of recording purchases, a Discounts Lost account is recorded for payments outside the discount period.

T F 10. Purchases discounts is considered a selling expense.

_____ 11. Which of the following appears on both the income statement and the balance sheet?
a. Merchandise inventory
b. Freight in
c. Freight out
d. Dividend income
e. Purchases

_____ 12. When a customer takes advantage of a discount available, the journal entry of the merchandiser would include a
a. credit to Purchases Discounts.
b. credit to Accounts Receivable.
c. credit to Cash.
d. credit to Sales Discounts.
e. debit to Purchases Discounts.

_____ 13. A company that returns goods previously purchased on credit would
a. debit Accounts Payable and Purchases.
b. debit Sales and credit Accounts Receivable.
c. debit Cash and credit Accounts Payable.
d. debit Accounts Payable and credit Purchases Returns and Allowances.
e. debit Accounts Receivable and credit Purchases Returns and Allowances.

_____ 14. Which of the following is closed with a debit?
a. Sales Discounts
b. Freight Out
c. Purchases
d. Purchases Returns and Allowances
e. Freight In

_____ 15. Which of the following companies would <u>most</u> likely use a perpetual inventory system?
a. A grain company
b. A grocery store
c. A clothing store
d. A fur dealer
e. A discount department store

_____ 16. Assuming that net purchases was $250,000 during the year, and ending inventory was $4,000 less than the beginning inventory of $30,000, how much was cost of goods sold?
a. $224,000
b. $246,000
c. $254,000
d. $276,000
e. $280,000

_____ 17. A net income will result if gross margin exceeds
a. cost of goods sold.
b. operating expenses.
c. purchases.
d. cost of goods sold plus operating expenses.
e. cost of goods available for sale.

_____ 18. At the end of the accounting period, beginning merchandise inventory and ending merchandise inventory are
a. debited and credited, respectively.
b. credited and debited, respectively.
c. both debited.
d. both credited.

_____ 19. A sale on October 21 with terms of n/10 eom is due to be collected
by
a. October 31.
b. November 1.
c. November 10.
d. November 21.
e. November 30.

_____ 20. Which of the following is not considered in computing net purchases?
a. Purchases Returns and Allowances
b. Purchases Discounts
c. Purchases
d. Freight paid on purchased goods
e. Freight paid on goods shipped to customers

ANSWERS TO TEN-MINUTE QUIZ

<u>True-False</u>

1. T
2. F
3. T
4. T
5. T
6. T
7. F
8. F
9. T
10. F

<u>Multiple-Choice</u>

11. a
12. b
13. d
14. d
15. d
16. c
17. b
18. b
19. c
20. e

CHAPTER SEVEN

ACCOUNTING SYSTEMS AND SPECIAL-PURPOSE JOURNALS

CHAPTER OUTLINE

Accounting Systems Installation
Principles of Systems Design
    Cost-Benefit Principle
    Control Principle
    Compatibility Principle
    Flexibility Principle
Data Processing: Three Perspectives
Computer Data Processing
    Hardware
    Software
    Personnel
    Configuration
Manual Data Processing: Journals and Procedures
    Sales Journal
        Controlling Accounts and Subsidiary Ledgers
        Summary of the Sales Journal Procedure
        Sales Taxes
    Purchases Journal
    Cash Receipts Journal
    Cash Payments Journal
    General Journal
    Flexibility of Special-Purpose Journals
Chapter Review
    Review of Learning Objectives
    Review Problem: Purchases Journal
    Answer to Review Problem
Chapter Assignments
    Questions
    Classroom Exercises
    Interpreting Accounting Information: B. Dalton and Waldenbooks
    Problem Set A
    Problem Set B
    Financial Decision Case 7-1: Buy-Rite Foods Company

LEARNING OBJECTIVES:

RESOURCE MATERIALS AND LECTURE OUTLINES

OBJECTIVE 1:   Describe the phases of systems installation and the principles of
              systems design (pp. 227-231)

Summary Statement

Accounting systems gather data from all areas of the business enterprise, trans-
form them into useful information, and communicate the results to management.
The installation of an accounting system consists of <u>system investigation</u>,
<u>system design</u>, and <u>system implementation</u>.

In designing an accounting system, the systems designer must adhere to four
general principles of systems design, as follows:

a. The <u>cost/benefit principle</u> states that the benefits derived from the accounting system must outweigh its cost.

b. The <u>control principle</u> states that the accounting system must contain the
   safeguards necessary to meet internal control requirements.

c. The <u>compatibility principle</u> states that the accounting system must be work-
   able by the personnel and within the organizational framework.

d. The <u>flexibility principle</u> states that the accounting system should be able
   to accommodate changes (as in volume of transactions) in the business.

<u>Data processing</u> involves gathering accounting information, working with the in-
formation, and communicating results to decision makers. There are several
types of data processing systems, many of which will be described in this
chapter.

New Words and Terms

system investigation (p. 228)
system design (p. 228)
system implementation (p. 228)
cost-benefit principle (p. 228)
control principle (p. 229)
compatibility principle (p. 229)

flexibility principle (p. 229)
data processing (p. 230)

<u>Related Text Illustrations</u>

Figure 7-1 Data Processing from Three Perspectives (p. 230)

<u>Lecture Outline</u>

A. The installation of an accounting system consists of three phases:

1. System investigation -- Study an existing system or the need for a new system.

2. System design -- Must conform to the principles listed below:

a. Cost/benefit principle

b. Control principle

c. Compatability principle

d. Flexibility principle

3. System implementation

B. Data processing involves gathering accounting information, working with the information, and communicating the results.

OBJECTIVE 2: Describe the basic features of computer systems and their application to data processing (pp. 231-234)

<u>Summary Statement</u>

A <u>computer data processing</u> system is made up of four basic elements: (a) hardware, (b) software, (c) procedures, and (d) personnel.

Computer <u>hardware</u> consists of all the equipment needed for the operation of a computer data processing system. It basically includes input devices, processing and memory units, and output devices. Some input devices are optical scanners, card and tape readers, and console typewriters. Some output devices are printers, cathode ray tubes, and card punches. The computer program is executed by the <u>central processor</u>, which consists of an <u>arithmetic/logic unit</u>, a <u>control unit</u>, and <u>storage</u> (memory) <u>units</u>.

Computer <u>software</u> consists of programs, instructions, and routines that make use of the hardware possible. A computer <u>program</u> is a sequence of instructions to the computer, and is written in one of several computer languages.

The procedures for a computer system are all the steps taken from data origination to output.

The key personnel in a computer system are the <u>systems analyst</u> (who designs the data processing system), the <u>programmer</u> (who writes the programs), and the <u>computer operator</u> (who runs the computer).

<u>Batch processing</u> is the processing of one job at a time, whereas <u>on-line processing</u> allows several jobs to be processed at once by means of remote terminals and random access of information.

<u>New Words and Terms</u>

hardware (p. 231)
central processor (p. 231)
control unit (p. 231)
arithmetic/logic unit (p. 231)
storage units (p. 233)
secondary or auxiliary storage (p. 233)
programs (p. 233)
software (p. 233)
systems analyst (p. 234)
programmer (p. 234)
computer operator (p. 234)
batch processing (p. 234)
on-line processing (p. 234)

<u>Related Text Illustrations</u>

Figure 7-2 Hardware Components for a Computer Data Processing System (p. 232)
Figure 7-3 Mainframe Computer System (p. 233)

<u>Lecture Outline</u>

A. A computer data processing system consists of four elements:

    1. Hardware -- the equipment

    a. Input devices

    b. Processing- and memory units

    c. Output devices

  2. Software -- Programs, instructions, and routines

  3. Procedures -- All steps from data origination to output.

  4. Personnel

    a. Systems analyst -- Designer of the system

    b. Programmer -- Writes the programs

    c. Operator -- Runs the computer

B. Batch processing is the processing of one job at a time.

C. On-line processing allows several jobs to be processed at once.

D. A computerized system is useful for functions such as purchasing, inventory, payroll, and production scheduling.

OBJECTIVE 3: Explain the objectives and uses of special-purpose journals
            (p. 235)

<u>Summary Statement</u>

Companies using <u>manual data processing</u> (maintaining hand-written accounting records) initially record an entry in one or more journals. A company can record all of its transactions in the general journal only. However, companies with a large number of transactions also use <u>special-purpose journals</u> to save time, effort, and money.

Most business transactions fall into one of four types, and are recorded in one of four special-purpose journals, as follows:

a. Sales of merchandise on credit are recorded in the <u>sales journal</u>.

b. Purchases of merchandise on credit are recorded in the <u>purchases journal</u>.

c. Receipts of cash are recorded in the <u>cash receipts journal</u>.

d. Disbursements of cash are recorded in the <u>cash payments journal</u>.

<u>New Words and Terms</u>

manual data processing (p. 234)
special-purpose journal (p. 235)

<u>Related Text Illustrations</u>

Figure 7-4 Steps and Devices in a Manual Accounting System (p. 235)

<u>Lecture Outline</u>

A. Special-purpose journals save time, effort, and money.

   1. Sales journal -- Record the sale of merchandise on credit.

   2. Purchases journal -- Record the purchase of merchandise on credit.

   3. Cash receipts journal -- Record the collection of cash.

   4. Cash payments journal -- Record the disbursement of cash.

OBJECTIVE 4: Construct and use the following types of special-purpose journals:
              sales journal, purchases journal, cash receipts journal, cash pay-
              ments journal, and others as needed (pp. 236-249)

<u>Summary Statement</u>

The <u>sales journal</u> saves time because (a) each entry requires only one line;
(b) account names need not be written out, since frequently occurring accounts
are used as column headings; (c) an explanation is not needed; and (d) only
total sales for the month are posted to the sales account, not each individual
sale. The same time-saving principles apply to other special-purpose journals.

Transactions that cannot be recorded in a special-purpose journal, such as the
purchase of office equipment on credit (assuming a single-column purchases

journal), are recorded in the general journal. Closing entries and adjusting entries are also made in the general journal. Postings are made at the end of each day, and in the case of Accounts Receivable and Accounts Payable, postings are made to both the controlling account and the subsidiary account.

Special-purpose journals of businesses may differ slightly from those used in the textbook, because the types of transactions may vary. However, an understanding of the general concepts and mechanics of special-purpose journals makes the adaptation to a different system relatively easy.

New Words and Terms

sales journal (p. 236)
purchases journal (p. 240)
cash receipts journal (p. 242)
cash payments journal (p. 245)

Related Text Illustrations

*Figure 7-5   Sales Journal and Related Ledger Accounts (p. 236)
*Figure 7-6   Relationship of Sales Journal, General Ledger, and Accounts Receivable Ledger and the Posting Procedure (p. 238)
Figure 7-7   Schedule of Accounts Receivable (p. 239)
Figure 7-8   Section of a Sales Journal with a Column for Sales Taxes (p. 239)
Figure 7-9   Relationship of Single-Column Purchases Journal to the General Ledger and the Accounts Payable Ledger (p. 241)
Figure 7-10   A Multicolumn Purchases Journal (p. 242)
*Figure 7-11   Relationship of the Cash Receipts Journal to the General Ledger and the Accounts Receivable Ledger (p. 243)
*Figure 7-12   Cash Payments Journal (p. 246)
Figure 7-13   Transactions Recorded in the General Journal (p. 248)

Lecture Outline

A. Refer to objective #3 for an explanation of special journals.

B. A general journal is used for transactions that cannot be accommodated by any special journal.

1. Postings are made daily.

2. Any account with a subsidiary ledger (such as accounts receivable and accounts payable) receives a "double posting."

C. Analyze several transactions in terms of which journal to use.

D. Explain line-by-line entries into journals, as well as postings to ledgers (refer to text illustrations).

E. A schedule of accounts receivable should be prepared.

F. A schedule of accounts payable should be prepared.

OBJECTIVE 5: Explain the purposes and relationships of controlling accounts and subsidiary ledgers (pp. 237-238)

Summary Statement

Most companies that sell to customers on credit keep an accounts receivable record for each customer, thereby enabling the company to determine how much a given customer owes at any time. All customer accounts are filed alphabetically in the Accounts Receivable <u>subsidiary ledger</u>.

The general ledger, however, contains an Accounts Receivable <u>controlling account</u>, which records the same accounts receivable but without the customers' names. The controlling account keeps a running total of *all* accounts receivable, and should equal the sum of all the accounts in the accounts receivable subsidiary ledger.

Most companies also use an Accounts Payable controlling account and subsidiary ledger, which function much like the Accounts Receivable controlling account and subsidiary ledger.

New Words and Terms

subsidiary ledger (p. 237)
controlling or control account (p. 237)

Related Text Illustrations

*Figure 7-6 Relationship of Sales Journal, General Ledger, and Accounts Receivable Ledger and the Posting Procedure (p. 238)
See also Figure 7-5 and Figures 7-7 through 7-13

Lecture Outline

A. A controlling account (found in the general ledger) is supported by individual accounts in the related subsidiary ledger.

    1. Accounts Receivable -- Usually contains a controlling account and related subsidiary ledger.

    2. Accounts Payable -- Usually contains a controlling account and related subsidiary ledger.

B. The sum of the subsidiary ledger account balances should equal the balance in the related controlling account.

    1. In theory, they should always be equal.

    2. In practice, they are equal only at the end of the month.

Chapter Seven Accounting Systems and Special-Purpose Journals

Learning Objectives	Questions	Exercises	A & B Problems	Case
1. Describe the phases of systems installation and the principles of systems design.	1, 2, 3, 4	IAI		
2. Describe the basic features of computer systems and their application to data processing.	5, 6, 7, 8, 9			
3. Explain the objectives and uses of special-purpose journals.	10,11	1, 2		1
4. Construct and use the following types of special-purpose journals: sales journal, purchases journal, cash receipts journal, cash payments journal, and others as needed.	11, 13	3, 4, 5, 6	1, 2, 3, 4, 5	1
5. Explain the purposes and relationships of controlling accounts and subsidiary ledgers.	12, 14		3, 4, 5	1

DIFFICULTY AND TIME CHART

A & B Problems	Difficulty	Time (in minutes)
1	easy	25
2	easy	20
3	easy	15
4	medium	20
5	medium	30
Case 7-1	medium	30

TEN-MINUTE QUIZ

T F   1. The cash receipts journal should have a column listing the names of all the payees.

T F   2. Cash sales should be recorded in the sales journal.

T F   3. Purchases discounts would appear as a Debit column in the cash payments journal.

T F   4. A debit in a Subsidiary Accounts Payable account would probably have been posted from the cash payments journal.

T F   5. The column totals in the general journal should be posted at the end of the month.

T F   6. Closing entries should be recorded in the general journal.

T F   7. The total in the Schedule of Accounts Receivable should equal the balance in the Accounts Receivable controlling account.

T F   8. The total of an Other Account column should be posted at the end of the month.

T F   9. Controlling accounts are always found in the general journal.

T F   10. Each account in a subsidiary ledger will have an account number.

_____ 11. The principle of systems design that involves safeguard of assets and the reliability of data is the
       a. flexiblity principle.
       b. planning principle.
       c. cost/benefit principle.
       d. compatibility principle.
       e. control principle.

_____ 12. A Purchases Discount column would most likely appear in the
       a. single-column purchases journal.
       b. multicolumn purchases journal.
       c. cash payments journal.
       d. cash receipts journal.
       e. sales journal.

      109

_____ 13. The type of data processing in which remote terminals provide direct access to the computer is
a. on-line processing.
b. remote processing.
c. batch processing.
d. central processing.
e. sequential processing.

_____ 14. The total of a single-column purchases journal is posted in the general ledger as a
a. debit to Purchases and a credit to Cash.
b. debit to Purchases and a credit to Accounts Payable.
c. debit to Accounts Payable and a credit to Purchases.
d. debit to Cash and a credit to Purchases.
e. debit to Purchases and a credit to Accounts Receivable.

_____ 15. A sales return for credit would be recorded in the
a. purchases journal.
b. sales journal.
c. general journal.
d. cash receipts journal.
e. cash payments journal.

_____ 16. The person who writes the instructions for the computer is a
a. systems analyst.
b. programmer.
c. hardware analyst.
d. computer operator.
e. central processor.

_____ 17. The entries in the sales journal must be posted individually to the
a. Sales account.
b. Accounts Receivable controlling account.
c. Accounts Receivable subsidiary ledger.
d. Accounts Payable subsidiary ledger.
e. Accounts Payable controlling account.

_____ 18. Which of the following is an example of computer software?
a. Card reader
b. Storage unit
c. Central processor
d. Printer
e. Computer program

_____ 19. Accounts Receivable and Accounts Payable are posted daily to <u>both</u> the general and subsidiary ledgers when entered in the
a. cash receipts journal.
b. cash payments journal.
c. general journal.
d. purchases journal.
e. sales journal.

_____ 20. Where would a check mark not be found?
    a. General journal
    b. Cash payments journal
    c. Accounts Payable subsidiary ledger
    d. Cash receipts journal

ANSWERS TO TEN-MINUTE QUIZ

<u>True-False</u>			<u>Multiple-Choice</u>	
1.	F		11.	e
2.	F		12.	c
3.	F		13.	a
4.	T		14.	b
5.	F		15.	c
6.	T		16.	b
7.	T		17.	c
8.	F		18.	e
9.	F		19.	c
10.	F		20.	c

CHAPTER EIGHT

INTERNAL CONTROL AND MERCHANDISING TRANSACTIONS

CHAPTER OUTLINE

Internal Control: Basic Principles and Policies
    Internal Control Defined
    Attributes of Internal Control
            Separation of Duties
            Sound Accounting System
            Sound Personnel Policies
            Reliable Personnel
            Regular Internal Review
    Limitations of Internal Control
Internal Control over Merchandising Transactions
    Control of Cash Sales Receipts
            Control of Cash Receipts Received Through the Mail
            Control of Cash Sales Received over the Counter
            Cash Over and Short
    Control of Purchases and Cash Disbursements
Banking Transactions
    Bank Account
    Deposits
    Bank Statement
    Preparing a Bank Reconciliation
            Steps in Reconciling the Bank Balance
            Illustration of a Bank Reconciliation
            Adjusting the Records After Reconciliation
Petty Cash Procedures
    Establishing the Petty Cash Fund
    Making Disbursements from the Petty Cash Fund
    Reimbursing the Petty Cash Fund
The Voucher System
    Vouchers
    Voucher Checks
    Voucher Register
    Check Register
    Operation of a Voucher System
            Preparing the Voucher
            Recording the Voucher
            Paying the Voucher
            Posting the Voucher and Check Registers
            Summarizing Unpaid Vouchers

     113

LEARNING OBJECTIVES:

RESOURCE MATERIALS AND LECTURE OUTLINES

OBJECTIVE 1: Define internal accounting control and state its four objectives
              (pp. 266-267)

Summary Statement

A business establishes a system of internal control to (a) safeguard its assets,
(b) check the accuracy and reliability of its accounting data, (c) promote oper-
ational efficiency, and (d) encourage adherence to prescribed managerial policies. The first two functions, which are referred to as internal accounting
controls, may include a system of authorization and approval as well as the
separation of duties. The last two functions, which are referred to as internal
administrative controls, may include employee training programs, performance
reports, quality control systems, statistical studies, time and motion studies,
and safety campaigns.

New Words and Terms

internal control (p. 267)
internal accounting controls (p. 267)
internal administrative controls (p. 267)

Lecture Outline

A. Internal control consists of internal accounting controls and internal administrative controls.

B. Internal accounting controls protect assets and promote accuracy and reliability of the accounting records.

C. There are four objectives of internal accounting control:

   1. Encourage adherence to managerial policy.

2. Financial statements are prepared in conformity with GAAP, and assets are accounted for.

3. Permission is required for access to assets.

4. Recorded assets are compared with existing assets.

OBJECTIVE 2: State five attributes of an effective system of internal control
(p. 268)

<u>Summary Statement</u>

To be effective, a system of internal control should consist of (a) separation of duties, (b) a sound accounting system, (c) sound personnel policies, (d) reliable personnel, and (e) regular internal review. <u>Bonding</u> an employee (an example of good internal control) means insuring the company against theft by that individual.

<u>New Words and Terms</u>

bonding (p. 268)

<u>Lecture Outline</u>

A. Discuss the attributes of an effective system of internal control.

   1. Separation of duties

   2. Sound accounting policy

   3. Sound personnel policies

   4. Reliable personnel

   5. Regular internal review

OBJECTIVE 3: Describe the inherent limitations of internal control (p. 268)

Summary Statement

To be effective, a system of internal control must rely on the people who perform the duties assigned. Thus, the effectiveness of internal control is limited by the people involved. For example, human error, collusion, and changing conditions can all contribute to the weakening of a system of internal control.

Lecture Outline

A. At least three factors contribute to the weakening of a system of internal control.

   1. Human error

   2. Collusion

   3. Changing conditions

OBJECTIVE 4: Apply the attributes of internal control to the control of certain merchandising transactions (pp. 269-276)

Summary Statement

Accounting controls over merchandising transactions help prevent losses from theft or fraud, and help assure accurate records of cash receipts, cash disbursements, and cash balances. Administrative controls over merchandising transactions serve to assure payment of debts when due, to maintain a reasonable cash balance for emergencies, to earn a reasonable return on excess cash, and to maintain appropriate inventory levels.

There are several procedures that should be followed to achieve effective internal control over sales and the exchange of cash.

Cash received by mail should be handled by two or more employees. Cash received by sales over the counter should be controlled through the use of cash registers and prenumbered sales tickets. At the end of each day, Cash is debited for cash receipts, and Sales is credited for the amount on the cash register tape. If the two amounts do not agree, Cash Over and Short is debited when there is a shortage and credited when there is an overage.

All cash disbursements for purchases should be made by check. However, before employees disburse cash, they should obtain autorization in the form of certain

signed documents. The system of authorization and the documents used will differ among companies, but the most common documents are described below.

a. A <u>purchase requisition</u> is completed by a department requesting that the company purchase something for the department.

b. A <u>purchase order</u> is completed by the department responsible for the company's
purchasing activities, and it is sent to the vendor.

c. An <u>invoice</u> is the bill sent to the buyer from the vendor.

d. A <u>receiving report</u> is completed by the receiving department, and contains information about the quantity and condition of goods received.

e. A <u>check authorization</u> is a document showing that the purchase order, purchase
requisition, receiving report, and invoice are in agreement, and that payment
is therefore approved.

f. When payment is approved, a <u>check</u> is issued to the vendor for the amount of
the invoice, less the appropriate discount. Remittance advice should be attached to the check, describing the articles being paid for.

New Words and Terms

Cash Over or Short (p. 271)
purchase requisition (p. 272)
purchase order (p. 272)
invoice (p. 273)
receiving report (p. 273)
check authorization (p. 275)
check (p. 276)

Related Text Illustrations

*Figure 8-1   Internal Control for Purchasing and Paying for Goods and Services
             (p. 272)
Table 8-1   Internal Control Plan for Cash Disbursements (p. 273)
Figure 8-2   Purchase Requisition (p. 274)
Figure 8-3   Purchase Order (p. 274)
Figure 8-4   Invoice (p. 275)
Figure 8-5   Check Authorization (p. 275)
Figure 8-6   Check with Attached Remittance Advice (p. 276)

Lecture Outline

A. Accounting controls helps prevent theft, and promote accurate cash records.

B. Administrative controls minimize credit losses and maintain adequate cash
   and inventory levels.

C. Cash received by mail should be handled by two or more persons.

D. Cash received over the counter should be controlled with cash registers or prenumbered sales tickets.

E. Discuss the use of Cash Over & Short.

F. Discuss the following documents that should be used when making a purchase:

1. Purchase requisition

2. Purchase order

3. Invoice

4. Receiving report

5. Check authorization

6. Check

OBJECTIVE 5: Describe a bank account and prepare a bank reconciliation
              (pp. 276-282)

Summary Statement

When a company opens a bank account, the official designated to sign the checks must also sign a _signature card_. The bank keeps the signature card as a record of the company's authorized signature.

Upon receipt of a check, the vendor compares its amount with the related invoice and then deposits the check in the bank. The vendor should retain the _deposit ticket_, which lists the cash and currency deposited as proof of deposit.

If the bank has honored the check, it returns the canceled check with the buyer's monthly _bank statement_. The bank statement shows the bank balance at the beginning of the month, all additions and deductions during the month, and the balance at the end of the month.

A bank statement's end-of-month balance will rarely agree with the balance in the company's books for that date. Thus the accountant must prepare a _bank_

     119

reconciliation to account for this difference and to locate any errors made by the bank or the company. The bank reconciliation begins with the "balance per books" and "balance per bank statement" figures as of the bank statement date. Each figure is adjusted by certain additions and deductions, resulting in two "adjusted cash balance" figures, which should agree. The "balance per books" figure is adjusted by information that the bank knew at the bank statement date but the company did not. The "balance per bank statement" figure is adjusted by information that the company knew at the bank statement date but the bank did not. Examples of adjustments follow.

a. Outstanding checks are a deduction from the balance per bank statement.

b. Deposits in transit are an addition to the balance per bank statement.

c. Service charges by the bank appear on the bank statement, and are a deduction from the balance per books.

d. A customer's NSF (not sufficient funds) check is deducted from the balance per books.

e. Miscellaneous charges are deducted from the balance per books. Miscellaneous credits are added to the balance per books.

f. Interest earned on a checking account is added to the balance per books.

After the bank reconciliation has been prepared, adjusting entries must be made so that the accounting records will reflect the new information supplied by the bank statement.

New Words and Terms

signature card (p. 277)
deposit ticket (p. 277)
bank statement (p. 277)
bank reconciliation (p. 277)

Related Text Illustrations

Figure 8-7 Deposit Ticket (p. 278)
Figure 8-8 Bank Statement (p. 279)
Figure 8-9 Bank Reconciliation (p. 281)

Lecture Outline

A. A bank reconciliation accounts for the difference between a company's records and the bank's.

   1. Outstanding checks are deducted from the balance per bank statement.

2. Deposits in transit are added to the balance per bank statement.

3. Service charges are deducted from the balance per books.

4. An NSF check is deducted from the balance per books.

5. Collection of a note by the bank is added to the balance per books.

6. An error may be placed anywhere in the bank reconciliation, depending on the nature of the error.

7. Interest earned is added to the balance per books.

B. The "adjusted cash balance" figures should be accurate and agree.

C. Formal adjusting entries must be prepared from information on the "book" side.

OBJECTIVE 6: Describe and record the related entries for a simple petty cash system (pp. 283-284)

Summary Statement

Although it is good practice for a company to pay for everything by check, an exception should be made for items of small value. Thus for items such as postage, donations, and taxi fare, many firms use a petty cash fund. One of the best ways of operating a petty cash fund is through the imprest system. Under this system, when the fund is established, Petty Cash is debited, and Cash is credited. When payment is made from the fund, the fund's custodian should prepare a petty cash voucher showing the date, amount, and purpose of the expenditure. The petty cash fund is replenished periodically and at the end of the accounting period. In each case, all of the expenses since the last replenishment are debited, and Cash is credited. Discrepancies are recorded as Cash Over and Short.

New Words and Terms

petty cash fund (p. 283)
imprest system (p. 283)
petty cash voucher (p. 283)

<u>Related Text Illustrations</u>

Figure 8-10 Petty Cash Voucher (p. 283)

<u>Lecture Outline</u>

A. Discuss the mechanics of a petty cash fund, as well as the internal control
   that should be exercised over it.

B. Journalize the establishment of a petty cash fund.

C. Journalize the replenishment of a petty cash fund, using Cash Over and Short,
   if necessary.

OBJECTIVE 7: Describe the components of a voucher system (pp. 284-288)

<u>Summary Statement</u>

The objective of a voucher system is to maintain maximum control over cash expenditures. Accordingly, each transaction requires the written approval of key
individuals, thus providing an audit trail. A voucher system consists of (a)
written authorizations called vouchers, (b) the form of payment called a voucher
check, (c) a special journal to record the vouchers, called the voucher register, and (d) a special journal to record the voucher checks, called the check
register.

<u>New Words and Terms</u>

voucher system (p. 284)
voucher (p. 285)
audit trail (p. 285)
voucher check (p. 285)
voucher register (p. 285)
check register (p. 288)

<u>Related Text Illustrations</u>

Figure 8-11 Front and Back of a Typical Voucher Form (pp. 286-287)
Figure 8-12 Voucher Register (pp. 286-287)
Figure 8-13 Check Register (p. 288)

Lecture Outline

A. A voucher system maintains maximum control over cash expenditures.

B. There are four components to a voucher system.

   1. Voucher

   2. Voucher check

   3. Voucher register

   4. Check register

OBJECTIVE 8: State and perform the five steps in operating a voucher system
(pp. 288-290)

Summary Statement

There are five steps in the operation of a voucher system, as follows:

a. Preparing the <u>voucher</u> (written authorization for an expenditure) for each liability incurred.

b. Recording the voucher in the <u>voucher register</u>.

c. Paying the voucher as it comes up in the unpaid voucher file by drawing either a check or a <u>voucher check</u> and recording it in the <u>check register</u>.

d. Posting the voucher and check registers. This process is very similar to posting any other special journals, except that Vouchers Payable takes the place of Accounts Payable.

e. Preparing a schedule of unpaid vouchers from the unpaid voucher file.

Related Text Illustrations

Figure 8-14 Schedule of Unpaid Vouchers (p. 290)

Lecture Outline

A. There are five steps in the operation of a voucher system.

    1. Prepare the voucher.

    2. Record the voucher in the voucher register.

    3. Pay the voucher and record it in the check register.

    4. Post the voucher register and check register.

    5. Prepare a schedule of unpaid vouchers.

Chapter Eight   Internal Control and Merchandising Transactions

Learning Objectives	Questions	Exercises	A & B Problems	Case
1. Define internal accounting control and state its four objectives.	1, 7			
2. State five attributes of an effective system of internal control.	2, 3, 9, 12			
3. Describe the inherent limitations of internal control.	9			
4. Apply the attributes of internal control to the control of certain merchandising transactions.	4, 5, 6, 8, 13	7, 8 IAI	4	1
5. Describe a bank account and prepare a bank reconciliation.	10, 11, 13	2, 3, 4	2, 3	
6. Describe and record the related entries for a simple petty cash system.	13, 14, 15, 16, 17	1	1	
7. Describe the components of a voucher system.	18, 19, 20, 21			
8. State and perform the five steps in operating a voucher system.	22	5, 6	5, 6	

DIFFICULTY AND TIME CHART

A & B Problems	Difficulty	Time (in minutes)
1	easy	10
2	easy	15
3	medium	25
4	difficult	20
5	medium	40
6	medium	40
Case 8-1	medium	60

TEN-MINUTE QUIZ

T F 1. When a petty cash fund is replenished, the journal entry requires a credit to Cash.

T F 2. An outstanding check that was also outstanding the previous month should not be included in the reconciliation of the bank statement.

T F 3. An effective system of internal control will centralize functions in the hands of a single capable individual.

T F 4. In a good system of internal control, the treasurer should prepare the check authorization and issue the checks.

T F 5. The voucher register is the book of original entry when a company uses the voucher system.

T F 6. In addition to keeping the records of a purchase transaction, the accounting department should also prepare and mail checks in payment.

T F 7. A company's signature card must be kept at the bank as proof of authorized signatures.

T F 8. Bonding an employee means insuring the company against theft by that employee.

T F 9. In a bank reconciliation, collection of a note receivable by the bank would be added to the balance per bank statement.

T F 10. The document prepared by a department asking the company to purchase something is called a purchase order.

_____ 11. In a voucher system, the equivalent to a cash payments journal is the
a. voucher check.
b. voucher register.
c. check register.
d. schedule of unpaid vouchers.
e. audit trail.

    12. Which of the following is involved in the last step in the operation of a voucher system?
- a. Voucher register
- b. Schedule of unpaid vouchers
- c. Voucher check
- d. Check register
- e. Posting

    13. The check register would not include
- a. a Debit column for Purchases.
- b. the name of the payee.
- c. a Debit column for Vouchers Payable.
- d. a credit for Cash.
- e. the check number.

    14. A $100 petty cash fund has cash of $15 and valid receipts for $82. The journal entry upon replenishment would include a
- a. credit to Cash for $82.
- b. credit to Petty Cash for $85.
- c. debit to Cash Over or Short for $3.
- d. debit to Cash for $82.
- e. credit to Cash Over or Short for $3.

    15. Which of the following is not an internal control procedure for cash?
- a. The functions of record keeping and keeping custody of cash should be combined.
- b. All cash disbursements should be made by check.
- c. Cash on hand should be kept to a minimum.
- d. Cash registers should be used.
- e. The number of persons who have access to cash should be limited.

    16. Each of the following is an attribute of internal control except
- a. separation of duties.
- b. sound personnel policies.
- c. a sound accounting system.
- d. a sound marketing plan.
- e. regular internal review.

    17. Which of the following documents would be sent to the treasurer?
- a. Invoice
- b. Purchase order
- c. Bank statement
- d. Check authorization
- e. Deposit ticket

    18. Which of the following items on a bank reconciliation would require an adjusting entry on the company's books?
- a. Outstanding checks
- b. Deposit in transit
- c. Bank error on the bank statement
- d. Cash on hand
- e. Bank service charge

_____ 19. A company issues a check for $56 but records it as $65. On the bank
reconciliation, the $9 should be
   a. added to the balance per books.
   b. added to the balance per bank statement.
   c. deducted from the balance per books.
   d. deducted from the balance per bank statement.

_____ 20. Which of the following is not a primary concern of internal accounting control?
   a. Safeguarding assets
   b. Accuracy of the accounting records
   c. Fairness of the financial statements
   d. Efficiency of company operations
   e. Adherence of transactions to policy

ANSWERS TO TEN-MINUTE QUIZ

True-False			Multiple-Choice	
1.	T		11.	c
2.	F		12.	b
3.	F		13.	a
4.	F		14.	c
5.	T		15.	a
6.	F		16.	d
7.	T		17.	d
8.	T		18.	e
9.	F		19.	a
10.	F		20.	c

CHAPTER NINE

GENERAL-PURPOSE EXTERNAL FINANCIAL STATEMENTS

CHAPTER OUTLINE

Objectives of Financial Information
Qualitative Characteristics of Accounting Information
    Understandability
    The Usefulness of Accounting Information
        Relevance
        Reliability
Conventions to Aid Interpretation of Financial Information
    Comparability and Consistency
    Materiality
    Conservatism
    Full Disclosure
    Cost-Benefit
Classified Balance Sheet
    Assets
        Current Assets
        Investments
        Property, Plant, and Equipment
        Intangible Assets
    Liabilities
        Current Liabilities
        Long-Term Liabilities
    Owner's Equity
        Sole Proprietorship
        Partnership
        Corporation
Forms of the Income Statement
Other Financial Statements
Chart of Accounts
Using Classified Financial Statements
    Evaluation of Liquidity
        Working Capital
        Current Ratio
    Evaluation of Profitability
        Profit Margin
        Return on Assets
        Debt to Equity
        Return on Equity

LEARNING OBJECTIVES:

RESOURCE MATERIALS AND LECTURE OUTLINES

OBJECTIVE 1: State the objectives of financial reporting (pp. 308-309)

Summary Statement

Financial reporting should fulfill three objectives. It should (a) provide information that is useful in investment and credit decisions; (b) provide information about the timing of cash flows; and (c) provide information about enterprise resources, claims to those resources, and changes in them. General-purpose external financial statements are the principal means of communicating financial information to interested parties, and consist of the balance sheet, income statement, statement of owner's equity, and statement of changes in financial position.

New Words and Terms

general-purpose external financial statements (p. 309)

Lecture Outline

A. Financial reporting should fulfill three objectives:

1. Provide useful information for investment and credit decisions.

2. Provide information about the timing of cash flows.

3. Provide information about enterprise resources.

B. General-purpose external financial statements consist of the balance sheet, income statement, statement of owner's equity, and statement of changes in financial position.

OBJECTIVE 2: State the qualitative characteristics of accounting information
and describe their interrelationships (pp. 310-311)

Summary Statement

Accounting attempts to provide decision makers with information that meets the
following qualitative characteristics or standards: relevance, reliability,
usefulness, understandability, cost/benefit, comparability, consistency, materiality, conservatism, and full disclosure.

a. Relevance encompasses the standards of predictive value, feedback value, and
timeliness; it means that the information is capable of influencing the
decision maker.

b. Reliability encompasses the standards of representational faithfulness, verifiability, and neutrality, and means that accounting information should accurately reflect what it is meant to represent.

c. Usefulness encompasses the qualitative characteristics of relevance and
reliability and means that accounting information is helpful to the decision
maker.

d. Understandability refers to the ease of interpretation by the decision maker.

New Words and Terms

understandability (p. 310)
qualitative characteristics (p. 310)
relevance (p. 311)
predictive value (p. 311)
feedback value (p. 311)
timeliness (p. 311)
reliability (p. 311)
representational faithfulness (p. 311)
verifiability (p. 311)
neutrality (p. 311)

Related Text Illustrations

*Figure 9-1 The Qualitative Characteristics of Accounting Information (p. 311)

Lecture Outline

A. Accounting information should meet the following qualitative characteristics:

   1. Relevance -- Encompasses predictive value, feedback value, and timeliness

2. Reliability -- Encompasses representational faithfulness, verifiability, and neutrality.

3. Usefulness

4. Understandability

OBJECTIVE 3:   Define and describe the use of the conventions of comparability and consistency, materiality, conservatism, full disclosure, and cost-benefit (pp. 312-314)

Summary Statement

The cost/benefit convention states that the cost of providing additional accounting information should not exceed the benefits derived from it.

Comparability means enabling the decision maker to make comparisons about the same company over two or more accounting periods, or among different companies for the same accounting period.

The consistency convention states that a particular accounting procedure, once adopted, should not normally be changed from period to period. However, if a company does change a procedure, it must disclose the dollar effect on the statements as well as justification for the change.

The materiality convention states that an item should be disclosed separately or treated specially if knowledge of it would probably influence the user's decision.

The conservatism convention states that an accountant who has a choice of acceptable accounting procedures should choose the one that would be the least likely to overstate assets and income. Applying the lower-of-cost-or-market rule to inventory valuation is an example of conservatism.

The full disclosure convention states that financial statements and their accompanying footnotes should contain all relevant information.

New Words and Terms

comparability (p. 312)
consistency (p. 312)
materiality (p. 313)
conservatism (p. 313)
full disclosure (p. 313)

<u>Lecture Outline</u>

A. The following conventions help interpret the qualitative characteristics discussed in objective 2:

   1. Cost/benefit

   2. Comparability and consistency

   3. Materiality

   4. Conservatism

   5. Full disclosure

OBJECTIVE 4:   Identify and describe the basic components of a classified
               balance sheet (pp. 315-319)

<u>Summary Statement</u>

<u>Classified financial statements</u> divide assets, liabilities, owner's equity,
revenues, and expenses into subcategories to provide more useful information to
the reader.

On a classified balance sheet, assets are usually divided into four categories:
(a) current assets; (b) investments; (c) property, plant, and equipment; and
(d) intangible assets. (Sometimes another category called other assets is
added for miscellaneous items.) These categories are usually listed in declining order of liquidity, the ease with which an asset can be converted into cash.

<u>Current Assets</u> comprise cash and assets that are expected to be converted into
cash or used up within the normal operating cycle of the company or one year,
whichever is longer (hereafter called the current period).

a. The normal operating cycle of a company is the average time span between the
   purchase of inventory and the ultimate cash collection after the sale of that
   inventory.

b. Cash, short-term investments, accounts receivable, notes receivable, prepaid
   expenses, supplies, and inventory are current assets.

<u>Investments</u> include stocks and bonds held for long-term investment, land held
for future use, plant and equipment not used in the business, special funds,
and a controlling interest in another company.

<u>Property</u>, <u>plant</u>, and <u>equipment</u> comprise land, buildings, delivery equipment, machinery, and office equipment. All except land are subject to depreciation.

<u>Intangible assets</u> have no physical substance, and represent certain long-lived rights or privileges. Examples are patents, copyrights, goodwill, franchises, and trademarks.

The liabilities of a classified balance sheet are usually divided into current and long-term liabilities.

a. <u>Current liabilities</u> are debts for which payment (or performance) is due in the current period, and are paid from current assets or by incurring new short-term liabilities. Examples are notes payable, accounts payable, taxes payable, and customer advances (unearned revenues).

b. <u>Long-term liabilities</u> comprise debts due beyond the current period and any debt payable from noncurrent assets. Examples are mortgage payable, long-term notes payable, bonds payable, employee pension obligations, and long-term leases.

The owner's equity section of a classified balance sheet is called owner's equity, partners' equity, or stockholders' equity depending on whether it refers to a sole proprietorship, partnership, or a corporation.

In a sole proprietorship or partnership, the owner's equity section provides the name of the owner or owners, each followed by the word *capital* and the dollar amount of investment as of the balance sheet date.

In a corporation, the stockholders' equity section consists of contributed capital (also called paid-in capital) and retained earnings.

a. <u>Contributed capital</u> represents the amount invested by the stockholders, and is further divided into legal capital (called face or par value) and contributed capital in excess of legal capital.

b. <u>Retained earnings</u> reflect the earnings record of the company since its inception. Dividends (assets distributed to stockholders) reduce the Retained Earnings account balance, as do net losses.

<u>New Words and Terms</u>

classified financial statements (p. 315)
current assets (p. 315)
investments (p. 317)
property, plant, and equipment (p. 317)
intangible assets (p. 317)
current liabilities (p. 318)
long-term liabilities (p. 318)
retained earnings (p. 319)

<u>Related Text Illustrations</u>

*Figure 9-2 Classified Balance Sheet for Shafer Auto Parts Company (p. 316)

Lecture Outline

A. A classified balance sheet divides assets, liabilities, and stockholders'
   equity into subcategories to facilitate decision-making.

B. Assets (listed in declining order of liquidity)

   1. Current assets. Discuss the concept of normal operating cycle.

   2. Long-term investments

   3. Property, plant, and equipment

   4. Intangible assets

C. Liabilities

   1. Current liabilities

   2. Long-term liabilities

D. Stockholders' equity (for a corporation only)

   1. Contributed capital

   2. Retained earnings

OBJECTIVE 5: Define comprehensive income and distinguish between the multistep
              and single-step types of classified income statements (pp. 319-
              323)

Summary Statement

The income statement measures comprehensive income, or the change in the
owner's equity of a business, exclusive of investments and withdrawals. A condensed income statement, which contains the statement's major categories with
little or no detail, may be presented in either multistep or single-step form.

a. The _multistep form_ is the more detailed of the two, containing several subtractions and subtotals; it has separate sections for cost of goods sold, operating expenses, and _other_ (nonoperating) _revenues and expenses_. One important subtotal is _income from operations_, which equals gross margin from sales minus operating expenses.

b. In the _single-step form_, the revenues section lists all revenues including other income, and the operating costs section lists all expenses including other expenses; the difference is labeled net income or net loss.

New Words and Terms

comprehensive income (p. 319)
income from operations (p. 320)
other revenues and expenses (p. 320)
condensed financial statements (p. 320)
multistep form (p. 320)
single-step form (p. 320)

Related Text Illustrations

*Figure 9-3   Income Statement for Shafer Auto Parts Company (p. 321)
*Figure 9-4   Condensed Multistep Income Statement for Shafer Auto Parts Company (p. 322)
 Figure 9-5   Condensed Single-Step Income Statement for Shafer Auto Parts Company (p. 322)
 Figure 9-6   Statement of Owner's Equity for Shafer Auto Parts Company (p. 323)

Lecture Outline

A. Explain how the income statement measures comprehensive income.

B. There are two condensed income statement forms:

1. Multistep form -- Contains several subtotals, including gross margin from sales and income from operations.

2. Single-step form -- Is a simple deduction of all expenses from all revenues.

OBJECTIVE 6: Relate a chart of accounts to classified financial statements
             (pp. 323-324)

<u>Summary Statement</u>

Ledger accounts are arranged in the order of their appearance in the financial
statements, with balance sheet accounts preceding income statement accounts.
The <u>chart of accounts</u> is a systematic numbering scheme for identifying the
accounts.

<u>New Words and Terms</u>

chart of accounts (p. 323)

<u>Related Text Illustrations</u>

Table 9-1 Shafer Auto Parts Company Chart of Accounts (p. 324)

<u>Lecture Outline</u>

A. Ledger accounts are listed in order of their appearance in the financial
   statements.

B. A chart of accounts is a numbering scheme for identifying the accounts.

OBJECTIVE 7: Use classified financial statements for the simple evaluation of
             liquidity and profitability (pp. 324-327)

<u>Summary Statement</u>

Classified financial statements help the reader evaluate liquidity and profitability.

<u>Liquidity</u> measures a company's ability to pay its bills when they are due and
to provide for unanticipated needs for cash. Two measures of liquidity are
working capital and the current ratio.

a. <u>Working capital</u> equals current assets minus current liabilities, thereby
   computing the current asset amount remaining if all the current debts were
   paid.

b. The <u>current ratio</u> equals current assets divided by current liabilities. A
   current ratio of 1:1, for example, shows that current assets are barely
   enough to settle current liabilities; a 3:1 current ratio would be considered more satisfactory.

<u>Profitability</u> measures more than just a company's net income, and such measurements must be compared with industry averages and past performance in order to draw conclusions. Four measures of profitability are the profit margin, return on assets, capital structure, and return on owner investment.

a. The <u>profit margin</u> equals net income divided by sales. A 12.5 percent profit margin, for example, means that 12½¢ has been earned on each dollar of sales.

b. <u>Return on assets</u> equals net income divided by average total assets, thereby showing how efficiently the company is using its assets.

c. The <u>debt to equity ratio</u> measures the proportion of a business financed by creditors relative to the proportion financed by owners. It equals total liabilities divided by owner's equity. A debt to equity ratio of 1.0 indicates equal financing by creditors and owners.

d. <u>Return on equity</u> shows what percentage was earned on the owner's investment. It equals net income divided by average owner's equity.

<u>New Words and Terms</u>

liquidity (p. 325)
working capital (p. 325)
current ratio (p. 325)
profitability (p. 325)
profit margin (p. 326)
return on assets (p. 326)
debt to equity (p. 326)
return on equity (p. 327)

<u>Lecture Outline</u>

A. Liquidity measures a company's ability to pay its bills when they fall due.

   1. Working capital = current assets minus current liabilities

   2. Current ratio = current assets divided by current liabilities

B. Profitability may be measured several ways:

   1. Profit margin = net income divided by sales

   2. Return on assets = net income divided by average total assets

   3. Debt to equity ratio = total liabilities divided by owner's equity

4. Return on equity = net income divided by average owner's equity

OBJECTIVE 8:   Identify the major components of a corporate annual report
(pp. 327-337)

<u>Summary Statement</u>

Financial statements of corporations are usually complicated and contain a number of features not found in a sole proprietorship's or partnership's statements. Published statements appear in the company's <u>annual report</u>, a publication distributed to stockholders annually and filled with nonfinancial information as well.

A company's financial statements of consecutive periods presented side by side for comparison are called <u>comparative financial statements</u>. <u>Consolidated</u> financial statements are the combined statements of a company and its controlled subsidiaries (chapter 20 explains consolidations in more detail).

The income statement of a corporation should disclose <u>provision for income taxes</u> (<u>income tax expense</u>) separately from the other expenses. Sole proprietorships and partnerships are not taxable units.

<u>Earnings per common share</u> (<u>net income per share</u>) equals net income divided by the number of shares of common stock; it usually appears below net income in the income statement and is a measure of the company's profitability.

A <u>summary of significant accounting policies</u> discloses the generally accepted accounting principles used in preparing the statements, and usually follows the last financial statement.

A section called <u>notes to the financial statements</u> is usually needed to help the reader interpret some of the complex financial statement items.

Corporations are frequently required to issue <u>interim financial statements</u>, consisting of financial information covering less than a year (for example, quarterly).

The <u>accountant's report</u> is issued by an independent auditor. It conveys to third parties that the financial statements were examined in accordance with generally accepted auditing standards (<u>scope section</u>), and expresses the auditor's opinion on how fairly the financial statements reflect the company's financial condition (<u>opinion section</u>).

<u>New Words and Terms</u>

annual report (p. 328)
consolidated (p. 328)
comparative financial statements (p. 329)
provision for income taxes (p. 329)

income tax expense (p. 329)
earnings per common share (p. 329)
net income per share (p. 329)
notes to the financial statements (p. 333)
summary of significant accounting policies (p. 334)
interim financial statements (p. 334)
accountants' report (p. 336)
scope section (p. 337)
opinion section (p. 337)

Related Text Illustrations

Lecture Outline

A. Formal financial statements appear in an annual report, usually in comparative form.

B. Consolidated financial statements are combined statements of affiliated
   companies.

C. A corporate income statement should disclose income tax expense separately.

D. Earnings per share is a measure of profitability, and should appear below
   net income.

E. A summary of significant accounting policies should accompany the financial
   statements.

F. Notes to the financial statements interpret portions of the financial statements.

G. The accountant's report accompanies the financial statements, and is issued
   by an independent auditor.

   1. The scope section describes the extent of the examination.

   2. The opinion section expresses the fairness of presentation of the finan-
      cial statements.

H. Corporations frequently issue interim financial statements to cover less than
   a year.

Chapter Nine   General-Purpose External Financial Statements

Learning Objectives	Questions	Exercises	A & B Problems	Case
1. State the objectives of financial reporting.	1, 4			
2. State the qualitative characteristics of accounting information and describe their interrelationships.	2			
3. Define and describe the use of the conventions of comparability and consistency, materiality, conservatism, full disclosure, and cost-benefit.	3	6	1	
4. Identify and describe the basic components of a classified balance sheet.	5, 6, 7, 8, 9, 10, 11, 12	1, 4	3, 6, 7	
5. Define comprehensive income and distinguish between the multistep and single-step types of classified income statements.	13, 14	2, 3	2, 5, 6, 7	
6. Relate a chart of accounts to classified financial statements.	15			
7. Use classified financial statements for the simple evaluation of liquidity and profitability.	16, 17, 18, 19, 20	5	4, 6, 7	1
8. Identify the major components of a corporate annual report.	21, 22, 23, 24	IAI		

145

DIFFICULTY AND TIME CHART

A & B Problems	Difficulty	Time (in minutes)
1	easy	20
2	easy	20
3	easy	25
4	easy	20
5	easy	15
6	medium	25
7	medium	30
Case 9-1	difficult	30

TEN-MINUTE QUIZ

T F   1. Verifiability means that accounting information can be confirmed or duplicated by independent parties.

T F   2. An advantage of the single-step income statement is that it is less complex than the multistep form.

T F   3. It is possible for an asset to be a current asset even though the expected realization of that asset into cash is to be longer than one year.

T F   4. The main difference between property, plant, and equipment and intangible assets is the length of the asset's life.

T F   5. Return on assets, because it takes into account the assets invested in the business, is a better measure of profitability than is profit margin.

T F   6. A single-step income statement will result in a different net income than would a multistep income statement.

T F   7. The opinion section of the accountants' report states which financial statements were examined.

T F   8. The purpose of the notes to the financial statements is to correct any errors made in the statements presented.

T F   9. Interim financial statements cover less than a year.

T F   10. A multistep income statement will show other (nonoperating) revenues and expenses separately, whereas a single-step income statement will not.

_____   11. The normal operating cycle helps define
         a. intangible assets.
         b. property, plant, and equipment.
         c. earnings per share.
         d. contributed capital.
         e. current assets.

_____ 12. One might ascertain the inventory and depreciation methods employed
by referring to the
a. accountants' report.
b. comparative financial statements.
c. summary of significant accounting policies.
d. chart of accounts.
e. consolidated statement of retained earnings.

_____ 13. Which of the following is not classified as a current asset?
a. Office supplies
b. Short-term investments
c. Prepaid rent
d. Inventory that will require 18 months to complete
e. Special fund to retire long-term bonds

_____ 14. Concealing information from the user of financial statements most
closely violates the standard or concept of
a. full disclosure.
b. representational faithfulness.
c. timeliness.
d. comparability.
e. verifiability.

_____ 15. A company would properly classify land held for a planned manufacturing facility as
a. a current asset.
b. an intangible asset.
c. property, plant, and equipment.
d. a long-term investment.
e. It should not appear on the balance sheet because it is not
presently being used.

_____ 16. Which of the following is properly classified as an intangible
asset?
a. Accounts Receivable
b. Accumulated Depreciation
c. Land held for resale
d. Oil wells
e. Franchises

_____ 17. Retained earnings
a. represents a cash account used to pay dividends.
b. generally represents earnings since inception, less dividends
paid.
c. exists for a sole proprietorship, partnership, and a corporation.
d. represents investments by the company's owners.
e. appears in the intangible assets section of the balance sheet.

_____ 18. Which of the following is a measure of liquidity?
a. Working capital
b. Profit margin
c. Return on assets
d. Debt to equity ratio
e. Return on equity

_____ 19. The accountants' report is largely for the benefit of
    a. investors and creditors.
    b. the Internal Revenue Service.
    c. the company's management.
    d. the Financial Accounting Standards Board.
    e. the Securities and Exchange Commission.

_____ 20. Which of the following appears in different sections of the income
        statement when prepared on a single-step and multistep basis?
    a. Dividend income
    b. Freight in
    c. Office salaries
    d. Purchases
    e. Sales

ANSWERS TO TEN-MINUTE QUIZ

<u>True-False</u>

1. T
2. T
3. T
4. F
5. T
6. F
7. F
8. F
9. T
10. T

<u>Multiple-Choice</u>

11. e
12. c
13. e
14. a
15. d
16. e
17. b
18. a
19. a
20. a

CHAPTER TEN

SHORT-TERM LIQUID ASSETS

CHAPTER OUTLINE

Accounting for Cash and Short-Term Investments
Accounting for Accounts Receivable
    Credit Policies and Uncollectible Accounts
    Matching Losses on Uncollectible Accounts with Sales
    Allowance for Uncollectible Accounts
    Estimating Uncollectible Accounts Expense
        Percentage of Net Sales Method
        Accounts Receivable Aging Method
        Comparison of the Two Methods
    Writing Off an Uncollectible Account
        Why Accounts Written Off Will Differ from Estimates
        Recovery of Accounts Receivable Written Off
    Direct Charge-off Method
    Credit Balances in Accounts Receivable
    Sales to and Purchases from the Same Firm
    Installment Accounts Receivable
    Credit Card Sales
    Other Accounts Receivable
Accounting for Notes Receivable
    Computations Associated with Promissory Notes
        Maturity Date
        Duration of Note
        Interest and Interest Rate
        Maturity Value
        Discount
        Proceeds from Discounting
    Illustrative Accounting Entries
        Receipt of a Note
        Collection of a Note
        Recording a Dishonored Note
        Discounting a Note
        Recording Adjusting Entries
Chapter Review
    Review of Learning Objectives
    Review Problem: Entries for Uncollectible Accounts Expense and
                     Notes Receivable Transactions
    Answer to Review Problem

Chapter Assignments
    Questions   .
    Classroom Exercises
    Interpreting Accounting Information: Chrysler Corporation
    Problem Set A
    Problem Set B
    Financial Decision Case 10-1: Elliot Electronics, Inc.

LEARNING OBJECTIVES:

RESOURCE MATERIALS AND LECTURE OUTLINES

OBJECTIVE 1: Describe accounting for cash and short-term investments
(pp. 358-361)

Summary Statement

Short-term liquid assets consist of cash, short-term investments, accounts receivable, and notes receivable.

Cash consists of coin and currency on hand, checks and money orders, and bank deposits. A company's cash account may include a compensating balance, which is a minimum amount required by the bank to remain in the bank account.

Companies frequently have excess cash on hand for short periods of time. To put this idle cash to good use, most companies purchase short-term investments (also called marketable securities).

a. Upon purchase, Short-term Investments is debited and Cash credited. When income on the investment is received, Cash is debited and Dividend Income or Interest Income is credited, depending on whether the investment consists of equity securities (such as stock) or debt securities (such as bonds). Upon the sale of a short-term investment, Cash is debited, Short-term Investments is credited, and a loss or gain is debited or credited, respectively, for any difference between original purchase price and sale price.

b. On the balance sheet, short-term investments in equity securities are presented at the lower-of-cost-or-market. This presentation is justified by the conservatism convention, which requires immediate recognition of some potential losses, but of no potential gains. Short-term investments in debt securities are presented on the balance sheet at cost, unless the value of the securities has been permanently impaired.

New Words and Terms

short-term liquid assets (p. 358)
compensating balance (p. 358)
short-term investments (p. 359)
marketable securities (p. 359)
accounts receivable (p. 361)

trade credit (p. 361)

<u>Lecture Outline</u>

A. Short-term liquid assets consist of cash, short-term investments, accounts receivable, and notes receivable.

B. Cash includes coin, currency, checks, money orders, and bank deposits.

C. Discuss the significance of a compensating balance.

D. Short-term investments are usually purchased with temporarily idle cash.

E. Journalize the purchase of short-term investments.

F. Journalize the receipt of dividends.

G. Journalize the sale of short-term investments, illustrating the possibility of a gain or a loss.

H. Illustrate the balance sheet presentation of short-term investments in equity securities, explaining the lower-of-cost-or-market convention.

OBJECTIVE 2: Explain why estimated losses from uncollectible accounts are important to income determination (pp. 361-364)

<u>Summary Statement</u>

<u>Accounts receivable</u> are classified as current assets and represent payment due from credit customers.

Wholesalers and retailers usually allow customers to pay for merchandise over a period of time (that is, they extend credit) because the customer cannot or will not make full payment immediately. This type of credit, often called <u>trade credit</u>, makes expensive items affordable and increases sales for the merchant. Most companies that sell on credit have credit departments, whose responsibility is to approve or refuse credit to individuals or companies. <u>Uncollectible accounts</u> (also called bad debts), the accounting term for nonpayment by customers, are an expense of selling on credit.

The matching rule requires that an uncollectible accounts expense must appear in the same income statement as the corresponding sale, even if the customer defaults in a future period. At the time of a credit sale, however, the company does not know which customers will or will not eventually pay. Therefore an estimate of uncollectible accounts must be made at the end of the accounting period. An adjusting entry is then made, debiting Uncollectible Accounts Expense and crediting Allowance for Uncollectible Accounts for the estimated amount. Uncollectible Accounts Expense is closed out in a manner similar to other expenses and appears in the income statement. <u>Allowance for Uncollectible Accounts</u> is a contra account to Accounts Receivable, reducing Accounts Receivable to the amount estimated to be collectible.

New Words and Terms

uncollectible accounts (p. 361)
allowance for uncollectible accounts (p. 362)

Related Text Illustrations

Figure 10-1 Partial Balance Sheet Showing Allowance for Uncollectible
            Accounts (p. 363)

Lecture Outline

A. Uncollectible accounts are an expense of selling on credit.

   1. The expense should be recorded in the same period as the related sale,
      to follow the matching rule.

   2. An estimate of bad debts must be made at the end of each year.

   3. Journalize the adjustment for bad debts.

      a. Illustrate the balance sheet presentation of Allowance for Bad Debts.

OBJECTIVE 3: Apply the percentage of net sales method and the accounts receivable aging method to accounting for uncollectible accounts
            (pp. 364-369)

Summary Statement

The two most common methods for estimating uncollectible accounts are the percentage of net sales method and the accounts receivable aging method.

Under the <u>percentage of net sales method</u>, the estimated percentage for uncollectible accounts is multiplied by net sales for the period. The resulting figure is then used in the above adjusting entry. Any previous balance in Allowance for Uncollectible Accounts represents estimates from previous years which have not yet been written off, and is irrelevant in making the adjusting entry under this method.

Under the <u>accounts receivable aging method</u>, customer accounts are placed into a "not yet due" category or into one of several "past due" categories. The amounts in each category are totaled, and each total is then multiplied by a different percentage for estimated bad debts. The sum of these products represents estimated bad debts on ending Accounts Receivable. Again, the debit is to Uncollectible Accounts Expense and the credit to Allowance for Uncollectible Accounts. However, the entry is for the amount that will bring Allowance for Uncollectible Accounts to the computed figure under the aging method.

New Words and Terms

percentage of net sales method (p. 364)
accounts receivable aging method (p. 365)
aging of accounts receivable (p. 365)

Related Text Illustrations

*Figure 10-2 Analysis of Accounts Receivable by Age (p. 366)
*Figure 10-3 Calculation of Estimated Uncollectible Accounts (p. 367)

Lecture Outline

A. Explain the percentage of net sales method.

   1. Any previous balance in Allowance for Uncollectible Accounts is <u>irrelevant</u> in making the adjusting entry.

B. Explain the accounts receivable aging method.

   1. Assign a probability of default to each age category.

   2. Any previous balance in Allowance for Uncollectible Accounts is <u>relevant</u> in making the adjusting entry.

OBJECTIVE 4: Journalize entries involving the allowance method of accounting for uncollectible accounts (pp. 365-369)

Summary Statement

When it becomes clear that a specific account will not be collected, it should be written off by a debit to Allowance for Uncollectible Accounts and a credit to Accounts Receivable. The debit is _not_ made to Uncollectible Accounts Expense. After a specific account is written off, Accounts Receivable and Allowance for Uncollectible Accounts decrease by the same amount, but the net figure for expected receivables stays the same.

When a customer whose account has been written off pays in full or in part, two entries must be made. First, the customer's receivable is reinstated by a debit to Accounts Receivable and a credit to Allowance for Uncollectible Accounts for the amount now considered collectible. Second, Cash is debited and Accounts Receivable is credited for each collection.

The direct charge-off method charges uncollectible accounts to an expense in the period of default, which may or may not coincide with the period of the related sale. There is no estimate for bad debts at the end of the period, and when an account is deemed uncollectible, a debit to Uncollectible Accounts Expense and a credit to Accounts Receivable are made. The direct charge-off method frequently violates the matching rule because accounts are often written off in periods subsequent to the sale.

New Words and Terms

direct charge-off method   (p. 369)

Lecture Outline

A. Journalize the write-off of a specific account.

   1. Uncollectible Accounts Expense is not involved in the entry.

   2. After the write-off, the account receivable net value does not change.

B. Journalize the collection of an account previously written off.

   1. Journalize the reinstatement of the receivable.

   2. Journalize the collection of cash.

C. Contrast the direct charge-off method with the allowance method.

OBJECTIVE 5:   Recognize types of receivables not classified as accounts receiv-
              able and specify their balance sheet presentation (pp. 369-371)

Summary Statement

When a customer overpays, his or her account will have a credit balance. When
a balance sheet is prepared, Accounts Receivable should be shown for the sum
of all accounts with debit balances. An account called Credit Balances in Customer Accounts should appear under current liabilities for the sum of all accounts with credit balances.

When a firm has made sales to and purchases from the same company, it should
maintain two separate accounts and should not offset them against each other.

Installment accounts receivable are receivables that will be collected in a
series of payments, and are usually classified on the balance sheet as current
assets.

Companies that allow customers to use national credit cards (such as Master
Card) must follow special accounting procedures. Operationally, the credit
card company reimburses the company for the sale, less a service charge. The
credit card company levies a service charge because it is responsible for establishing credit and collecting the money from the customer.

When loans and sales are made to the company's officers, employees, or stockholders, they should be shown separately in the balance sheet with a title such
as "Receivables from Employees and Officers."

New Words and Terms

installment accounts receivable (p. 370)

Lecture Outline

A. Credit balances in customers' accounts should be shown as a current
   liability.

B. Installment accounts receivable are classified as a current asset.

C. Discuss accounting for credit card sales.

D. Receivables from employees and officers should be disclosed separately on
   the balance sheet.

OBJECTIVE 6: Define and describe a promissory note (pp. 371-372)

Summary Statement

A **promissory note** is a written promise to pay a definite sum of money on demand or at a future date. The person who signs the note and thereby promises to pay is called the maker of the note. The person to whom money is owed is called the payee. The payee records long- or short-term Notes Receivable and the maker records long- or short-term Notes Payable.

New Words and Terms

promissory note (p. 371)

Lecture Outline

A. A promissory note is a written promise to pay a sum of money on a certain date.

1. The maker of the note records notes payable.

2. The payee of the note records notes receivable.

OBJECTIVE 7: Make calculations involving promissory notes (pp. 372-375)

Summary Statement

The **maturity date** and **duration of note** must either be stated on the promissory note or be determinable from the information on the note.

To the borrower, **interest** is the cost of borrowing money. To the lender, it is the reward for lending money. The principal is the amount of money borrowed or loaned. The interest rate is the annual charge for borrowing money, and is expressed as a percentage. A note may be either interest-bearing or noninterest-bearing.

Interest (not interest rate) is a dollar figure, which is computed as follows:

$$\text{interest} = \text{principal} \times \text{interest rate} \times \text{time (length of loan)}$$

For example, interest on $800 at 5 percent for 90 days is $10, which is computed by solving ($800/1) x (5/100) x (90/360). A 360-day year is commonly used to simplify the computation. If the length of the note were expressed in months, then the number of months divided by 12 would constitute the third fraction.

Interest of 12 percent for 30 days can quickly be determined by moving the decimal point of the principal two places to the left. This 12 percent method can also be modified to deal with variations from 30 days and 12 percent.

Maturity value (of an interest-bearing note) is the face value of the note (principal) plus interest.

It is common practice for banks to deduct the interest in advance when lending money on promissory notes. This practice is called discounting a note. The discount is the amount of interest deducted, and it is computed as follows:

$$\text{discount} = \text{maturity value} \times \text{discount rate} \times \text{discount period}$$

The proceeds from discounting are the amount received by the borrower, and equal the maturity value minus the discount.

New Words and Terms

maturity date (p. 372)
duration of note (p. 372)
interest (p. 373)
maturity value (p. 374)
discount (p. 374)
proceeds from discounting (p. 374)

Lecture Outline

A. Calculate the maturity date of a note, if not specifically stated.

B. Calculate the duration of a note, if not specifically stated.

C. Interest = principal x rate x time (length of note).

D. Discuss the 30-day, 12 percent shortcut method.

E. Maturity value = principal plus interest.

F. A company may discount a note to receive money prior to maturity.

1. The discount = maturity value x discount rate x discount period.

2. Proceeds from discounting = maturity value minus discount.

OBJECTIVE 8: Journalize entries involving notes receivable (pp. 376-379)

Summary Statement

A _dishonored note_ is one that is not paid at maturity date. The payee would debit Accounts Receivable for the principal plus interest plus _protest fee_, credit Notes Receivable, and credit Interest Earned.

Companies often sell notes receivable to banks or financing companies prior to maturity to obtain immediate cash. This practice is called discounting because the bank deducts the interest from the maturity value of the note to determine the proceeds. The company then debits Cash for the proceeds, credits Notes Receivable for the principal, and credits Interest Earned for the difference.

On the maturity date, the maker of a note that has been discounted must pay the bank or financing company directly. The original payee must make good on the note if the maker does not, and is therefore said to have a _contingent liability_.

End-of-period adjustments must be made for notes that apply to both the current and future periods, so that interest may be properly apportioned among the periods.

New Words and Terms

dishonored note (p. 376)
contingent liability (p. 377)
notice of protest (p. 378)
protest fee (p. 378)

Lecture Outline

A. Journalize a dishonored note.

B. Journalize the receipt of cash upon the discount of a note.

  1. Discuss the contingent liability that exists until the maturity date.

2. Journalize the dishonor of a discounted note.

C. Journalize the adjusting entry for accrued interest receivable on a note.

Chapter Ten   Short-Term Liquid Assets

Learning Objectives	Questions	Exercises	A & B Problems	Case
1. Describe accounting for cash and short-term investments.	1, 2	1		1
2. Explain why estimated losses from uncollectible accounts are important to income determination.	3, 4, 6, 7, 8, 11	IAI		1
3. Apply the percentage of net sales method and the accounts receivable aging method to accounting for uncollectible accounts.	9, 10	2	1, 2	
4. Journalize entries involving the allowance method of accounting for uncollectible accounts.	5, 12, 13	2, 3, 4	1, 2	
5. Recognize types of receivables not classified as accounts receivable and specify their balance sheet presentation.	14	8		
6. Define and describe a promissory note.	15			
7. Make calculations involving promissory notes.	16, 17, 18, 19	5, 6	3, 4, 5	
8. Journalize entries involving notes receivable.	17, 18, 19	7, 9	3, 4, 5	

DIFFICULTY AND TIME CHART

A & B Problems	Difficulty	Time (in minutes)
1	easy	20
2	medium	25
3	medium	30
4	medium	35
5	medium	25
Case 10-1	difficult	30

TEN-MINUTE QUIZ

T F   1. The aging method is an application of the direct charge-off method.

T F   2. Short-term investments are always reported on the balance sheet at market value, not cost.

T F   3. The maker of a note would record Notes Receivable.

T F   4. When a note is discounted at the bank, the maker of the note would pay the bank directly on the maturity date.

T F   5. A note dated May 14 and due in 60 days would be due on July 14.

T F   6. When a customer overpays, the customer's account will have a credit balance.

T F   7. The maturity value of a note equals the face value of the note minus the interest.

T F   8. The allowance method for uncollectible accounts violates the matching principle.

T F   9. Interest of 8% on $500 for 30 days would be computed by multiplying $500 x .08 x 30.

T F   10. When a year-end adjustment is made regarding a note, the payee would record Accrued Interest Receivable.

_______ 11. A company performs the aging of ending accounts receivable calculation and arrives at the figure of $800. If the account Allowance for Uncollectible Accounts has a debit balance of $300 prior to the year-end adjustment, how much should the adjustment be journalized for?
a. $300
b. $500
c. $800
d. $1,100
e. $0

_____ 12. The longer a company holds a note before it is discontinued,
a. the more the discount by the bank.
b. the more the proceeds from the bank.
c. the less chance there is of discounting the note.
d. the more the interest expense on the discount.
e. the higher the maturity value of the note.

_____ 13. When a note is discounted at the bank, and the proceeds are greater than the principal, the journal entry would include a
a. credit to Cash.
b. debit to Interest Expense.
c. debit to Interest Earned.
d. debit to Notes Payable.
e. credit to Notes Receivable.

_____ 14. Under the allowance method, when a specific account is written off the entry is
a. a debit to Uncollectible Accounts Expense and a credit to Accounts Receivable.
b. a debit to Allowance for Uncollectible Accounts and a credit to Accounts Receivable.
c. a debit to Uncollectible Accounts Expense and a credit to Allowance for Uncollectible Accounts.
d. a debit to Accounts Receivable and a credit to Uncollectible Accounts Expense.
e. No entry would be made under this method.

_____ 15. A company has net sales of $100,000 during the year. At year-end (before the adjustment is made), the account Allowance for Uncollectible Accounts has a credit balance of $5,000. If the company estimates that 3% of net sales is uncollectible, what will be the balance in the allowance account after the year-end adjustment has been made?
a. $8,000 credit balance
b. $3,000 credit balance
c. $3,000 debit balance
d. $2,000 debit balance
e. $2,000 credit balance

_____ 16. The account Allowance for Uncollectible Accounts is classified as a(n)
a. contra account to Sales.
b. expense.
c. liability.
d. contra account to Uncollectible Accounts Expense.
e. contra account to Accounts Receivable.

_____ 17. Under the direct charge-off method, when a specific account is
written off the entry is
a. a debit to Uncollectible Accounts Expense and a credit to
Accounts Receivable.
b. a debit to Allowance for Uncollectible Accounts and a credit to
Accounts Receivable.
c. a debit to Uncollectible Accounts Expense and a credit to
Allowance for Uncollectible Accounts.
d. a debit to Accounts Receivable and a credit to Uncollectible
Accounts Expense.
e. No entry would be made under this method.

_____ 18. The maturity value of a $10,000, 60-day, 9% note is
a. $150.
b. $540.
c. $10,000.
d. $10,150.
e. $10,540.

_____ 19. A company makes $10,000 in credit card sales, but must mail the in-
voices to the credit card company, which will then forward the cash.
Upon receipt of the cash, the company's entry would include a
a. credit to Cash.
b. debit to Credit Card Discount Expense.
c. debit to Accounts Receivable.
d. credit to Credit Card Discount Expense.
e. credit to Sales.

_____ 20. When a discounted note has been dishonored, the company that discounted the note must make payment and would
a. debit Notes Receivable and credit Notes Payable.
b. debit Cash and credit Protest Fee.
c. debit Accounts Receivable and credit Cash.
d. debit Protest Fee and credit Cash.
e. debit Accounts Receivable and credit Notes Payable.

ANSWERS TO TEN-MINUTE QUIZ

<u>True-False</u>			<u>Multiple-Choice</u>	
1.	F		11.	d
2.	F		12.	b
3.	F		13.	e
4.	T		14.	b
5.	F		15.	a
6.	T		16.	e
7.	F		17.	a
8.	F		18.	d
9.	F		19.	b
10.	T		20.	c

CHAPTER ELEVEN

INVENTORIES

CHAPTER OUTLINE

Nonmonetary Assets and the Matching Rule
Inventories and Income Determination
    Objective of Inventory Measurement
    Review of Gross Margin and Cost of Goods Sold Computations
    Effects of Errors in Inventory Measurement
Inventory Measurement
    Merchandise in Transit
    Sold Merchandise on Hand
Pricing the Inventory at Cost
    Cost Defined
    Methods of Pricing Inventory at Cost
        Specific Identification Method
        Average-Cost Method
        First-In, First-Out (FIFO) Method
        Last-In, First-Out (LIFO) Method
    Comparison of the Alternative Methods of Pricing Inventory
        Effect on the Financial Statements
        Effect on Income Taxes
Valuing the Inventory at the Lower-of-Cost-or-Market (LCM)
    Methods of Applying LCM
        Item-by-Item Method
        Major Category Method
        Total Inventory Method
A Note on Inventory Valuation and Federal Income Taxes
Valuing the Inventory by Estimation
    Retail Method of Inventory Estimation
    Gross Profit Method of Inventory Estimation
Periodic and Perpetual Inventory Systems
    Handling Inventory Systems in the Accounts
    Need for Physical Inventories Under the Perpetual Inventory System
Chapter Review
    Review of Learning Objectives
    Review Problem: Periodic and Perpetual Inventory Methods
    Answer to Review Problem
Chapter Assignments
    Questions
    Classroom Exercises
    Interpreting Accounting Information: Iowa Beef Processors
    Problem Set A
    Problem Set B
    Financial Decision Case 11-1: RTS Company

LEARNING OBJECTIVES:

RESOURCE MATERIALS AND LECTURE OUTLINES

OBJECTIVE 1: Define nonmonetary assets and state their relationship to the matching rule (pp. 392-393)

Summary Statement

Monetary assets consist of cash and assets that represent the right to receive cash. Nonmonetary assets are unexpired costs that will become expenses in the periods that they benefit; they comprise all assets except cash, temporary investments, receivables, and long-term investments. Short-term nonmonetary assets are classified as current assets, and include inventory, supplies, and prepaid expenses. Long-term nonmonetary assets benefit more than the current period, and include property, plant, equipment, natural resources, and intangibles.

To measure income properly and observe the matching rule, the following two questions must be answered:

a. How much of the nonmonetary asset has been used up (expired) during the current period and should be transferred to expense?

b. How much of the nonmonetary asset is unused (unexpired) and should remain on the balance sheet as an asset?

New Words and Terms

monetary assets (p. 392)
nonmonetary assets (p. 392)
short-term nonmonetary assets (p. 392)
long-term nonmonetary assets (p. 392)

Lecture Outline

A. Nonmonetary assets are unexpired costs that will eventually become expenses.

1. Short-term nonmonetary assets include inventory, supplies, and prepaid expenses.

2. Long-term nonmonetary assets include property, plant, equipment, natural resources, and intangibles.

B. Nonmonetary assets should be expensed in the period benefitted, according to the matching rule.

C. Nonmonetary assets with future benefits should be placed on the balance sheet.

OBJECTIVE 2: Define merchandise inventory and show how inventory measurement affects income determination (pp. 393-398)

Summary Statement

Merchandise inventory consists of all goods held for sale in the regular course of business. It appears in the current asset section of the balance sheet below receivables.

Beginning inventory plus purchases equals cost of goods available for sale. Cost of goods sold is indirectly determined by deducting ending inventory from cost of goods available for sale.

Because the cost of ending inventory is needed to compute cost of goods sold, it affects net income dollar for dollar. It is most important to match cost of goods sold with sales so that a proper determination of net income will result.

This year's ending inventory automatically becomes next year's beginning inventory. Because beginning inventory also affects net income dollar for dollar, an error in this year's ending inventory will result in misstated net income for both this year and next year.

a. When ending inventory is understated, net income for the period will be understated.

b. When ending inventory is overstated, net income for the period will be overstated.

c. When beginning inventory is understated, net income for the period will be overstated.

d. When beginning inventory is overstated, net income for the period will be understated.

Ending inventory is computed by (a) counting the items on hand, (b) determining the cost of each item, and (c) multiplying unit cost by quantity. Inventory comprises all items to which a company has title, regardless of the location of the items.

Goods in transit should be included in inventory only if the company has title to the goods. When goods are sent FOB shipping point, title passes to the buyer when the goods reach the common carrier. When goods are shipped FOB destination, title passes when the goods reach the buyer. Goods that have been sold but are still on hand should not be included in the seller's inventory count.

Related Text Illustrations

*Figure 11-1 Effect of Error in Ending Inventory on Current and Succeeding
            Year (p. 397)

Lecture Outline

A. Merchandise inventory consists of all goods held for sale in the ordinary
   course of business.

B. Beginning and ending inventory are an integral part of the calculation of
   cost of goods sold, and therefore of net income.

   1. When ending inventory is under- or overstated, net income will be under-
      or overstated, respectively.

   2. When beginning inventory is under- or overstated, net income will be
      under- or overstated, respectively.

C. Discuss the concept of a counterbalancing error.

D. Discuss goods in transit and the F.O.B. point.

OBJECTIVE 3a: Calculate the pricing of inventory, using the cost basis accord-
              ing to the specific identification method (pp. 398-401)

Summary Statement

The <u>inventory cost</u> is defined as the purchase price plus any charges incurred in bringing the inventory to its existing condition and location.

When identical items of merchandise are purchased at different prices during the year, it is usually impractical to monitor the actual goods flow and record their corresponding costs. Instead, the accountant will make an assumption of the cost flow, and will use one of the following methods: (a) specific identification, (b) average cost, (c) first-in, first-out, or (d) last-in, first-out.

Under the specific identification method, the units of ending inventory can be identified as having come from specific purchases. The flow of costs reflects the actual flow of goods in this case.

New Words and Terms

inventory cost (p. 399)
goods flow (p. 399)
cost flow (p. 399)
specific identification method (p. 400)

Related Text Illustrations

Figure 11-2 Inventory Cost Methods Used by 600 Large Companies (p. 400)

Lecture Outline

A. Under this method, ending inventory can be identified as having come from specific purchases.

B. (At this point, it might be helpful to set up a problem that will illustrate the four inventory methods discussed in objective 3.)

OBJECTIVE 3b: Calculate the pricing of inventory, using the cost basis according to the average-cost method (pp. 400-402)

Summary Statement

Under the average-cost method, the average cost per unit is first computed for the goods available for sale during the period. This is accomplished by dividing the cost of goods available for sale by the units available for sale. Then, the average cost per unit is multiplied by the number of units in ending inventory to obtain the cost of ending inventory.

New Words and Terms

average-cost method (p. 400)

CHAPTER ELEVEN

<u>Lecture Outline</u>

A. Under this method, a weighted-average per unit is calculated on goods available for sale to determine ending inventory and cost of goods sold.

OBJECTIVE 3c: Calculate the pricing of inventory, using the cost basis according to the first-in, first-out (FIFO) method (pp. 400-402)

<u>Summary Statement</u>

Under the <u>first-in, first-out (FIFO) method</u>, the cost of the first items purchased is assigned to the first items sold. Therefore, ending inventory is costed at the prices of the most recent purchases. During periods of rising prices, FIFO yields the highest net income of the four methods.

<u>New Words and Terms</u>

first-in, first-out (FIFO) method (p. 400)

<u>Lecture Outline</u>

A. Under FIFO, the goods purchased first are <u>assumed</u> to be the first sold.

OBJECTIVE 3d: Calculate the pricing of inventory, using the cost basis according to the last-in, first-out (LIFO) method (pp. 400-403)

<u>Summary Statement</u>

Under the <u>last-in, first-out (LIFO) method</u>, the last items purchased are assumed to be the first items sold. Therefore, the ending inventory is assumed to consist of items from the earliest purchases. During periods of rising prices, LIFO yields the lowest net income of the four methods, but it best matches current merchandise costs with current sales prices.

<u>New Words and Terms</u>

last-in, last-out (LIFO) method (p. 400)

<u>Lecture Outline</u>

A. Under LIFO, the goods purchased most recently are <u>assumed</u> to be the first sold.

OBJECTIVE 4: Recognize the effects of each method on income determination in
periods of changing prices (pp. 403-405)

Summary Statement

During periods of rising prices, FIFO will produce a higher net income than
LIFO, and the average cost and specific identification methods will produce net
income figures that are somewhere between those of FIFO and LIFO. During periods of falling prices, the reverse is true for all of the above. Even though
LIFO best follows the matching rule, FIFO provides a more up-to-date ending
inventory figure for balance-sheet purposes.

Lecture Outline

A. During periods of rising prices, FIFO will produce a higher net income than
   LIFO. Also, the average cost and specific identification methods will produce figures that are between FIFO and LIFO.

B. During periods of falling prices, LIFO will produce a higher net income than
   FIFO.

C. In general, LIFO best follows the matching rule.

D. In general, FIFO provides a more up-to-date ending inventory figure for
   balance sheet purposes.

OBJECTIVE 5: Apply the lower-of-cost-or-market (LCM) rule to inventory valuation (pp. 405-406)

Summary Statement

The market value of inventory may fall below its cost, owing to physical deterioration, obsolescence, or decline in price level. Accordingly, it should be
valued at the lower-of-cost-or-market. The three basic methods of valuing inventory at lower-of-cost-or-market are the item-by-item method, the major category method, and the total inventory method.

New Words and Terms

market (p. 405)
lower-of-cost-or-market (LCM) rule (p. 405)
item-by-item method (p. 406)
major category method (p. 406)
total inventory method (p. 406)

Lecture Outline

A. Inventory should be valued at lower-of-cost-or-market, according to one of three methods:

  1. Item-by-item

  2. Major category

  3. Total inventory

B. First, cost is determined by applying FIFO, LIFO, etc.

C. Market is defined as replacement cost.

D. Cost is compared with market.

OBJECTIVE 6a: Estimate the cost of ending inventory by using the retail inventory method (pp. 407-408)

Summary Statement

The retail method of inventory estimation may be used when there is an overall constant relationship between cost and sales price for goods over a period of time. It may be used whether or not the business makes a physical count of goods. To apply the retail method, goods available for sale are first determined at cost and at retail. Then, a cost-to-retail ratio can be computed. Sales for the period are then subtracted from goods available for sale at retail to produce ending inventory at retail. Finally, ending inventory at retail is multiplied by the cost-to-retail ratio to produce an estimate of ending inventory at cost.

New Words and Terms

retail method (p. 407)

Lecture Outline

A. May be used when the relationship between cost and selling price is relatively constant.

B. Records must be kept at cost and at retail.

C. First, compute goods available for sale at cost and at retail.

D. Compute a cost-to-retail ratio.

E. Subtract sales to obtain ending inventory at retail.

F. Multiply "E" by the cost-to-retail ratio for ending inventory at cost.

OBJECTIVE 6b: Estimate the cost of ending inventory by using the gross profit
                method (pp. 408-409)

Summary Statement

The gross profit method of inventory estimation assumes that the ratio of gross
profit for a business remains relatively stable from year to year. It is used
when inventory records are lost or destroyed, and when records of beginning inventory and purchases are not kept at retail.

To apply the gross profit method, cost of goods available for sale is first
determined by adding purchases to beginning inventory. Then cost of goods sold
is estimated by multiplying sales by (1 minus the gross profit percentage).
The resulting estimated cost of goods sold is subtracted from cost of goods
available for sale to arrive at estimated ending inventory.

New Words and Terms

gross profit method (p. 408)

Lecture Outline

A. May be used when the gross profit ratio remains relatively constant.

B. Is usually used when inventory is destroyed or stolen.

C. Inventory records are not kept at retail.

D. First, compute goods available for sale (at cost).

E. Compute estimated cost of goods sold by multiplying sales by (1 minus the gross profit percentage).

F. Subtract "E" from "D" to obtain estimated ending inventory.

OBJECTIVE 7: Distinguish between perpetual and periodic inventory systems (409-411)

Summary Statement

When the <u>periodic inventory method</u> is used, a physical inventory is taken only at the end of the period, and cost of goods sold is derived by subtracting ending inventory from cost of goods available for sale.

The <u>perpetual inventory method</u> is used by companies that want more control over their inventories. A continuous record is kept of the balance in each inventory item, thus eliminating the need for a physical count (although one should be taken periodically to confirm the perpetual records).

The journal entries for the cost of merchandise purchased and sold are different for the periodic and perpetual systems. The periodic system records all purchases of goods in a Purchases account, closes out Purchases and beginning inventory at the end of the period, and records ending inventory. The perpetual system records all purchases of goods with a debit to Merchandise Inventory, and records Cost of Goods Sold and a reduction in Merchandise Inventory after each sale. No Purchases account is needed, and the only merchandise-related entry made at the end of the period is to close out Cost of Goods Sold.

New Words and Terms

periodic inventory method (p. 409)
perpetual inventory method (p. 409)

Related Text Illustrations

Figure 11-3 Perpetual Inventory Record Card, FIFO (p. 410)

Lecture Outline

A. Periodic inventory method -- A physical count is taken at the end of the period; a continuous record is not kept for each inventory item.

1. Purchased goods are recorded in a Purchases account.

2. Cost of goods sold is <u>not</u> recorded upon the sale of inventory.

3. Beginning inventory is closed out, and ending inventory established at year-end.

B. Perpetual inventory method -- Inventory records are updated with every purchase and every sale.

1. Purchased goods are recorded in a Merchandise Inventory account.

2. Cost of goods sold <u>is</u> recorded upon the sale of inventory.

3. The inventory account is not involved in closing entries, though cost of goods sold is closed out.

Chapter Eleven Inventories

Learning Objectives	Questions	Exercises	A & B Problems	Case
1. Define nonmonetary assets and state their relation- ship to the matching rule.	1			
2. Define merchandise inventory and show how inventory measurement affects income determination.	2, 3, 4, 5, 6	2		
3. Calculate the pricing of inventory, using the cost basis according to the (a) specific identification method; (b) average cost method; (c) first-in, first-out method; (d) last-in, first-out method.	9, 10, 11	1, 3	1	
4. Recognize the effects of each method on income determination in periods of changing prices.	7, 8	IAI		1
5. Apply the lower-of-cost-or-market rule to inventory valuation.	12, 13, 14	6	2	
6. Estimate the cost of ending inventory by using the (a) retail inventory method and (b) gross profit method.	15, 16, 20	4, 5	5, 6	
7. Distinguish between perpetual and periodic inventory systems.	17, 18, 19, 20		3, 4	

DIFFICULTY AND TIME CHART

A & B Problems	Difficulty	Time (in minutes)
1	medium	25
2	easy	25
3	medium	35
4	medium	35
5	medium	20
6	medium	20
Case 11-1	medium	30

TEN-MINUTE QUIZ

T   F   1.   An inventory error will correct itself over a two-year period.

T   F   2.   The retail method and the gross profit method are both methods of inventory estimation.

T   F   3.   Goods in transit would not be included in the ending inventory of the buyer or the seller.

T   F   4.   Under the retail inventory method, Sales is not involved in the cost-to-retail percentage computation.

T   F   5.   When the cost of inventory is $100 and market at year-end is $140, the balance sheet should show $140.

T   F   6.   We can use the FIFO inventory method only if we observe that the oldest units are always sold first.

T   F   7.   Under the perpetual inventory method, the purchase of merchandise is recorded with a debit to Merchandise Inventory.

T   F   8.   When beginning inventory is overstated, net income will be understated.

T   F   9.   Cost of goods available for sale minus the cost of goods sold equals ending inventory.

T   F   10.   When prices are falling, FIFO results in a higher ending inventory than LIFO.

_____   11.   Double-counting an inventory item will result in
               a.   understated net income.
               b.   understated beginning inventory for the next period.
               c.   overstated tax liability.
               d.   overstated cost of goods sold.
               e.   understated total assets.

_____   12.   Which of the following methods would probably be used when inventory is destroyed or stolen?
               a.   Gross profit method
               b.   Retail inventory method
               c.   First-in, first-out
               d.   Last-in, first-out
               e.   Perpetual method

_____ 13. Under the perpetual inventory system, the sale of goods is recorded
with two entries. The first entry debits Cash or Accounts Receivable and credits Sales. The second entry
a. debits Inventory and credits Cost of Goods Sold.
b. debits Cost of Goods Sold and credits Purchases.
c. debits Purchases and credits Inventory
d. debits Cost of Goods Sold and credits Inventory.
e. debits Accounts Payable and credits Inventory.

_____ 14. Which of the following is not a short-term monetary asset?
a. Inventory
b. Short-term investments
c. Notes receivable
d. Cash
e. Accounts receivable

_____ 15. A retail company has goods available for sale of $500,000 at retail
and $300,000 at cost, and ending inventory of $50,000 at retail.
What is the estimated cost of goods sold?
a. $30,000
b. $50,000
c. $270,000
d. $450,000
e. $150,000

The following information relates to questions 16 through 18:

Beginning inventory	100 units @ $2.00
Purchase – May	200 units @ $1.50
Purchase – July	100 units @ $3.00

A periodic inventory system is used; ending inventory is 150 units.

_____ 16. What is the ending inventory under the average cost method?
a. $75   b. $125   c. $300   d. $500   e. $800

_____ 17. What is the cost of goods sold under LIFO?
a. $375   b. $275   c. $425   d. $525   e. $300

_____ 18. What is the ending inventory under FIFO?
a. $375   b. $275   c. $425   d. $525   e. $300

_____ 19. A company has cost of goods available for sale of $500,000, sales
of $600,000, and a gross profit percentage of 30%. Using the gross
profit method, what is the ending inventory?
a. $80,000
b. $320,000
c. $420,000
d. $350,000
e. $70,000

_____ 20. Under rising prices
   a. FIFO will result in a lower net income than LIFO.
   b. LIFO will result in a lower cost of goods sold than FIFO.
   c. FIFO will result in a higher tax liability than LIFO.
   d. LIFO will result in a higher ending inventory than FIFO.
   e. None of the above.

     184

ANSWERS TO TEN-MINUTE QUIZ

<u>True-False</u>

1. T
2. T
3. F
4. T
5. F
6. F
7. T
8. T
9. T
10. F

<u>Multiple-Choice</u>

11. c
12. a
13. d
14. a
15. c
16. c
17. d
18. a
19. a
20. c

CHAPTER TWELVE

CURRENT LIABILITIES AND PAYROLL ACCOUNTING

CHAPTER OUTLINE

Nature and Measurement of Liabilities
    Recognition of Liabilities
    Valuation of Liabilities
    Classification of Liabilities
Common Categories of Current Liabilities
    Definitely Determinable Liabilities
        Trade Accounts Payable
        Notes Payable
        Dividends Payable
        Sales and Excise Taxes Payable
        Current Portions of Long-Term Debt
        Accrued Liabilities
        Payroll Liabilities
        Unearned or Deferred Revenues
    Estimated Liabilities
        Income Tax
        Property Taxes Payable
        Product Warranty Liability
        Vacation Pay Liability
Contingent Liabilities
Introduction to Payroll Accounting
    Liabilities for Employee Compensation
    Liabilities for Employee Payroll Withholdings
        FICA Tax
        Federal Income Tax
        State Income Tax
        Other Withholdings
    Computation of an Employee's Take-Home Pay: An Illustration
        Employee Earnings Record
        Payroll Register
        Recording the Payroll
    Liabilities for Employer Payroll Taxes
        FICA Tax
        Federal Unemployment Insurance Tax
        State Unemployment Insurance Tax
        Recording Payroll Taxes
    Payment of Payroll and Payroll Taxes

LEARNING OBJECTIVES:

RESOURCE MATERIALS AND LECTURE OUTLINES

OBJECTIVE 1: Define liability and explain how the problems of recognition, valuation, and classification apply to liabilities (pp. 425-426)

Summary Statement

Liabilities are present obligations requiring either future payment of assets or future performance of services. A liability generally should be recorded when an obligation arises, but it is also necessary to make end-of-period adjustments for accrued and estimated liabilities. On the other hand, contracts representing future obligations are not recorded as liabilities until they become current obligations.

Liabilities are valued at the actual or estimated amount due, or at the fair market value of goods or services which must be delivered.

Current liabilities are present obligations that are expected to be satisfied within one year or the normal operating cycle, whichever is longer. Payment is expected to be out of current assets or through the incurrence of another current liability. Long-term liabilities are obligations that are not expected to be satisfied in the current period.

Current liabilities consist of definitely determinable liabilities and estimated liabilities.

New Words and Terms

liabilities (p. 425)
current liabilities (p. 426)
long-term liabilities (p. 426)

Lecture Outline

A. Liabilities are present obligations that must be satisfied with the future payment of assets or the performance of services.

1. A liability should be recognized when incurred; end-of-period adjustments may be necessary.

2. Liabilities are valued at the amount due, or at the fair market value of goods or services that must be delivered.

3. Liabilities are classified as current or long-term.

   a. A current liability is a liability due within one year or the normal operating cycle, whichever is longer.

   b. A long-term liability is a liability due beyond the current period.

OBJECTIVE 2: Identify, compute, and record definitely determinable and estimated current liabilities (pp. 427-434)

Summary Statement

Definitely determinable liabilities are obligations that can be precisely measured, and include trade accounts payable, short-term notes payable, dividends payable, sales and excise taxes payable, current portions of long-term debt, accrued liabilities, payroll liabilities, and deferred revenues.

a. Trade accounts payable are current obligations due to suppliers of goods and services.

b. Short-term notes payable are current obligations evidenced by promissory notes. Interest may be either stated on the face of the note or deducted in advance (discounted).

c. Dividends payable represent an obligation to distribute earnings of a corporation to its stockholders, and arise only when the board of directors declares a dividend.

d. Most states and many cities levy a sales tax on retail transactions, and the federal government also charges an excise tax on some products. The merchant must collect the taxes at the time of the sale, and would record the receipt of cash, and the proper tax liabilities.

e. An accrued liability is an actual or estimated liability that exists at the balance sheet date but is unrecorded. An end-of-period adjustment is needed to record both the expenses and the accrued liabilities.

f. Deferred revenues represent obligations to deliver goods or services in return for advance payment. When delivery takes place, Deferred Revenue is debited and a revenue account is credited.

<u>Estimated liabilities</u> are definite obligations. However, the amount of the obligation must be estimated at the balance sheet date because the exact figure will not be known until a future date. Examples of estimated liabilities are income taxes, property taxes, product warranties, and vacation pay.

a. A corporation's income tax is dependent on its net income, a figure that often is not determined until well after the balance sheet date.

b. Property taxes are taxes levied on real and personal property. Very often a company's accounting period ends before property taxes have been assessed. Therefore, it must make an estimate, and would debit Property Taxes Expense and credit Estimated Property Taxes Payable.

c. When a company sells its products, many of the warranties will still be in effect during the next accounting period. However, the warranty expense and liability must be recorded in the period of the sale regardless of when the company makes good on the warranty. Therefore, at the end of each accounting period, the company should make an estimate of future warranty expense that applies to the present period's sales.

d. In most companies, employees earn vacation pay for working a certain length of time. Therefore, the company must estimate vacation pay applicable to each payroll period, and would debit Vacation Pay Expense and credit Estimated Liability for Vacation Pay.

New Words and Terms
<u>New Words and Terms</u>

definitely determinable liabilities (p. 427)
unearned or deferred revenues (p. 431)
estimated liabilities (p. 431)

<u>Related Text Illustrations</u>

Figure 12-1   Two Promissory Notes: One with Interest Stated Separately; One
              with Interest in Face Amount (p. 427)
*Figure 12-2   Growth in Liability of Interest-bearing Note, with Interest
              Expense Allocated to Two Accounting Periods (p. 430)

<u>Lecture Outline</u>

A. Current liabilities consist of definitely determinable liabilities and estimated liabilities.

B. A definitely determinable liability can be precisely measured. Examples follow.

   1. Trade accounts payable.

2. Short-term notes payable.

3. Dividends payable.

4. Sales and excise taxes payable.

5. Current portion of a long-term debt.

6. Accrued liabilities (such as interest payable).

7. Payroll liability.

8. Deferred revenue.

C. Estimated liabilities are definite obligations whose amounts will not be known precisely until after the balance sheet date. Examples follow.

1. Income taxes

2. Property taxes

3. Product warranties

4. Vacation pay

OBJECTIVE 3: Define a contingent liability (pp. 434-435)

Summary Statement

A contingent liability is a potential liability that may or may not become an actual liability. The uncertainty regarding its outcome is resolved by the occurrence or nonoccurrence of a future event. Contingent liabilities arise from pending lawsuits, tax disputes, discounted notes receivable, the guarantee of indebtedness of others, and failure to comply with pollution regulations.

New Words and Terms

contingent liability (p. 434)

Lecture Outline

A. A contingent liability is a potential liability which may or may not become an actual liability. Examples follow.

1. Pending lawsuits

2. Tax disputes

3. Discounted notes receivable

4. Guarantee of indebtedness of others

5. Failure to comply with pollution regulations

OBJECTIVE 4: Identify and compute the liabilities associated with payroll accounting (pp. 435-438)

Summary Statement

The three general types of liabilities associated with payroll accounting are (a) liabilities for employee compensation, (b) liabilities for employee payroll withholding, and (c) liabilities for employer payroll taxes. An employee is one who is under the direct supervision and control of the firm; an independent contractor (such as a lawyer or a CPA) is one who is not, and who therefore is not accounted for under the payroll system.

Wages are hourly or piecework compensation, whereas salaries are the monthly or yearly rate paid generally to administrative or managerial employees.

The employer is required by law to withhold certain taxes from the employee's wages and to remit those taxes to government agencies. The employer also makes other withholdings for the employee's benefit.

a. FICA taxes provide for retirement and disability benefits, survivor's bene-fits, and medical benefits.

b. Federal income taxes depend on (1) the amount that the employee earns, and (2) the number of exemptions claimed on his or her W-4 form (Employee's Withholding Exemption Certificate). The amount that the employer withholds and remits to the government should approximate the employee's actual federal income tax liability. State income taxes require similar withholding pro-cedures.

c. Withholdings may also be made for pension plans, insurance premiums, union dues, and savings plans.

<u>New Words and Terms</u>   <u>Related Text Illustrations</u>

wages (p. 435)   Figure 12-3 Wage-Bracket Table (p. 438)
salaries (p. 435)

<u>Lecture Outline</u>

A. There are three types of payroll liabilities:

  1. Liabilities for employee compensation.

  2. Liabilities for payroll withholding.

  3. Liabilities for employer payroll taxes.

B. Distinguish between an employee and an independent contractor.

C. Distinguish between wages and salaries.

D. Discuss FICA taxes.

E. Federal taxes and withholdings depend on earnings and exemptions (discuss W-4 form).

F. "Non-tax" withholdings may also be made.

OBJECTIVE 5: Record transactions associated with payroll accounting
              (pp. 438-442)

<u>Summary Statement</u>

An employee's take-home pay equals his or her gross earnings less total with-holdings. To facilitate payroll procedures, the company must maintain a sep-arate <u>employee earnings record</u> for each employee, listing all pertinent payroll data (earnings, deductions, and payment). Each year, the firm must inform the employee of his or her yearly earnings and withholdings on a W-2 form (Wage and Tax Statement) needed for completing the individual tax return.

The <u>payroll register</u> is a detailed listing of the company's total payroll each
payday. Each employee's name, regular and overtime hours, gross earnings,
deductions, net pay, and payroll classification are listed for that payroll
period. The journal entry for recording the payroll is based on the column
totals of the payroll register.

Independent of employee's taxes, the employer must pay (a) FICA taxes, (b) federal unemployment insurance taxes (FUTA), and (c) state unemployment compensation taxes. These taxes are considered operating expenses, and require a debit
to Payroll Tax Expense and a credit to each of the three tax liabilities.

To pay salaries, many companies use a special payroll bank account against
which payroll checks are drawn. In addition, monthly or quarterly payments
must be made to the proper agencies for withholdings.

<u>New Words and Terms</u>   <u>Related Text Illustrations</u>

employee earnings record (p. 439)   Figure 12-4   Employee Earnings Record
payroll register (p. 439)   (p. 440)
                                       Figure 12-5   Payroll Register (p. 440)

<u>Lecture Outline</u>

A. Take-home pay equals gross earnings minus total withholdings.

B. An employee earnings record is maintained for each employee.

C. Explain the significance of the W-2 form.

D. The payroll register is a detailed payroll listing on payday.

E. Make the journal entry to record the payroll.

F. Make the journal entry to record the employer's payroll taxes.

   1. FICA taxes are shared by employer and employee.

   2. Federal unemployment taxes are paid by the employer.

   3. State unemployment taxes are paid by the employer.

OBJECTIVE 6: Apply internal control to the payroll system (pp. 442-443)

Summary Statement

It is important to maintain adequate internal control over payroll to minimize
the possibility of payroll fraud. For this reason, the business should separate
the duties of (a) the personnel function, (b) the timekeeping function, (c) the
accounting function, and (d) the distribution function.

Lecture Outline

A. To maintain adequate internal control over payroll, the business should
   separate the duties of the following functions:

   1. Personnel function.

   2. Timekeeping function.

   3. Accounting function.

   4. Distribution function.

Chapter Twelve Current Liabilities and Payroll Accounting

Learning Objectives	Questions	Exercises	A & B Problems	Case
1. Define liability and explain how the problems of recognition, valuation, and classification apply to liabilities.	1, 2, 3, 4, 5			1
2. Identify, compute, and record definitely deter-minable and estimated current liabilities.	6, 7, 8, 9, 10, 11	1, 2, 3, 7, 8	2, 3, 4	1
3. Define a contingent liability.	12, 13			
4. Identify and compute the liabilities associated with payroll accounting.	14, 15, 16, 17, 18, 19	4, 5, 6	1, 5, 6	1
5. Record transactions associated with payroll accounting.	20, 21	4, 5, 6	1, 6	
6. Apply internal control to the payroll system.	22			

DIFFICULTY AND TIME CHART

A & B Problems	Difficulty	Time (in minutes)
1	easy	15
2	easy	15
3	medium	25
4	medium	25
5	easy	20
6	medium	30
Case 12-1	medium	20

TEN-MINUTE QUIZ

T F   1. A liability must never be classified as current if it is due in
            more than one year.

T F   2. Recording a discount on a note is appropriate when the interest on
            the note is stated separately from its face value.

T F   3. When a business sells an item and collects a state sales tax on it,
            a current liability to the state arises.

T F   4. A deferred revenue would arise from the acceptance of payment in
            advance for a service to be performed.

T F   5. When the maker borrows money on a note that has the interest in-
            cluded in the face value, the amount of cash received will be less
            than the face value.

T F   6. Taxes for the social security system (FICA) must be paid by both the
            the employee and the employer.

T F   7. An independent lawyer providing a service for a company would not
            be accounted for under the company's payroll system.

T F   8. Vacation pay is properly charged as an expense in the month in
            which the employee takes the vacation.

T F   9. Property Tax Expense should only be recorded when payment is made.

T F   10. A washing machine is sold in year 1, but a repair is made in year
            2. The company's entry upon making the repair would include a
            debit to Estimated Product Warranty Liability.

_____ 11. A time card for a nonexistent employee is turned in and the payroll
            check collected by a supervisor. The best control to prevent this
            fraud would be to
            a. have a separate department distribute paychecks upon proper
                identification.
            b. have the supervisor distribute all paychecks.
            c. have the payroll records maintained by the accounting depart-
                ment.
            d. have the supervisor approve all time cards.
            e. have one department administer the payroll, from time cards to
                check distribution.

_____ 12. A listing of payroll data for all employees for one payday can be
found on
a. the employee earnings record.
b. the payroll register.
c. a time card.
d. a W-2 form.
e. a W-4 form.

_____ 13. The account Discount on Notes Payable
a. has a normal credit balance.
b. is considered a miscellaneous revenue account.
c. involves an interest-bearing note.
d. would be recorded by the payee of the note.
e. is a contra account to Notes Payable.

_____ 14. Recording estimated warranty expense in the year of the sale best
follows which accounting principle?
a. Consistency
b. Matching
c. Full disclosure
d. Historical cost
e. Materiality

_____ 15. Incorrectly paying an employee a much higher hourly rate than was
contracted for suggests a flaw in which function?
a. Accounting function
b. Distribution function
c. Timekeeping function
d. Personnel function
e. Payroll function

_____ 16. Which of the following is not a contingent liability?
a. Pending lawsuit
b. Discounted note receivable
c. Income tax dispute
d. Dividends declared

_____ 17. Which of the following is not an estimated liability?
a. Vacation pay
b. Property taxes
c. Product warranties
d. Income taxes
e. Sales taxes

_____ 18. Which of the following would not typically be an employee payroll
withholding?
a. Medical insurance premiums
b. Unemployment taxes
c. Union dues
d. Federal income taxes
e. Charitable donations

_____ 19. Of a company's employees, 50 percent typically qualify to receive two weeks' paid vacation per year. What is the amount of estimated vacation pay liability for a week in which the total payroll is $3,400?
a. $34   b. $68   c. $136   d. $850   e. $1,700

_____ 20. Each year a ceiling exists for the amount that is subject to all of the following except:
a. state unemployment taxes payable
b. FICA taxes payable
c. federal income taxes payable
d. federal unemployment taxes payable

ANSWERS TO TEN-MINUTE QUIZ

True-False   Multiple-Choice

1.   F   11.   a
2.   F   12.   b
3.   T   13.   e
4.   T   14.   b
5.   T   15.   d
6.   T   16.   d
7.   T   17.   e
8.   F   18.   b
9.   F   19.   b
10.   T   20.   c

CHAPTER THIRTEEN

PROPERTY, PLANT, AND EQUIPMENT

CHAPTER OUTLINE

Long-Term Nonmonetary Assets
    Life of Long-Term Nonmonetary Assets
    Types of Long-Term Nonmonetary Assets
    Problems of Accounting for Long-Term Nonmonetary Assets
Acquisition Cost of Property, Plant, and Equipment
    Land
    Building
    Equipment
    Land Improvements
    Group Purchases
Accounting for Depreciation
    Causes of Limited Useful Life
        Physical Deterioration
        Obsolescence
    Recording Depreciation in the Accounts
    Factors That Affect the Computation of Depreciation
        Cost
        Residual Value
        Depreciable Cost
        Estimated Useful Life
Methods of Computing Depreciation
    Straight-Line Method
    Production Method
    Sum-of-the-Years'-Digits Method
    Declining-Balance Method
    Comparing the Four Methods
Special Problems of Depreciating Plant Assets
    Depreciation for Partial Years
    Revision of Depreciation Rates
    Accounting for Assets of Low Unit Cost
    Group Depreciation
Income Taxes and Plant Assets
Disposal of Depreciable Assets
    Assumptions for the Comprehensive Illustration
    Depreciation for Fractional Period Prior to Disposal
    Recording Discarded Plant Assets
    Recording Plant Assets Sold for Cash
    Recording Exchanges of Similar Plant Assets
        Loss Recognized on the Exchange

LEARNING OBJECTIVES:

RESOURCE MATERIALS AND LECTURE OUTLINES

OBJECTIVE 1: Describe the nature, types, and problems of long-term nonmonetary assets (pp. 457-460)

Summary Statement

Long-term nonmonetary assets (also called fixed assets) are assets that (a) have a useful life of more than one year, (b) are acquired for use in the operation of the business, and (c) are not intended for resale to customers. Property, plant, and equipment is the balance sheet classification representing tangible nonmonetary assets such as land, buildings, equipment, and natural resources. Intangible assets is the balance sheet classification representing intangible nonmonetary assets such as patents, trademarks, goodwill, copyrights, lease-holds, franchises, and organization costs.

In dealing with long-term nonmonetary assets, the major accounting problem is to determine how much of the asset has benefited the current period, and how much should be carried forward as an asset to benefit future periods. This alloca-tion of costs to different accounting periods is called depreciation in the case of plant and equipment (plant assets), depletion in the case of natural re-sources, and amortization in the case of intangible assets. Because land has an unlimited useful life, its cost is never converted into an expense.

To account for long-term nonmonetary assets, one must determine (a) the cost of the asset, (b) the method of matching the cost with revenues, (c) the treatment of subsequent expenditures such as repairs and maintenance, and (d) the treat-ment of asset disposal.

New Words and Terms

long-term nonmonetary assets (p. 457)
fixed assets (p. 457)
tangible assets (p. 458)
depreciation (p. 458)
natural resources (p. 458)
depletion (p. 458)
intangible assets (p. 459)
amortization (p. 459)

<u>Related Text Illustrations</u>

*Figure 13-1 Problems of Accounting for Long-Term Assets (p. 459)

<u>Lecture Outline</u>

A. Long-term nonmonetary assets have three characteristics in common:

   1. They have a useful life of more than one year.

   2. They are used in the operations of the business.

   3. They are not intended for resale.

B. Tangible nonmonetary assets consist of property, plant, and equipment.

C. Intangible nonmonetary assets consist of such items as patents, copyrights, goodwill, etc.

D. The major accounting problem is how much asset cost to allocate as expenses to accounting periods.

   1. Property, plant, and equipment are subject to depreciation (except for land).

   2. Natural resources are subject to depletion.

   3. Intangible assets are subject to amortization.

OBJECTIVE 2: Account for the cost of long-term nonmonetary assets
              (pp. 460-462)

<u>Summary Statement</u>

The cost of a long-term nonmonetary asset includes the purchase cost, freight charges, insurance while in transit, installation, and other costs involved in the acquisition of the asset. Interest incurred during the construction of a plant asset is included in the cost of the asset, whereas interest incurred for the purchase of a plant asset is expensed when incurred.

When land is purchased, the Land account should be debited for the price paid for the land, real estate commissions, lawyers' fees, back taxes assumed, draining, clearing, and grading costs, assessments for local improvements, and the cost (less salvage value) of razing (tearing down) a building situated on the property.

Land improvements, such as driveways, parking lots, and fences, are subject to depreciation and require a separate Land Improvements account.

When long-term nonmonetary assets are purchased for a lump sum, the cost should be allocated to the assets acquired in proportion to their appraisal values.

Lecture Outline

A. The cost of a long-term nonmonetary asset includes the purchase cost, freight-in, installation, and any other costs required prior to operation.

1. Discuss as specifically related to land, buildings, and equipment.

2. The cost of razing a building is debited to the Land account.

3. Interest during construction is capitalized.

B. Land improvements (driveways, etc.) are subject to depreciation.

C. When a lump-sum purchase is made, the cost should be allocated based on the assets' relative fair market values.

OBJECTIVE 3:   Define depreciation, show how to record it, and state the factors that affect its computation (pp. 462-464)

Summary Statement

Depreciation, as used in accounting, refers to the allocation of the cost (less the residual value) of a plant asset to the periods benefited by the asset. It does not refer to the physical deterioration or the decrease in market value of the asset, for it is a process of allocation, not valuation.

A plant asset should be depreciated over its estimated useful life in a systematic and rational manner. Plant assets have limited useful lives because of physical deterioration and obsolescence (becoming out-of-date).

Depreciation is recorded by debiting Depreciation Expense and crediting Accumulated Depreciation. Accumulated Depreciation is a contra asset account, and

its balance is deducted from the corresponding plant asset in the balance sheet.
The difference is called the book value or _carrying value_, and represents the
unexpired cost of the asset. Generally, separate Depreciation Expense and Accumulated Depreciation accounts are maintained for each type of plant asset.

Depreciation may be computed after determining the cost, residual value, depreciable cost, and estimated useful life. The _residual value_ is the estimated
value at the disposal date, and is often referred to as _salvage value_ or _dis-
posal value_. The _depreciable cost_ equals the cost less its residual value. The
estimated useful life may be measured in time or in units, and requires careful
consideration by the accountant.

New Words and Terms

obsolescence (p. 463)
carrying value (p. 464)
residual value (p. 464)
salvage value (p. 464)
disposal value (p. 464)
depreciable cost (p. 464)
estimated useful life (p. 464)

Lecture Outline

A. Depreciation is the logical allocation of asset cost to the periods benefitted.

B. Record the adjusting entry for depreciation.

   1. Distinguish between Depreciation Expense and Accumulated Depreciation.

   2. Define and illustrate carrying value (book value).

C. Several factors affect the computation of depreciation:

   1. Cost

   2. Residual (salvage) value

   3. Depreciable cost

   4. Estimated useful life (in time or in units)

OBJECTIVE 4:   Compute periodic depreciation under each of four methods
                (pp. 464-465)

Summary Statement

The most common depreciation methods are (a) straight-line, (b) production, (c) sum-of-the-years'-digits, and (d) declining balance. The last two are examples of accelerated methods because depreciation is greatest in the first year and declines each year thereafter.

New Words and Terms

straight-line method (p. 465)
production method (p. 465)
accelerated methods (p. 465)

Related Text Illustrations

Figure 13-2 Depreciation Methods Used by 600 Large Companies (p. 465)

Lecture Outline

A. List the four most common depreciation methods:

   1. Straight-line -- Depreciation is based on the passage of time

   2. Production -- Depreciation is based on units produced, miles driven, etc.

   3. Sum-of-the-years'-digits (an accelerated method)

   4. Double-declining balance (an accelerated method)

B. Accelerated depreciation takes higher depreciation in the early years when
   assets are more productive.

OBJECTIVE 4a: Compute periodic depreciation under the straight-line method
                 (p. 466)

<u>Summary Statement</u>

Under the <u>straight-line method</u>, the depreciable cost is spread uniformly over the life of the asset. Under this method, depreciation for each year is computed as follows:

$$\frac{\text{cost} - \text{residual value}}{\text{estimated useful life in years}}$$

<u>Lecture Outline</u>

A. Provide the formula, and work a simple problem.

OBJECTIVE 4b:　Compute periodic depreciation under the production method
(pp. 466-467)

<u>Summary Statement</u>

Under the <u>production method</u>, depreciation is based not on time but on use of the asset in units. Under this method, depreciation for each year is computed as follows:

$$\frac{\text{cost} - \text{residual value}}{\text{estimated useful life in years}} \times \text{ actual units of output}$$

<u>Lecture Outline</u>

A. Provide the formula, and work a simple problem.

OBJECTIVE 4c(1):　Compute periodic depreciation under the sum-of-the years'-digits method (pp. 467-468)

<u>Summary Statement</u>

Under the <u>sum-of-the-years'-digits method</u>, depreciation is calculated by multiplying depreciable cost by a fraction that changes every year. Under this method, depreciation for the first year (where n = estimated useful life) is computed as follows:

$$(\text{cost} - \text{residual value}) \times \frac{n}{1 + 2 + \ldots + n}$$

In each succeeding year, the numerator decreases by one, but the denominator remains the same.

New Words and Terms

sum-of-the-years'-digits method (p. 467)

Lecture Outline

A. Provide the formula, and work a simple problem.

B. Discuss the formula for computing the denominator quickly.

OBJECTIVE 4c(2): Compute periodic depreciation under the declining-balance method (pp. 468-470)

Summary Statement

Under the declining-balance method, depreciation is computed by multiplying the existing carrying value of the asset by a fixed percentage. The double-declining-balance method is a form of the declining-balance method, and uses a fixed percentage that is twice the straight-line percentage. Under the double-declining-balance method, depreciation for each year is computed as follows:

$$\text{existing carrying value} \times \frac{100\%}{\text{useful life in years}} \times 2$$

Under the declining-balance or double-declining-balance method, the asset may not be depreciated below its residual value.

New Words and Terms

declining-balance method (p. 468)
double-declining-balance method (p. 468)

Related Text Illustrations

*Figure 13-3 Graphical Comparison of the Four Methods of Determining Depreciation (p. 469)

Lecture Outline

A. Provide the formula, and work a simple problem.

B. Residual value is ignored initially, but the asset may not be depreciated below its residual value.

OBJECTIVE 5: Apply depreciation methods to problems of partial years, revised rates, items of small unit value, and groups of similar items (pp. 470-474)

Summary Statement

When an asset is purchased after the beginning of the year or is discarded before the end of the year, depreciation should be recorded for only part of the year. This is done by computing the year's depreciation and multiplying this figure by the fraction of the year that the asset was in use.

When the estimated useful life or residual value is found to be over- or understated after some depreciation has been taken, the accountant must produce a revised figure for the remaining useful life or remaining depreciable cost. Future depreciation is then calculated by spreading the remaining depreciable cost over the remaining useful life, leaving previous depreciation unchanged.

Assets of low unit cost, such as small tools, generally are not depreciated on an individual basis. Instead, they are either charged as expenses or recorded in an inventory account when purchased. In the latter case, an inventory of small tools must be taken at the end of each period to determine the amount consumed in that period.

When a company has several plant assets that are similar, it will probably use group depreciation rather than individual depreciation. Under group depreciation, the original cost of all similar assets are accumulated in one summary account. Then depreciation is computed for the assets as a whole, using the straight-line or declining-balance method.

Under the accelerated cost recovery system (ACRS), each depreciable asset is placed in one of four categories for tax purposes (3, 5, 10, and 15 years), and depreciated in accordance with percentages established by Congress. Automobiles, trucks, and small tools typically fall in the 3-year category, whereas depreciable real estate typically falls in the 15-year category.

New Words and Terms

group depreciation (p. 473)
accelerated cost recovery system (ACRS) (p. 473)

Lecture Outline

A. When an asset is used for less than a year, only partial year's depreciation
   should be taken.

B. Under certain circumstances, the depreciation computed should be revised.

   1. Leave previously-taken depreciation unchanged.

   2. The useful life or residual value is revised.

   3. The remaining depreciable cost is allocated over the remaining useful life.

C. When small tools are purchased, they are expensed either upon purchase or
   upon disposal (i.e., they are not depreciated).

D. Group depreciation saves time by depreciating a group of similar assets taken
   as a whole.

E. Explain the accelerated cost recovery system (ACRS) used for tax purposes.

OBJECTIVE 6: Account for disposal of depreciable assets (pp. 474-479)

Summary Statement

When an asset is still in use after it has been fully depreciated, no more depreciation should be taken, and the asset should not be written off until its
disposal. Disposal occurs when the asset is discarded, sold, or traded in.

When a business disposes of an asset, depreciation should be recorded for the
period preceding disposal. This will bring the asset's Accumulated Depreciation
account up to the date of disposal.

When a machine, for example, is discarded (thrown out), Accumulated Depreciation,
Machinery is debited and Machinery is credited for their present balances. If
the machine has not been fully depreciated, then Loss on Disposal of Machinery
must be debited for the carrying value to balance the entry.

When a machine, for example, is sold for cash, Accumulated Depreciation, Machinery is debited, Cash is debited, and Machinery is credited. If cash received is
less than the carrying value of the machine, then Loss on Sale of Machinery
would also be debited. On the other hand, if cash received is greater than the

carrying value, then Gain on Sale of Machinery would instead be credited to balance the entry.

When an asset is traded in (exchanged) for a similar one, the gain or loss should first be computed, as follows:

    Trade-in allowance
    − Carrying value of asset traded in
    = Gain (loss) on trade-in

a. For financial reporting purposes, losses should be recognized (recorded) on the exchange of similar assets, but gains should not be. When there is a loss, the asset acquired should be debited for its list price (cash paid plus trade-in allowance). When there is a gain, however, the asset acquired should be debited for the carrying value of the asset traded in plus cash paid (this will result in nonrecognition of the gain).

b. For income tax purposes, no gain or loss should be recognized on the exchange of similar assets. All assets acquired should be recorded at the carrying value of the asset traded in plus cash paid.

Lecture Outline

A. An asset is disposed of when it is discarded, sold, or traded in.

B. Record depreciation for the period preceding disposal.

C. Journalize the disposal of an asset.

   1. Debit accumulated depreciation and credit the asset account.

   2. Debit any receipt of cash.

   3. Debit or credit a loss or gain on disposal, if cash received differs from the carrying value.

D. Account for a similar asset received from a trade-in.

   1. For reporting purposes, losses are recognized, but gains are not.

   2. For tax purposes, no gain or loss should be recognized.

OBJECTIVE 7: Record property, plant, and equipment transactions in the plant
              asset records (pp. 479-481)

Summary Statement

Most companies maintain a subsidiary ledger for each type of asset, detailing
the purchase, depreciation, and disposal of each particular asset within that
asset group. This practice enables the company to exercise adequate control
over the assets and to provide tax, insurance, and depreciation information to
the accounting department.

Related Text Illustrations

Figure 13-4   Illustration of Plant Asset Subsidiary Records and Controlling
              Accounts (pp. 480-481)

Lecture Outline

A. Property, plant, and equipment should be recorded in subsidiary ledgers, detailing the accounting for each asset.

OBJECTIVE 8: Identify the accounting issues associated with natural resources
              and compute depletion (pp. 481-484)

Summary Statement

Natural resources are tangible nonmonetary assets containing valuable substances
that may be extracted and sold. They are sometimes referred to as wasting assets, and include standing timber, oil and gas fields, and mineral deposits.

Depletion refers to the allocation of a natural resource's cost to accounting
periods based upon the amount extracted each period. Depletion for each year is
computed as follows:

$$\frac{\text{cost} - \text{residual value}}{\text{estimated units to be extracted}} \times \text{actual units extracted during period}$$

Units extracted but not sold in that year are recorded as inventory, to be
charged as expense in the year sold.

Assets that are acquired in conjunction with the natural resource, and that cannot be used after the natural resource is depleted, should be depreciated on the
same basis as depletion is computed.

In accounting for the exploration and development of oil and gas resources, two
methods have been used. The full costing method, which is no longer acceptable,

capitalizes and depletes costs of both successful and dry wells. Under <u>success-ful efforts accounting</u>, the method now required, the cost of a dry well is written off immediately as a loss.

The SEC has rejected both of the above methods and has proposed <u>reserve recognition accounting</u>, a method that emphasizes the current value of reserves discovered. It may be a long while, however, before the issue of oil and gas accounting is resolved.

<u>New Words and Terms</u>

wasting assets (p. 481)
successful efforts accounting (p. 483)
full costing (p. 483)
reserve recognition accounting (p. 483)

<u>Lecture Outline</u>

A. Depletion is the allocation of the cost of a natural resource over the periods benefitted.

B. Compute depletion expense, using the depletion formula.

   1. The estimated life in units, as well as the residual value are difficult to determine.

C. Units extracted but unsold are recorded as inventory.

D. Depreciation, not depletion, should be taken on tangible assets used with natural resources.

E. Two methods have been used in accounting for oil and gas resources:

   1. Full-costing method -- No longer acceptable

   2. Successful efforts accounting -- Dry wells are expensed immediately

F. The SEC has proposed reserve recognition accounting for oil and gas.

Chapter Thirteen Property, Plant, and Equipment

Learning Objectives	Questions	Exercises	A & B Problems	Case
1. Describe the nature, types, and problems of long-term nonmonetary assets.	1, 2, 3, 4			
2. Account for the cost of long-term nonmonetary assets.	5, 6, 7	1	2, 4, 5, 6, 7	
3. Define depreciation, show how to record it, and state the factors that affect its computation.	8, 12			
4. Compute periodic depreciation under the (a) straight-line method, (b) production method, and (c) accelerated methods, including (1) sum-of-the-years'-digits method and (2) declining-balance method.	9, 10, 11, 13, 14, 15	2, 3, 4, 5, 9	1, 2, 3, 5, 6, 7	1
5. Apply depreciation methods to problems of partial years, revised rates, items of small unit value, and groups of similar items.	16, 17, 18, 19	4, 5, 6	3, 4	
6. Account for disposal of depreciable assets.	21, 22, 23	7, 8	5, 6	1
7. Record property, plant, and equipment transactions in the plant asset records.	24		5	
8. Identify the accounting issues associated with natural resources and compute depletion.	25, 26	9, IAI	7	

DIFFICULTY AND TIME CHART

A & B Problems	Difficulty	Time (in minutes)
1	easy	30
2	medium	30
3	medium	20
4	medium	30
5	medium	40
6	difficult	45
7	difficult	35
Case 13-1	difficult	30

TEN-MINUTE QUIZ

T   F   1.   One argument in favor of accelerated depreciation is that repair and maintenance tends to be greater in later years.

T   F   2.   Under the double-declining method of depreciation, an asset may not be depreciated below its estimated residual value.

T   F   3.   Natural resources are included in the intangible asset classification in the balance sheet.

T   F   4.   The group depreciation method would probably be used by a taxi company that owns several hundred taxis.

T   F   5.   Depreciation, as the term is used in accounting, refers to the physical deterioration of an asset.

T   F   6.   When the estimated residual value is changed after some depreciation has been taken on an asset, corrections must be made to the prior periods in which depreciation was taken.

T   F   7.   Driveways and parking lots are properly included in the Land account because they are not subject to depreciation.

T   F   8.   The unexpired cost of a plant asset is referred to as its carrying value.

T   F   9.   A machine's estimated life in years is irrelevant in computing its depreciation under the production method.

T   F   10. The depreciable cost of an asset equals its original cost minus accumulated depreciation.

_____ 11. A company purchases land and a building on the land for a total of $80,000. The fair market value of the land and building are $25,000 and $75,000, respectively. The land and building should be recorded at
a. $40,000 each.
b. $25,000 and $75,000, respectively.
c. $20,000 and $60,000, respectively.
d. $80,000 each.
e. $26,667 and $53,333, respectively.

_____ 12. The cost of tearing down a building would properly be
a. debited to the Building account.
b. expensed immediately.
c. debited to the Land account.
d. debited to the Land Improvements account.
e. debited to an Intangible Assets account.

_____ 13. An asset that cost $6,000 and has accumulated depreciation of $4,500 is sold for $1,300. The journal entry would include a
a. debit to Loss on Sale of Asset for $4,700.
b. credit to Gain on Sale of $1,300.
c. credit to the asset account for $1,500.
d. credit to Accumulated Depreciation for $4,500.
e. debit to Loss on Sale of Asset for $200.

_____ 14. An important way of maintaining control over plant assets is to keep a separate record card on each plant asset in
a. the general ledger.
b. the subsidiary ledger.
c. the controlling account.
d. the depreciation ledger.
e. the voucher register.

_____ 15. Equipment costing $8,000 with accumulated depreciation of $6,700 is traded for equipment priced at $15,000 minus a trade-in allowance of $3,000. Under the income tax method of recording no gain or loss, the new equipment would be recorded at
a. $12,000.
b. $15,000.
c. $16,300.
d. $13,300.
e. $13,700.

The following information relates to questions 16 through 18:

On January 1, a machine with a useful life of 5 years and a residual value of $2,000 was purchased for $10,000.

_____ 16. What is the depreciation expense in year 3 under straight-line depreciation?
a. $2,000 b. $6,000 c. $1,600 d. $4,800 e. $4,000

_____ 17. What is the depreciation expense in year 4 under sum-of-the-years' digits?
a. $1,600 b. $533 c. $1,067 d. $2,000 e. $1,333

_____ 18. What is the depreciation expense in year 2 under double-declining balance?
a. $4,000 b. $3,200 c. $2,400 d. $2,720 e. $1,920

_____ 19. In oil and gas accounting, the method that requires the cost of dry
holes to be written off immediately as a loss is
a. successful efforts accounting.
b. reserve recognition accounting.
c. the current operating method.
d. the accrual method.
e. the full costing method.

_____ 20. A company purchases an oil well for $200,000. It estimates that the
well contains 500,000 barrels, has a 10-year life, and has no salvage value. If the company extracts and sells 40,000 barrels during
the first year, how much depletion expense should be recorded?
a. $16,000
b. $40,000
c. $20,000
d. $100,000
e. $24,000

ANSWERS TO TEN-MINUTE QUIZ

True-False		Multiple-Choice	
1.	T	11.	c
2.	T	12.	c
3.	F	13.	e
4.	T	14.	b
5.	F	15.	d
6.	F	16.	c
7.	F	17.	c
8.	T	18.	c
9.	T	19.	a
10.	F	20.	a

CHAPTER FOURTEEN

REVENUE AND EXPENSE ISSUES AND INFLATION ACCOUNTING

CHAPTER OUTLINE

Applying the Matching Rule to Revenue Recognition
    Point of Sale Basis
    Cash Basis
Applying the Matching Rule to Allocation of Expired Costs
    Capital Expenditures and Revenue Expenditures
    Intangible Assets
        Research and Development Costs
        Goodwill
    Arbitrary Allocation Procedures
The Nature of Inflation
    Price Indexes
    General Price Indexes
Reporting the Effects of Price Changes
    Constant Dollar Accounting
        Purchasing Power Gains and Losses
        Balance Sheet Restatement
        Arguments for and Against Restatement
    Current Value Accounting
        Arguments for Replacement Cost Disclosure
        Arguments Against Replacement Cost Disclosure
    The FASB Position
Chapter Review
    Review of Learning Objectives
    Review Problem: Comprehensive Capital and Revenue Expenditure Entries
    Answer to Review Problem
Chapter Assignments
    Questions
    Classroom Exercises
    Interpreting Accounting Information
    Problem Set A
    Problem Set B
    Financial Decision Case 14-1

LEARNING OBJECTIVES:

RESOURCE MATERIALS AND LECTURE OUTLINES

OBJECTIVE 1: Apply the matching rule to revenue recognition (pp. 502–503)

Summary Statement

Applying the matching rule involves (a) recognition of the revenue earned in the period, and (b) allocation of the expired costs to the period.

The following two bases are commonly used to determine when revenue should be recognized: (a) point-of-sale basis and (b) cash basis.

a. Under the point-of-sale basis, revenue is recognized when title to the goods sold passes to the buyer, or when services are rendered completely.

b. Under the cash basis, revenue is recognized when cash is received, regardless of when the sale is made.

New Words and Terms

point of sale basis (p. 503)
cash basis (p. 503)

Lecture Outline

A. The matching rule has two requirements:

   1. Recognize revenue earned during the period.

   2. Recognize an expense in the same period as the revenue that was generated by that expense.

B. Revenue is recognized under the point-of-sale basis or the cash basis.

1. Under the point-of-sale basis, revenue is recognized when title passes or when services are rendered.

2. Under the cash basis, revenue is recognized when cash is received.

OBJECTIVE 2: Apply the matching rule to the allocation of expired costs as it relates to capital expenditures and revenue expenditures (pp. 503-505)

Summary Statement

Capital expenditures are expenditures (payments or incurrence of liabilities) for plant and equipment, additions (as a building wing), betterments (as the installation of an air-conditioning system), and intangible assets. A capital expenditure is recorded as an asset because it will benefit several accounting periods. Revenue expenditures are expenditures for repairs, maintenance, fuel, and anything else necessary to maintain and operate the plant and equipment. A revenue expenditure is charged as expense in the period incurred, under the theory that it benefits only the current accounting period. For the sake of convenience, however, many companies establish a dollar amount above which all expenditures are considered capital expenditures and below which they are considered revenue expenditures.

Ordinary repairs are expenditures necessary to maintain an asset in good operating condition, and are charged as expense in the period incurred. Extraordinary repairs are expenditures (as for a major overhaul) that either increase the asset's residual value or lengthen its useful life. They are recorded by debiting Accumulated Depreciation and crediting Cash.

New Words and Terms

expenditure (p. 503)
capital expenditure (p. 503)
revenue expenditure (p. 504)
additions (p. 504)
betterments (p. 504)
ordinary repairs (p. 505)
extraordinary repairs (p. 505)

Lecture Outline

A. Any expenditure for plant and equipment is considered either a capital expenditure or a revenue expenditure.

1. A capital expenditure significantly improves or adds to an asset, and should be capitalized (recorded as an asset).

   a. Capital expenditures have definite future benefit, and should be allocated as expense in accordance with the matching principle.

   b. Examples are additions, betterments, and acquisitions of intangibles, plant, and equipment.

2. A revenue expenditure merely maintains the asset in good working condition.

   a. Revenue expenditures are expensed in the period incurred.

B. Extraordinary repairs are recorded with a debit to accumulated depreciation and a credit to cash.

C. For convenience, companies will expense all items under a certain dollar amount.

OBJECTIVE 3: Apply the matching rule to the accounting problems associated with intangible assets, including research and development costs and goodwill (pp. 505-509)

Summary Statement

Intangible assets are long-term nonmonetary assets that have no physical substance and that represent certain rights and advantages available to their owner. Examples of intangible assets are patents, copyrights, trademarks, goodwill, leaseholds, leasehold improvements, franchises, licenses, brand names, formulas, and processes. An intangible asset should be written off over its useful life (not to exceed 40 years) through a process called amortization.

Research and development involves developing new products, testing existing ones, and doing pure research. The costs associated with these activities should normally be charged to expense in the period incurred.

Goodwill, as the term is used in accounting, refers to the ability of a company to earn more than is normal for its particular industry and/or for the amount of its capitalization (net assets). Goodwill should be recorded only when a company is purchased, and equals the excess of the purchase cost over the fair market value of the net assets. There are several methods available to place a cost value on goodwill when a business is purchased. It often is (a) arbitrarily set by the buyer and seller, (b) arbitrarily valued at some multiple of the expected superior earnings, or (c) determined by capitalizing superior earnings at the industry's average rate of return. Once it is recorded, goodwill should be amortized over its estimated useful life, not to exceed 40 years.

New Words and Terms

goodwill (p. 508)

Related Text Illustrations

Table 14-1 Accounting for Intangible Assets (p. 507)

Lecture Outline

A. Intangible assets represent rights and privileges extended to the owner.
   List examples.

B. Intangible assets should usually be capitalized, and expensed over their
   useful lives (not to exceed 40 years) in accordance with the matching rule.

C. However, most research and development costs should be expensed in the period
   incurred, regardless of future benefit.

D. Goodwill is the excess of the purchase cost over the fair market value of
   the net assets purchased.

   1. For financial reporting purposes, goodwill should be amortized over its
      useful life (not to exceed 40 years).

   2. Goodwill may be estimated for negotiation purposes, usually based on
      superior past earnings.

OBJECTIVE 4: Demonstrate the effects of arbitrary allocation procedures on
              reported net income (pp. 509-510)

Summary Statement

Net income is affected to a great extent by the accounting estimates and procedures chosen when applying the matching principle. These choices must be
made when dealing with uncollectible accounts, inventory, depreciation, depletion, and amortization.

<u>Lecture Outline</u>

A. Net income is affected by the choice of one acceptable estimate or procedure chosen over another.

   1. Uncollectible accounts

      a. Allowance vs. direct charge-off method

      b. Default-percentage estimate

   2. Inventory

      a. FIFO, LIFO, etc.

      b. Periodic vs. perpetual

      c. Valuing inventory individually, by category, or in total

   3. Depreciation

      a. Straight-line, etc.

      b. Estimate of useful life and residual value

   4. Depletion -- Estimate of useful life in tons, barrels, etc.

   5. Amortization -- Estimate of useful life is difficult

OBJECTIVE 5: Identify the two principal types of price changes (pp. 510-513)

<u>Summary Statement</u>

One of the most difficult challenges in accounting is dealing effectively with changes in the <u>purchasing power</u> of the dollar. Changes in <u>specific price levels</u> relate to a specific commodity or item, whereas changes in <u>general price levels</u> relate to a group of goods and services. <u>Inflation</u> refers to an increase in the general price level, while <u>deflation</u> refers to a decrease in the general price level.

A <u>price index</u> shows the relative price (between periods) of the same group of goods and services. The percentage change in the index from one year to the next is computed as follows:

$$\frac{\text{change in index}}{\text{previous year's index}}$$

The Price Index for All Urban Consumers (CPI-U) is the index used in adjusting financial statements for changes in the general price level.

The two methods of accounting for changing prices are constant dollar accounting and current value accounting.

<u>New Words and Terms</u>

specific price levels (p. 511)
general price levels (p. 511)
inflation (p. 511)
purchasing power (p. 511)
deflation (p. 511)
price index (p. 511)

<u>Related Text Illustrations</u>

*Table 14-2 Construction of a Price Index (p. 512)
*Table 14-3 Consumer Price Index for Urban Consumers (p. 513)

<u>Lecture Outline</u>

A. There are two types of price changes:

   1. A specific price level change relates to a specific item.

   2. A general price level change relates to a <u>group</u> of items.

      a. The CPI-U measures general price level changes.

B. There are two methods of accounting for changing prices:

   1. Constant dollar accounting (see objective 6)

   2. Current value accounting (see objective 6)

OBJECTIVE 6:   Using constant dollar accounting, compute purchasing power gains and losses, and restate a balance sheet for changes in the general price level (pp. 513-519)

Summary Statement

Constant dollar accounting involves restating historical cost statements for changes in the general price level. That is, all amounts are stated in dollars of uniform general purchasing power.

a. Changes in the general price level affect monetary and nonmonetary items differently. Monetary items (cash, receivables, and liabilities) are stated in terms of current dollars at all times. Since these items are fixed in dollar amount regardless of inflation or deflation, purchasing power gains and losses will occur. On the other hand, nonmonetary items (inventory, investments, plant assets, intangibles, owners' equity, revenues, and expenses) are sensitive to changes in the general price level and therefore do not create purchasing power gains and losses.

b. To restate an amount in terms of current dollars, use this formula:

$$\text{recorded amount} \times \frac{\text{current price level}}{\text{price level when item originated}}$$

Nonmonetary items on the balance sheet are adjusted for changes in the price level since the item's origin, except for retained earnings, which is computed as a balancing figure.

Current value accounting represents a departure from historical cost accounting, and involves disclosure of current value information. Current value may be measured in terms of net realizable value (the amount a company could sell its assets for) or replacement cost (the cost of buying equivalent, new assets).

New Words and Terms

constant dollar accounting (p. 513)
purchasing power gains and losses (p. 514)
current value accounting (p. 518)
net realizable value (p. 519)
replacement cost (p. 519)

Related Text Illustrations

*Figure 14-1 Calculation of Purchasing Power Gain or Loss (p. 516)
*Figure 14-2 Restatement of Balance Sheet (p. 517)

Lecture Outline

A. Constant dollar accounting restates historical cost financial statements for general price level changes.

1. Monetary items are stated in terms of current dollars.

   a. Monetary items include cash, receivables, and payables.

   b. They are fixed in dollar amount, regardless of general price level changes.

   c. Purchasing power gains and losses should be recorded.

2. Nonmonetary items (all accounts not mentioned above) must be restated.

   a. They are sensitive to general price level changes.

   b. They do not create purchasing power gains and losses.

   c. Balance sheet items should be restated (see formula in summary or text).

B. Current value accounting represents a departure from historical cost accounting.

1. General price level changes are irrelevant.

2. Values are based on net realizable value or replacement cost.

OBJECTIVE 7: Describe the FASB's approach to accounting for changing prices
             (pp. 519-522)

Summary Statement

The FASB requires that certain large publicly held companies disclose supplemental information (for the current year and the most recent five years) on both a constant dollar and current value basis. The current value is the lower of net realizable value or replacement cost at the balance sheet date.

<u>Related Text Illustrations</u>

Figure 14-3   Disclosure for Current Year from Annual Report of Westinghouse
              Electric Corporation (p. 520)
Figure 14-4   Disclosure for Most Recent Five Years from Annual Report of
              Westinghouse Electric Corporation (p. 521)

<u>Lecture Outline</u>

A. The FASB requires <u>supplemental</u> information:

   1. For the current and most recent five years

   2. Based on both constant dollar and current value accounting

      a. For current value accounting, use the lower of net realizable value
         and replacement cost.

Chapter Fourteen   Revenue and Expense Issues and Inflation Accounting

Learning Objectives	Questions	Exercises	A & B Problems	Case
1. Apply the matching rule to revenue recognition.	1, 2			
2. Apply the matching rule to the allocation of expired costs as it relates to capital expenditures and revenue expenditures.	1, 3, 4 5, 6	4	5	
3. Apply the matching rule to the accounting problems associated with intangible assets, including research and development costs and goodwill.	8, 9, 10, 11, 12	2, 3	2, 3, 6	
4. Demonstrate the effects of arbitrary allocation procedures on reported net income.	7	5	1	1
5. Identify the two principal types of price changes.	13, 14			
6. Using constant dollar accounting, compute purchasing power gains and losses, and restate a balance sheet for changes in the general price level.	15, 16	1, 6, IAI	4	
7. Describe the FASB's approach to accounting for changing prices.	17			

DIFFICULTY AND TIME CHART

A & B Problems	Difficulty	Time (in minutes)
1	easy	35
2	easy	25
3	easy	15
4	medium	30
5	difficult	50
6	medium	35
Case 14-1	medium	25

TEN-MINUTE QUIZ

T   F   1.   Under the point of sale basis, revenue should be recognized when cash is received from the sale.

T   F   2.   Current value accounting makes use of the general price index.

T   F   3.   Leasehold improvements become the property of the landlord upon expiration of the lease.

T   F   4.   Purchasing power gains and losses should be included in an income statement adjusted for changing prices.

T   F   5.   When an expenditure extends the life of an asset, the journal entry should include a debit to Accumulated Depreciation.

T   F   6.   Current value accounting represents a departure from historical cost accounting.

T   F   7.   When preparing a balance sheet adjusted for general price level changes, both Retained Earnings and Accumulated Depreciation are subject to restatement.

T   F   8.   Net realizable value is the cost of buying equivalent new assets.

T   F   9.   Constant dollar accounting does not represent a departure from historical cost accounting.

T   F   10.   Under constant dollar accounting, each nonmonetary item in the balance sheet is restated based upon the changes in the specific item's price level.

_____   11.   The cash basis of accounting
      a.   records revenue when earned.
      b.   is theoretically preferable to the accrual basis.
      c.   is justified when there is considerable doubt as to ultimate collection on a sale.
      d.   may not be used by individuals who file income tax returns.
      e.   always violates the matching principle.

_____ 12. A company purchases for $24,000 an asset that has a useful life of six years and no salvage value. After two years, the company spent $4,000 for a major overhaul that would extend the machine's useful life four years beyond the original six. Assuming straight-line depreciation, how much depreciation should be taken in year 3?
   a. $2,800
   b. $2,000
   c. $2,500
   d. $4,000
   e. $1,600

_____ 13. During deflationary periods, a purchasing power gain arises when
   a. monetary assets exceed monetary liabilities.
   b. monetary liabilities exceed monetary assets.
   c. nonmonetary assets exceed nonmonetary liabilties.
   d. nonmonetary liabilities exceed nonmonetary assets.
   e. monetary assets exceed nonmonetary assets.

_____ 14. A long-term note for $20,000 was received by XYZ Company when the general price index was 90. What amount should be used in restating the note receivable (under constant dollar accounting) when the index is 135?
   a. $18,000
   b. $20,000
   c. $27,000
   d. $27,300
   e. $30,000

_____ 15. Which of the following intangible assets should be expensed in the year incurred, regardless of the extent of future benefit?
   a. Leasehold improvements
   b. Goodwill
   c. Research and development
   d. Leaseholds
   e. Patents

_____ 16. Which of the following would not be considered a capital expenditure?
   a. Addition of a building wing
   b. Complete overhaul of an air-conditioning system
   c. The cost to install a piece of equipment
   d. Tune-up of the company vehicle
   e. Replacing an old motor with a new one in a piece of equipment

_____ 17. A company earns an average of $13,000 on net assets of $100,000, in an industry that normally earns 8% on its net assets. If goodwill is computed by capitalizing average superior earnings at 20%, what is goodwill?
   a. $1,000
   b. $5,000
   c. $25,000
   d. $57,000
   e. $65,000

_____ 18. The exclusive right to publish and sell literary, artistic, or musical work is called a
    a. copyright.
    b. patent.
    c. trademark.
    d. franchise.
    e. license.

_____ 19. An asset purchased for $1,000 in 1970, when the Consumer Price Index was 116 (1967 = 100), would be restated to what amount today (in constant dollars) assuming today's CPI is 200?
    a. $580
    b. $1,000
    c. $1,160
    d. $1,724
    e. $2,000

_____ 20. Holding which of the following assets during a period of inflation will result in a purchasing power loss?
    a. Accounts Receivable
    b. Inventory
    c. Machinery
    d. Notes Payable
    e. Copyrights

ANSWERS TO TEN-MINUTE QUIZ

True-False		Multiple-Choice	
1.	F	11.	c
2.	F	12.	c
3.	T	13.	a
4.	T	14.	b
5.	T	15.	c
6.	T	16.	d
7.	T	17.	c
8.	F	18.	a
9.	T	19.	d
10.	F	20.	a

CHAPTER FIFTEEN

ACCOUNTING FOR PARTNERSHIPS

CHAPTER OUTLINE

Partnership Characteristics
    Voluntary Association
    Partnership Agreement
    Limited Life
    Mutual Agency
    Unlimited Liability
    Co-ownership of Partnership Property
    Participation in Partnership Income
    Summary of the Advantages and Disadvantages of Partnerships
Accounting for Partners' Equity
Distribution of Partnership Income and Losses
    Stated Ratio
    Capital Investment Ratio
    Salaries, Interest, and Stated Ratio
Dissolution of a Partnership
    Admission of a New Partner
    Withdrawal of a Partner
    Death of a Partner
Liquidation of a Partnership
    Gain on Sale of Assets
    Loss on Sale of Assets
Chapter Review
    Review of Learning Objectives
    Review Problem: Distribution of Income and Admission of Partner
    Answer to Review Problem
Chapter Assignments
    Questions
    Classroom Exercises
    Interpreting Accounting Information: Meriweather Clinic
    Problem Set A
    Problem Set B
    Financial Decision Case 15-1: L & T Oyster Bar

LEARNING OBJECTIVES:

RESOURCE MATERIALS AND LECTURE OUTLINES

OBJECTIVE 1: Identify the major characteristics of a partnership (pp. 540-542)

Summary Statement

A partnership is "an association of two or more persons to carry on as co-owners a business for profit." Its chief characteristics are as follows:

a. Voluntary association: Partners choose each other when they form their business.

b. Partnership agreement: Partners may have either an oral or a written agreement.

c. Limited life: Certain events may dissolve the partnership.

d. Mutual agency: Each partner may bind the partnership to outside contracts.

e. Unlimited liability: Each partner is personally liable for all debts of the partnership.

f. Co-ownership of partnership property: Business property is jointly owned by all partners.

g. Participation in partnership income: Each partner shares income and losses of the business.

New Words and Terms

partnership (p. 540)
partnership agreement (p. 541)
limited life (p. 541)
mutual agency (p. 541)
unlimited liability (p. 541)

CHAPTER FIFTEEN

<u>Lecture Outline</u>

A. Define partnership, and discuss the following characteristics:

1. Voluntary association

2. Partnership agreement

3. Limited life

4. Mutual agency

5. Unlimited liability

6. Co-ownership of partnership property

7. Participation in partnership income

OBJECTIVE 2:   Identify the advantages and disadvantages of the partnership form
of business (p. 542)

<u>Summary Statement</u>

The advantages of a partnership are (a) ease of formation and dissolution, (b)
ability to pool capital and individual talents, (c) avoidance of the corporation's tax burden, and (d) freedom and flexibility of its partners' actions.

The disadvantages of a partnership are (a) limited life, (b) mutual agency, (c)
unlimited liability, (d) capital limitation, and (e) difficulty of transferring
ownership interest.

<u>Lecture Outline</u>

A. There are several advantages of the partnership form of business:

1. Ease of formation and dissolution.

240

2. Ability to pool capital and individual talents

3. Avoidance of the corporation's tax burden

4. Freedom and flexibility of partners' actions

B. There are several disadvantages of the partnership form of business:

1. Limited life

2. Mutual agency

3. Unlimited liability

4. Capital limitation

5. Difficulty of transferring ownership interest

OBJECTIVE 3:   Record investments of cash and of other assets by the partners in forming a partnership (pp. 542-544)

<u>Summary Statement</u>

The owners' equity section of a partnership's balance sheet is called <u>Partners' Equity</u>, and a separate capital and withdrawals account must be maintained for each partner. When a partner makes an investment, the assets contributed are debited at their fair market value, and the partner's capital account is credited.

<u>New Words and Terms</u>

partners' equity (p. 542)

<u>Lecture Outline</u>

A. A separate capital and withdrawals account is maintained for each partner.

B. Journalize the investment by a partner.

   1. Assets are recorded at their fair market value.

   2. Liabilities assumed by the partnership are deducted from the assets
      invested.

OBJECTIVE 4:   Compute the income or losses that partners share, based on a
stated ratio, the capital investment ratio, and salaries and interest to partners (pp. 544–550)

Summary Statement

The method of distributing partnership income and losses should be specified in
the partnership agreement. The most common methods base distribution on (a) a
stated ratio only, (b) a capital investment ratio only, and (c) a combination
of fixed "salaries," interest on each partner's capital, and the stated ratio.
Net income is distributed to partners' equity by debiting Income Summary and
crediting each partner's capital account; the reverse is done for a net loss.

When income and losses are based upon a stated income ratio only, partnership
income or loss for the period is multiplied by each partner's ratio (stated as
a fraction or percentage) to obtain each partner's share.

When income and losses are based upon a capital investment ratio only, partnership income or loss for the period is multiplied by each partner's proportion
of total capital invested either (a) at the beginning of the period or (b) during the period on the average.

When income and losses are based upon "salaries," interest, and a stated ratio,
a certain procedure must be followed. First, "salaries" and interest must be
allocated to the partners regardless of the net income figure for the period.
Then, any excess of net income over the salary and interest allocation must
also be allocated to the partners, in the stated ratio. On the other hand, if
the salary and interest allocation exceeds net income, then this excess must be
deducted from each partner's allocation, in the stated ratio.

Lecture Outline

A. Illustrate the distribution of partnership income and losses, using the following methods:

   1. Based on a stated ratio only

2. Based on capital investment ratio only

3. Based on salaries, capital investments, and stated ratio

B. Journalize the distribution of income and losses.

OBJECTIVE 5:   Record a person's admission to or withdrawal from a partnership
               (pp. 551-558)

Summary Statement

When a partnership is legally dissolved, it loses the authority to continue
business as a going concern. Dissolution of a partnership occurs upon the (a)
withdrawal of a partner, (b) bankruptcy of a partner, (c) incapacity of a partner, (d) death of a partner, (e) admission of a new partner, (f) retirement of
a partner, or (g) expiration of the partnership agreement.

A new partner may be admitted into a partnership by either (a) purchasing an
interest in the partnership from one or more of the original partners or (b)
investing assets into the partnership.

a. When a new partner purchases an interest from another partner, the selling
   partner's capital account is debited and the buying partner's account credited for the interest in the business sold; the purchase price is ignored in
   making this entry.

b. When a new partner invests his or her own assets in the partnership, the contributed assets are debited and the new partner's capital account is credited; the amount of the debit and credit may or may not equal the value of
   the assets, depending upon the value of the business and the method applied.
   When the partners feel that the business is worth more than its net assets
   indicate, they will probably ask the entering partner to pay them a bonus.
   Under the opposite set of circumstances, a partnership may give the new
   partner a greater interest in the business than the value of the assets contributed.

A partner may withdraw from (leave) a partnership by either (a) taking assets
from the partnership at greater than, less than, or equal to the capital investment, or (b) selling his or her interest to new or existing partners.

New Words and Terms

dissolution (p. 551)
bonus (p. 552)

Related Text Illustrations

Figure 15-1 Alternative Ways for a Partner to Withdraw (p. 555)

Lecture Outline

A. List some causes of partnership dissolution.

B. There are two ways a new partner may be admitted:

1. The new partner purchases an interest from existing partner(s).

2. The new partner invests assets into the partnership, possibly resulting in a bonus.

C. There are two ways a partner may withdraw from a partnership:

1. The partner withdraws partnership assets (equal to, greater than, or less than his or her capital interest).

2. The partner sells his or her interest to new or existing partners.

OBJECTIVE 6: Compute the distribution of assets to partners when they liquidate their partnership (pp. 558-564)

Summary Statement

Liquidation of a partnership is the process of (a) selling partnership assets, (b) paying off partnership liabilities, and (c) distributing the remaining assets to the partners. The liquidation transactions are summarized in a statement of liquidation.

a. The sale of partnership assets is recorded by debiting Cash, crediting the assets, and debiting or crediting Gain or Loss from Realization for the difference. The gain or loss must then be distributed to the partners in their stated ratio. If a partner's account results in a deficit after the distribution of a loss, then he or she must contribute personal assets to the business to cover the deficit. Otherwise, the remaining partners must absorb the deficit, in their stated ratio.

b. The payment of liabilities is recorded by debiting the liabilities and crediting Cash.

c. The distribution of cash to the partners is recorded by crediting Cash and debiting the partners' capital accounts for their remaining balances (not in their stated ratio).

New Words and Terms

liquidation (p. 558)

Related Text Illustrations

*Figure 15-2 Statement of Liquidation Showing Gain on Sale of Assets (p. 560)
*Figure 15-3 Statement of Liquidation Showing Loss on Sale of Assets (p. 562)

Lecture Outline

A. There are three steps in a partnership liquidation:

1. Sale of partnership assets, distributing the gains and losses to the partners (in their stated ratio)

2. Payment of liabilities

3. Distribution of remaining cash to the partners (not in stated ratio)

B. Discuss the disposition of a deficit in a partner's capital account.

Chapter Fifteen Accounting for Partnerships

Learning Objectives	Questions	Exercises	A & B Problems	Case
1. Identify the major characteristics of a partner-ship.	1, 2, 3			
2. Identify the advantages and disadvantages of the partnership form of business.	5			
3. Record investments of cash and of other assets by the partners in forming a partnership.	6	1	1, 5, 6	
4. Compute the income or losses that partners share, based on a stated ratio, the capital investment ratio, and salaries and interest to partners.	4, 7, 10, 13	2, 3	1, 2, 6	1
5. Record a person's admission to or withdrawal from a partnership.	8, 9	4, 6	6	1
6. Compute the distribution of assets to partners when they liquidate their partnership.	11, 12	5	4, 5	

DIFFICULTY AND TIME CHART

A & B Problems	Difficulty	Time (in minutes)
1	medium	35
2	medium	30
3	medium	25
4	medium	20
5	medium	45
6	difficult	55
Case 15-1	difficult	60

TEN-MINUTE QUIZ

T F   1. A partner can bind a partnership to outside contracts only after receiving permission from the other partners.

T F   2. A partner is liable for more than just his or her investment in the partnership.

T F   3. When a partnership agreement does not specify the method of profit distribution, profits and losses shall be distributed based on the ratio of capital investment by each partner.

T F   4. The admission of a partner will change the composition of partners' equity if the new partner purchases the old partner's interest by paying the old partner directly.

T F   5. If the liquidation of a partnership results in a negative balance in a partner's account, the other partners may have to absorb the negative balance from their capital accounts.

T F   6. In a partnership, when profits and losses are based upon salaries, interest, and a stated ratio, if the salary and interest allocation exceeds net income, then in fact a net loss has occurred.

T F   7. A partnership may be formed either orally or in writing.

T F   8. After selling all the assets in a liquidation, the partners share the remaining cash in their stated ratio.

T F   9. There is no income tax on a partnership, though the individual partners must pay a tax on their individual earnings.

T F 10. In a partnership, each partner has his or her own capital account and withdrawals account.

_____ 11. Which of the following will not result in dissolution of a partnership?
           a. Admission of a new partner
           b. Withdrawal of a partner
           c. Death of a partner
           d. Sale of partnership assets
           e. Bankruptcy of a partner

_____ 12. Smith invests $80,000 for a one-fourth interest in a partnership in which the other partners have capital totaling $160,000 before admitting Smith. After distribution of the bonus, what would Smith's capital be?
a. $20,000   b. $40,000   c. $60,000   d. $80,000   e. $100,000

_____ 13. James invests $20,000 for a 10% interest in a partnership that has total capital of $150,000 after admitting James. Which of the following is true?
a. James's capital is $20,000.
b. James's capital is $13,000.
c. James received a bonus of $5,000.
d. The original partners' capital in the business was $135,000 before admitting James.
e. The original partners received a bonus of $5,000.

_____ 14. In a liquidation, the liabilities of the partnership should be paid
a. before any sales of assets.
b. before the distribution of gains and losses on disposal of assets.
c. after a revaluation of assets.
d. before the distribution of cash to partners.
e. before a revaluation of assets.

_____ 15. A partnership agreement would most likely stipulate that assets be reappraised when
a. a new partner is admitted to the partnership.
b. a partner leaves the partnership.
c. profits and losses are being distributed.
d. the partnership is liquidated.
e. more than one new partner is admitted to the partnership.

_____ 16. Partners X and Y receive a salary allowance of $3,000 and $7,000, respectively, and share the remainder equally. If the company earned $4,000 during the period, what is the effect on Y's capital?
a. $2,000 increase
b. $3,000 decrease
c. $5,000 increase
d. $9,000 increase
e. $4,000 increase

_____ 17. Partners M and N receive an interest allowance of $10,000 and $15,000, respectively, and divide the remaining profits and losses in a 3:1 ratio. If the company sustained a net loss of $11,000 during the year, what is the effect on M's capital?
a. $17,000 decrease
b. $8,250 decrease
c. $10,500 decrease
d. $12,000 decrease
e. $2,667 decrease

_____ 18. The division of partnership profits on the basis of salaries, interest, and stated ratios is usually necessary because
a. most states require this method of distribution.
b. it reflects the amount of time devoted to the partnership by the partners.
c. partners seldom contribute time, effort, and resources equally.
d. it prevents arguments among the partners.
e. this is the required method of distribution when no partnership agreement exists.

_____ 19. The ability of a partner to enter into a contract on behalf of all partners is called
a. voluntary association.
b. mutual agency.
c. unlimited liability.
d. limited liability.
e. voluntary agency.

_____ 20. A liquidation differs from a dissolution in that in a liquidation
a. there may be an adjustment of partners' capital accounts.
b. assets may be revalued.
c. gains and losses are distributed according to the partnership agreement.
d. the business will not continue.
e. a new partnership agreement must be prepared.

ANSWERS TO TEN-MINUTE QUIZ

<u>True-False</u>   <u>Multiple-Choice</u>

1.   F   11.   d
2.   T   12.   c
3.   F   13.   e
4.   F   14.   d
5.   T   15.   b
6.   F   16.   e
7.   T   17.   a
8.   F   18.   c
9.   T   19.   b
10. T   20.   d

CORPORATIONS: ORGANIZATION AND CONTRIBUTED CAPITAL

CHAPTER OUTLINE

LEARNING OBJECTIVES:

RESOURCE MATERIALS AND LECTURE OUTLINES

OBJECTIVE 1:   Define a corporation and describe its basic organization and key
personnel (pp. 577-579)

<u>Summary Statement</u>

A <u>corporation</u> is a business organization authorized by the state to conduct business, and considered a separate legal entity from its owners. It is the dominant form of American business because it makes possible the accumulation of large quantities of capital.

Before a corporation may do business, it must apply for and obtain a charter from the state. The state must approve the <u>articles of incorporation</u>, which describe the basic purpose and structure of the proposed corporation.

The articles of incorporation will indicate the number of <u>shares of stock</u> that a corporation is authorized to issue. Stock that has been <u>issued</u> to stockholders and has not been bought back by the corporation is called <u>outstanding stock</u>.

Management of a corporation consists of the board of directors, who determine corporate policy, and the officers, who carry on the daily operations. The board is elected by the stockholders, and the officers are appointed by the board.

The stockholders usually meet once a year to elect directors and to carry on other important business. Each share of voting stock entitles its owner to one vote. A stockholder unable to attend the meeting can legally authorize another to vote his or her shares, called voting by <u>proxy</u>.

Some specific duties of the board of directors are to (a) declare <u>dividends</u>, (b) authorize contracts, (c) determine executive salaries, (d) arrange major loans with banks, and (e) appoint an <u>audit committee</u> to serve as a channel of communication between the corporation and the independent auditor. Management's primary means of reporting the corporation's financial position and results of operations is its annual report.

<u>New Words and Terms</u>

corporation (p. 577)
articles of incorporation (p. 577)

share of stock (p. 578)
proxy (p. 579)
audit committee (p. 579)

Related Text Illustrations

*Figure 16-1 The Corporate Form of Business (p. 578)

Lecture Outline

A. A corporation is a business organization authorized by the state, and considered a separate legal entity from its owners.

B. The state must approve the articles of incorporation and grant a charter before the corporation can do business.

C. A corporation must obtain permission to issue a certain amount of stock.

D. Outstanding stock is stock purchased by stockholders, but not bought back
   by the corporation.

E. Officers carry on the everyday operations of a corporation, and are appointed
   by the board.

F. The board of directors sets corporate policy (list other duties); it is
   elected by the stockholders.

G. The audit committee is the channel of communication between the corporation
   and the independent auditor.

H. The annual report includes the corporation's financial statements, as well
   as other information about the business.

OBJECTIVE 2: State the advantages and disadvantages of the corporate form of
              business (pp. 579-581)

Summary Statement

The corporate form of business has several advantages over the sole proprietorship and partnership: separate legal entity, limited liability of owners, ease
of capital generation, ease of transfer of ownership, lack of mutual agency,

continuous existence, centralized authority and responsibility, and professional management.

The corporate form of business has several disadvantages compared with the sole proprietorship and partnership: government regulation, double taxation, limited liability of owners, and separation of ownership and control.

Lecture Outline

A. There are several advantages to the corporate form of business:

1. Separate legal entity

2. Limited liability of owners

3. Ease of capital generation

4. Ease of transfer of ownership

5. Lack of mutual agency

6. Continuous existence

7. Centralized responsibility

8. Professional management

B. There are several disadvantages of the corporate form of business:

1. Government regulation

2. Double taxation

3. Limited liability of owners

4. Separation of ownership and control

OBJECTIVE 3: Account for organization costs (pp. 581-582)

Summary Statement

The costs of forming a corporation (such as attorneys' fees and incorporation
fees) are debited to an intangible asset account called organization costs.
These costs are amortized over the early period of the corporation's life, usually five years.

New Words and Terms

organization costs (p. 581)

Lecture Outline

A. Organization costs (an intangible asset) consist of all costs of forming a
   corporation.

B. Organization costs are usually amortized over five years.

OBJECTIVE 4: Identify the components of stockholders' equity (pp. 582-584)

Summary Statement

A corporation's balance sheet contains assets, liabilities, and a stockholders'
equity section. Stockholders' equity is composed of contributed capital, representing the stockholders' investment, and retained earnings, representing earnings that have remained in the business.

Ownership in a corporation is evidenced by a document called a stock certificate. A stockholder sells stock by endorsing the stock certificates and send-
ing them to the corporation's secretary or its transfer agent. The secretary
or transfer agent is responsible for transferring the corporation's stock, maintaining stockholders' records, and preparing a list of stockholders for stockholders' meetings and for the payment of dividends. In addition, corporations
often engage an underwriter to assist in the initial issue of stock.

When only one type of stock is issued, it is called common stock. A second
type of stock, called preferred stock, may also be issued. Preferred stockholders receive prior claim over common stockholders to dividends when declared
and to assets when distributed at liquidation. In addition, preferred stock
(a) is cumulative or noncumulative, (b) is participating or nonparticipating,
(c) is convertible or nonconvertible, (d) may be callable, and (e) usually has
no voting rights. Because common stockholders' claim to assets upon liquidation ranks behind that of creditors and preferred stockholders, common stock is
considered the residual equity of a company.

New Words and Terms

stockholders' equity (p. 582)
contributed capital (p. 582)
stock certificate (p. 583)
authorized stock (p. 583)
par value (p. 583)
issued stock (p. 584)
outstanding stock (p. 584)
common stock (p. 584)
residual equity (p. 584)
preferred stock (p. 584)

Lecture Outline

A. Stockholders' equity is composed of contributed capital and retained earnings.

B. When one type of stock is issued, it is called common stock.

C. Preferred stockholders receive preference over common stockholders, under two circumstances:

   1. To receive dividends

   2. Upon liquidation of the corporation

D. Preferred stock has several features:

   1. It is cumulative or noncumulative.

   2. It is participating or nonparticipating.

   3. It is convertible or nonconvertible.

   4. It may be callable.

   5. It usually has no voting rights.

OBJECTIVE 5: Calculate the division of dividends between common and preferred
             stockholders (pp. 585-588)

Summary Statement

Each share of preferred stock entitles its owner to a dollar amount or percentage of par value each year before common stockholders are to receive anything.
Once the preferred stockholders have received the annual dividends to which they
are entitled, however, the common stockholders generally receive the remainder.

When the preferred stockholders do not receive the full amount of their annual
dividend, the unpaid amount is carried over to the next year when the preferred
stock is cumulative. Unpaid back dividends are called dividends in arrears,
and should be disclosed either in the balance sheet or as a footnote. When the
preferred stock is noncumulative, unpaid dividends are not carried over to the
next period.

When a dividend is declared by the board of directors, Dividends Declared is
debited, and Dividends Payable is credited.

When preferred stock is participating, its holders are entitled to more than the
annual fixed amount, once the common stockholders have also received an equal
percentage on their total par value. Preferred stock is fully participating
when no limit is placed on additional dividends, and is partially participating
when a limit does exist for additional dividends. Holders of nonparticipating
preferred stock, on the other hand, are limited to their annual fixed amount.

An owner of convertible preferred stock has the option to exchange each share of
preferred stock for a set number of common stock shares.

Some preferred stock is callable, meaning that the corporation has the right to
buy it back for cancellation at a specified call or redemption price. Convertible preferred stock can instead be converted to common stock if its holder so
desires.

New Words and Terms

noncumulative preferred stock (p. 585)
cumulative preferred stock (p. 585)
dividends in arrears (p. 585)
nonparticipating (p. 586)
participating (p. 586)
convertible preferred stock (p. 587)
callable preferred stocks (p. 588)

Lecture Outline

A. Compute the distribution of dividends to common and preferred shareholders,
   assuming the different features of preferred.

B. Dividends in arrears are unpaid back dividends when preferred stock is cumulative.

C. Journalize the declaration of a dividend.

OBJECTIVE 6:   Account for the issuance of common and preferred stock for cash and other assets   (pp. 589-593)

<u>Summary Statement</u>

<u>Par value</u> is a legal value established for a share of stock. Capital stock (common or preferred) may or may not have a par value, depending upon the specifications in the charter. When par-value stock is issued, the Capital Stock account is credited for the <u>legal capital</u> (par value), and any excess is recorded as Paid-in Capital in Excess of Par Value. In the stockholders' equity section of the balance sheet, the entire amount is labeled Total Contributed Capital. On rare occasions, stock is issued at a discount (less than par value), thereby creating a contingent liability (for the amount of the discount) for those stockholders upon liquidation.

<u>No-par stock</u> is stock for which par value has not been established, and it may be issued with or without a <u>stated value</u>. Stated value (when established by the board of directors) constitutes the legal capital for a share of no-par stock, and is set by the board of directors. The total stated value is recorded in the Capital Stock account. Any amount received in excess of stated value is recorded as Paid-in Capital in Excess of Stated Value. If no stated value is set, however, the entire amount received constitutes legal capital and is credited to Capital Stock.

When stock is issued in exchange for assets or for services rendered, the stock should be recorded at the fair market value of the assets or services, unless the fair market value of the stock is more easily determinable.

<u>New Words and Terms</u>

legal capital (p. 589)
no-par stock (p. 589)
stated value (p. 589)

<u>Lecture Outline</u>

A. Common and preferred stock may or may not have a par value.

B. Journalize the issue of par value stock at greater than par value.

C. Journalize the issue of par value stock at a discount.

D. Journalize the issue of no-par stock with a stated value.

E. Journalize the issue of no-par stock with no stated value.

F. Discuss the issue of stock in exchange for assets or services.

OBJECTIVE 7: Account for stock subscriptions (pp. 593-595)

Summary Statement

An investor who signs a stock subscription agrees to pay for a certain amount of stock at some later date or in installments. When subscriptions are received, Subscriptions Receivable is debited, and Capital Stock Subscribed (a contributed capital account) and Paid-in Capital in Excess of Par Value are credited. Upon collection, Cash is debited and Subscriptions Receivable is credited. When the stock is issued upon full payment, Capital Stock Subscribed is debited and Capital Stock is credited.

New Words and Terms

stock subscription   (p. 593)

Lecture Outline

A. Subscribed stock is paid for in installments.

   1. Journalize the receipt of subscriptions.

   2. Journalize the collection of cash.

   3. Journalize the issue of stock.

OBJECTIVE 8:   Account for the retirement of stock and donations of stock and
               other assets (pp. 595-597)

Summary Statement

When stock is retired, all of the contributed capital associated with the retired shares must be removed from the accounts. When less is paid than was
originally contributed, the difference is credited to Paid-in Capital, Retirement of Stock. When more is paid, the difference is debited to Retained Earnings.

When stock is donated to a corporation by its stockholders, only a memorandum
entry should be made because assets, liabilities, and stockholders' equity are
unaffected. In addition, the balance sheet should disclose the number of
shares now in the treasury.

When assets are donated to a corporation, they are debited at their fair market
value, and a contributed capital account is credited.

Lecture Outline

A. Journalize the retirement of stock at the original issue price.

B. Journalize the retirement of stock at less than the original issue price.

C. Journalize the retirement of stock at greater than the original issue price.

D. When stock is donated by its stockholders, only a memorandum entry is needed.

E. Donated assets are recorded at their fair market value.

OBJECTIVE 9:   Calculate book value per share, and distinguish it from market
               value (pp. 598-600)

Summary Statement

The book value of a share of stock equals the net assets represented by one
share of a company's stock. If the company has common stock only, the book
value per share is calculated by dividing stockholders' equity by the number of
outstanding and subscribed shares. When the company also has preferred stock,
the liquidating value of the preferred stock plus any dividends in arrears are
deducted from stockholders' equity in calculating book value per share of common stock.

<u>Market value</u> is the highest price that investors are willing to pay for a share of stock on the open market.

<u>New Words and Terms</u>

book value (p. 598)
market value (p. 600)

<u>Lecture Outline</u>

A. Calculate book value per share when there is no preferred stock.

B. Calculate book value per share when there <u>is</u> preferred stock.

   1. Liquidating value is deducted from stockholders' equity in the numerator.

   2. Dividends in arrears are also deducted.

C. Market value is the price that the willing buyer and seller will agree upon.

Chapter Sixteen   Corporations: Organization and Contributed Capital

Learning Objectives	Questions	Exercises	A & B Problems	Case
1. Define a corporation and describe its basic organization and key personnel.	1, 2, 3			
2. State the advantages and disadvantages of the corporate form of business.	4, 5			
3. Account for organization costs.	6, 7	7		
4. Identify the components of stockholders' equity.	8, 9, 15	2, IAI		1
5. Calculate the division of dividends between common and preferred stockholders.	14	3, 6	3	
6. Account for the issuance of common and preferred stock for cash and other assets.	10, 11, 13	1, 4, 8	1, 2, 5	
7. Account for stock subscriptions.	12	9	2, 5	
8. Account for the retirement of stock and donations of stock and other assets.		10	5	
9. Calculate book value per share, and distinguish it from market value.	16	5	4, 5	

DIFFICULTY AND TIME CHART

A & B Problems	Difficulty	Time (in minutes)
1	easy	20
2	easy	25
3	medium	25
4	medium	15
5	medium	45
Case 16-1	medium	30

TEN-MINUTE QUIZ

T   F   1.   Donations of assets by nonstockholders should not be recorded on the balance sheet because nothing was paid for the assets.

T   F   2.   When stock is retired for more than the original issue price, Retained Earnings is debited for the difference.

T   F   3.   The cumulative and participation features of stock do not apply to common stock.

T   F   4.   Stockholders' liability is generally limited to the amount of their investment.

T   F   5.   Corporate income is taxed only when it is distributed to the stockholders as dividends.

T   F   6.   A corporation will not be bound to a contract entered into by one of its stockholders.

T   F   7.   The costs of organizing a corporation are properly expensed in the first year of operation.

T   F   8.   Discount on Capital Stock refers to stock that is issued at less than its par value.

T   F   9.   Partially participating stock sets a limit on the amount that holders of common stock may receive when a dividend is paid.

T   F   10.   When computing book value per share, both the call value of preferred stock and any dividends in arrears are relevant.

_____   11.   A corporation has 10,000 shares of 8% cumulative and nonparticipating preferred stock and 20,000 shares of common stock outstanding. Par value for each is $100. No dividends were paid last year, but this year a $200,000 dividend is paid. How much of this $200,000 would go to the holders of common stock?
a.   None
b. $184,000
c. $160,000
d. $120,000
e. $40,000

_____ 12. Assume the same facts as in question 11, except that the preferred stock is noncumulative and fully participating, and that a $300,000 cash dividend is paid. How much of the $300,000 would go to the holders of preferred stock?
a. $100,000
b. $200,000
c. $150,000
d. $120,000
e. $180,000

_____ 13. The journal entry to record stock subscriptions <u>before</u> cash is received would include a
a. credit to Subscriptions Receivable.
b. credit to Cash.
c. credit to Common Stock Subscribed.
d. debit to Paid-in Capital in Excess of Par.
e. credit to Common Stock.

_____ 14. Book value per share refers to
a. the net assets represented by one share of a company's stock.
b. the highest price that investors will pay for a share of stock.
c. the par or stated value of a share of stock.
d. the issue price of the stock, less any market decline since issuance.
e. preferred stock, but not to common stock.

_____ 15. Which of the following is not a right given to common stockholders?
a. The right to vote for the board of directors
b. The right to participate in the daily operations of the business
c. The right to sell their stock at their own discretion
d. The right to purchase additional shares when issued
e. The right to vote by proxy

_____ 16. Dividends in arrears
a. should be shown on the balance sheet as a current liability.
b. should be disclosed as a footnote.
c. should be shown on the income statement as an expense.
d. should not be disclosed in the financial statements, nor as a footnote.

_____ 17. Par value
a. represents what a share of stock is worth.
b. represents the original selling price for a share of stock.
c. is established for a share of stock after it is issued.
d. is the legal capital established for a share of stock.

_____ 18. Which of the following classifications would represent the most shares of common stock?
a. Issued shares
b. Outstanding shares
c. Treasury shares
d. Unissued shares
e. Authorized shares

_____ 19. Preferred stock would <u>least</u> likely contain which characteristic?
   a. Preference as to assets upon liquidation of the corporation
   b. Preference as to dividends
   c. The right of the holder to convert to common stock
   d. The right of the holder to vote at stockholders' meetings
   e. The right of the corporation to redeem or retire the stock

_____ 20. Which of the following features applies to both common and preferred stock?
   a. The cumulative feature
   b. Voting rights
   c. The participation feature
   d. Legal capital
   e. Convertability

ANSWERS TO TEN-MINUTE QUIZ

<u>True-False</u>   <u>Multiple-Choice</u>

1.   F   11.   e
2.   T   12.   a
3.   T   13.   c
4.   T   14.   a
5.   F   15.   b
6.   T   16.   b
7.   F   17.   d
8.   T   18.   e
9.   F   19.   d
10.   T

CHAPTER SEVENTEEN

RETAINED EARNINGS AND CORPORATE INCOME STATEMENTS

CHAPTER OUTLINE

Retained Earnings Transactions
    Income and Losses of a Corporation
    Dividends
        Cash Dividends
        Stock Dividends
        Stock Splits
    Treasury Stock Transactions
        Purchase of Treasury Stock
        Reissuance of Treasury Stock
    Prior Period Adjustments
    Statement of Retained Earnings
Appropriation of Retained Earnings
Corporate Income Statements
    Income Tax Expense
        Dividends Received Deduction
        Net Operating Loss Deduction
        Charitable Contributions
        Capital Gains and Losses
        Corporate Tax Rates
        Investment Tax Credit and Other Tax Credits
        Corporate Tax Illustration
    Net of Taxes
    Discontinued Operations
    Extraordinary Items
    Accounting Changes
    Earnings per Share
Chapter Review
    Review of Learning Objectives
    Review Problem: Statement of Retained Earnings and Corporate Income
                     Statement
Chapter Assignments
    Questions
    Classroom Exercises
    Interpreting Accounting Information: Lockheed Corporation
    Problem Set A
    Problem Set B
    Financial Decision Case 17-1: Metzger Steel Corporation

LEARNING OBJECTIVES:

RESOURCE MATERIALS AND LECTURE OUTLINES

OBJECTIVE 1: Define and explain the significance of retained earnings
(pp. 615-616)

Summary Statement

The stockholders' equity section of a corporation's balance sheet is composed of contributed capital and retained earnings. Contributed capital represents the owners' capital investment, whereas retained earnings represents profits that have accumulated since a corporation's inception, minus any losses, dividends declared, or other transfers out of retained earnings.

Ordinarily, Retained Earnings will have a credit balance. However, when a debit balance exists, the corporation is said to have a deficit.

The Retained Earnings account may be increased through (a) net income from operations, and (b) certain prior period adjustments. It may be decreased through (a) net loss from operations, (b) cash dividend declarations, (c) stock dividend declarations, (d) certain prior period adjustments, and (e) certain treasury stock transactions. A corporation's net income is closed at the end of the period by debiting Income Summary and crediting Retained Earnings; the reverse is journalized for a net loss.

New Words and Terms

retained earnings (p. 615)
deficit (p. 616)

Related Text Illustrations

Figure 17-1 A Simplified Statement of Retained Earnings (p. 616)

<u>Lecture Outline</u>

A. Retained earnings is (for the most part) cumulative profits and losses, less
   dividends declared.

B. Negative retained earnings are considered a deficit.

C. Retained earnings may be increased in two ways:

   1. Net income

   2. Certain prior period adjustments

D. Retained earnings may be decreased in five ways:

   1. Net loss

   2. Cash dividends declared

   3. Stock dividends declared

   4. Certain prior period adjustments

   5. Certain treasury stock transactions

OBJECTIVE 2:   Account for cash dividends, stock dividends, and stock splits
               (pp. 616-622)

<u>Summary Statement</u>

A <u>dividend</u> is a distribution of assets by a corporation to its stockholders,
normally in cash. Dividends are usually stated as a specified dollar amount
per share of stock and are declared by the board of directors. Dividends are
declared on the date of declaration, specifying that the owners of the stock on
the date of record will receive the dividends on the date of payment.

When cash dividends are declared, the Dividends Declared account is debited and
Cash Dividends Payable is credited; when they are paid, Cash Dividends Payable
is debited and Cash is credited. The Dividends Declared account is closed to
Retained Earnings at the end of the year. No journal entry is made on the date

of record. A <u>liquidating dividend</u> is the return of contributed capital to the stockholders, and is normally paid when a company is going out of business.

A <u>stock dividend</u> is a pro rata distribution of shares of stock to a corporation's stockholders. Stock dividends are declared to (a) effect a noncash distribution, (b) reduce the stock's market price, and (c) allow a nontaxable distribution. The result of a stock dividend is the transfer of a portion of retained earnings to contributed capital. For a small stock dividend (less than 20-25 percent), the market value of the shares distributed is transferred from retained earnings. For a large stock dividend (greater than 20-25 percent), the par or stated value is transferred. A stock dividend does not change total stockholders' equity, nor does it change each stockholder's proportionate equity in the company.

A <u>stock split</u> is an increase in the number of shares of stock outstanding, with a corresponding decrease in the par or stated value of the stock. For example, a 3 for 1 split on 40,000 shares of $30 par value stock would result in the distribution of 80,000 additional shares (that is, a former owner of one share now owns two more shares) and the reduction of par value to $10. The amount for each component of stockholders' equity would not be affected.

The purpose of a stock split is to improve the stock's marketability by effecting a decrease in the stock's market price. In the above example, if the stock were selling for $180 per share, a 3 for 1 split would probably cause the market price to decline to approximately $60 per share. A memorandum entry should be made for a stock split, disclosing the decrease in par or stated value as well as the increase in shares of stock outstanding.

<u>New Words and Terms</u>

dividend (p. 616)
liquidating dividend (p. 617)
stock dividend (p. 618)
stock split (p. 621)

<u>Lecture Outline</u>

A. There are three dates associated with a cash dividend:

1. Date of declaration (discuss the journal entry)

2. Date of record (no entry)

3. Date of payment (discuss the journal entry)

B. A stock dividend is the proportional distribution of additional stock to its present shareholders.

   1. It conserves cash.

   2. The stock's market price will probably decline.

   3. It allows for a nontaxable distribution.

C. A stock dividend transfers a portion of retained earnings to contributed capital.

D. Journalize the declaration and distribution of a small and a large stock dividend.

   1. Observe stockholders' equity before and after the dividend.

E. A stock split is a distribution of additional stock for the purpose of effecting a decline in market price.

   1. Par or stated value will decrease.

   2. At most, a memorandum entry is needed.

OBJECTIVE 3: Account for treasury stock transactions (pp. 622-624)

Summary Statement

Treasury stock is common or preferred stock that has been issued and reacquired by the issuing company. That is, it is issued but no longer outstanding stock. Treasury stock is purchased (a) to distribute to employees through stock option plans, (b) to maintain a favorable market for the company's stock, (c) to increase earnings per share, and (d) to use in purchasing other companies.

Treasury stock may be held indefinitely, reissued, or canceled, and has no rights until reissued. Treasury stock appears on the balance sheet as the last item in the stockholders' equity section, as a deduction.

When treasury stock is purchased, it is debited for the purchase cost. It may be reissued at cost, above cost, or below cost. When cash received from reissuance exceeds the cost, the difference is credited to Paid-in Capital, Treasury Stock Transactions. When cash received is less than cost, the difference is debited to Paid-in Capital, Treasury Stock Transactions (and Retained Earnings if needed). In no instance should a gain or loss account be established.

New Words and Terms

treasury stock (p. 622)

Lecture Outline

A. Treasury stock is issued stock that has been reacquired by the issuing corporation, for the following reasons:

   1. Stock may be used for stock option plans.

   2. To maintain a favorable market for the company's stock.

   3. To increase earnings per share.

   4. Stock may be used to purchase other companies.

B. Treasury stock is the last item in stockholders' equity (as a deduction)

C. Journalize the purchase of treasury stock.

D. Journalize the reissuance of treasury stock (at cost, above cost, and below cost).

E. Gains and losses are not recognized during treasury stock transactions.

OBJECTIVE 4: Define prior period adjustments and prepare a statement of retained earnings (pp. 624-626)

Summary Statement

Prior period adjustments are entries made in the current period for certain transactions that relate to, but were not determinable in, prior accounting periods. A prior period adjustment can be made only (a) to correct an error in the financial statements of a prior period, or (b) to record a tax adjustment resulting from realization of income tax benefits of a preacquisition operating loss carry-forward of purchased subsidiaries. They appear in the current period's retained earnings statement as an adjustment to the beginning balance, but not in its income statement. All other items of income and loss during the period that do not qualify as a prior period adjustment must appear in the income statement.

The <u>statement of retained earnings</u> is a labeled calculation of the changes in retained earnings during the accounting period.

New Words and Terms

prior period adjustments (p. 624)
statement of retained earnings (p. 625)

Related Text Illustrations

*Figure 17-2 A Statement of Retained Earnings (p. 626)

Lecture Outline

A. Discuss the criteria for prior period adjustments, as well as their disclosure in the statement of retained earnings.

B. A statement of retained earnings is a labeled calculation of the changes in retained earnings during the period.

OBJECTIVE 5: Account for the appropriation of retained earnings (pp. 626-628)

Summary Statement

Retained earnings consist of appropriated and unappropriated retained earnings. Unappropriated retained earnings dictate the asset amount (if available) that may be distributed to stockholders as dividends. <u>Appropriated retained earnings</u> dictate the asset amount that is to be retained in the business for other purposes. Retained earnings are appropriated for contractual, legal, or voluntary reasons, and by the board of directors only. Retained Earnings is not a cash account, but is merely a guide to asset distribution.

Appropriations of retained earnings should be disclosed in the retained earnings portion of the balance sheet or as notes to the financial statements.

New Words and Terms

appropriated retained earnings (p. 626)

Lecture Outline

A. Retained earnings (not a cash account) may be appropriated (restricted) or unappropriated.

B. Retained earnings is appropriated to restrict dividend payments so that funds may be used for other purposes.

C. Appropriations may be contractual, legal, or voluntary.

D. Journalize the appropriation of retained earnings (e.g., for plant expansion).

E. Journalize the elimination of a retained earnings appropriation.

OBJECTIVE 6: Define the basic terms of corporate income tax liability, and calculate corporate tax liability (pp. 628-634)

Summary Statement

Corporate taxable income is determined by subtracting allowable business deductions from includable gross income. Some special features of corporate tax provisions are a special dividends-received deduction, carry-forwards and carry-backwards for net operating loss deductions and net capital losses, a limit on the deduction for charitable contributions, and tax credits for certain expenditures.

Capital assets comprise stocks and bonds owned by individuals, as well as certain business property. Capital assets are classified as long-term or short-term depending upon whether they have been held for more or less than one year. The combined total for all gains and losses on short-term capital assets during a tax year is called the net short-term capital gain (or loss). The combined total for all gains and losses on long-term capital assets is called the net long-term capital gain (or loss). An excess of net long-term capital gain over net short-term capital loss is termed net capital gain. A corporation's net long-term capital gain is taxed at 28 percent, whereas a net capital loss may be used only to offset net capital gains in the three preceding and five successive years.

Tax credits are dollar-for-dollar deductions from the computed tax liability. An investment tax credit of 6 to 10 percent is allowed on certain expenditures for plant assets.

Corporations are subject to a tax rate that ranges from 15 percent to a 46 percent marginal tax rate.

<u>New Words and Terms</u>

capital assets (p. 630)
net short-term capital gain (or loss) (p. 631)
net long-term capital gain (or loss) (p. 631)
net capital gain (p. 631)
tax credits (p. 631)
investment tax credit (p. 631)

<u>Related Text Illustrations</u>

*Figure 17-3   A Corporate Income Statement (p. 630)
*Table 17-1   Tax Rate Schedule for Corporations (p. 631)
 Figure 17-4   The Computation of Corporate Tax Liability (p. 633)

<u>Lecture Outline</u>

A. Corporate taxable income = Gross income minus business deductions.

B. Capital assets consist of stocks and bonds.

   1. Capital assets are classified as short-term or long-term.

   2. Define net short-term capital gain (or loss).

   3. Define net long-term capital gain (or loss).

   4. The net capital gain (or loss) = The combined figure for "2" and "3"
      above.

   5. Net capital gains are treated differently from net capital losses.

C. Tax credits are dollar-for-dollar deductions from the tax liability.

D. An investment tax credit of six or ten percent is allowed for certain plant
   assets.

E. The corporate tax rate ranges from a 15% to a 46% marginal rate. Illustrate
   this computation.

OBJECTIVE 7: Describe the disclosure on the income statement of discontinued
              operations, extraordinary items, and accounting changes
              (pp. 634-636)

Summary Statement

An income statement should contain all revenues and expenses of the period, as
well as discontinued operations, extraordinary items, accounting changes, and
earnings per share. These items should be disclosed (net of tax) after Income
from Continuing Operations.

The results of operations for the period and any gains or losses from the discontinued operations of a segment of a business should be disclosed (net of tax)
after Income from Continuing Operations. A segment is defined as a separate
major line of business or class of customer.

An extraordinary item is an event that is unusual and occurs infrequently. Extraordinary items should be disclosed separately in the income statement (net of
tax) after Discontinued Operations.

A company may change from one accounting principle to another (as from FIFO to
LIFO) only if it can be justified as better accounting practice. Once an accounting change is made, the nature and justification for the change, as well as
its effect on income before extraordinary items, net income, and earnings per
share, should be disclosed. In addition, the cumulative effect of the change on
prior years (net of tax) should be included on the income statement after extraordinary items.

New Words and Terms

discontinued operations (p. 634)
extraordinary items (p. 634)

Lecture Outline

A. In addition to revenue and expenses, an income statement should contain the
   following:

   1. Discontinued operations of a segment of a business

   2. Extraordinary gains and losses -- from unusual and infrequent items

   3. The cumulative effect of an accounting change on prior years

   4. Earnings per share (see objective 8)

B. All of the above should be disclosed net of tax.

OBJECTIVE 8:   Compute primary and fully diluted earnings per share
              (pp. 636-639)

Summary Statement

The earnings per share figure is used by investors to evaluate the performance
of a company, to estimate future earnings, and to evaluate their investment op-
portunities. Earnings per share figures should be disclosed for income from
continuing operations, income before extraordinary items, cumulative effect of
accounting changes, and net income, and should appear on the face of the income
statement.

When a company has issued no securities that are convertible into common stock,
a simple capital structure exists. In this instance, earnings per share is
computed by dividing net income applicable to common stock by the weighted-
average shares outstanding.

When a company has issued securities that may be converted into common stock, a
complex capital structure exists. In this instance, a dual presentation of
primary and fully diluted earnings per share is required. Primary earnings per
share is computed as follows:

    net income applicable to common stock
       weighted-average common shares
         plus common stock equivalents

Fully diluted earnings per share is computed as follows:

    net income applicable to common stock
       weighted-average common shares
         plus common stock equivalents
      plus other potentially dilutive securities

Common stock equivalents are convertible securities that are in substance common stock when they meet certain criteria.

New Words and Terms

simple capital structure (p. 637)
complex capital structure (p. 637)
common stock equivalents (p. 637)
primary earnings per share (p. 637)
fully diluted earnings per share (p. 637)

Lecture Outline

A. Earnings per share is a measure of performance, and may be composed of several parts.

B. A simple capital structure requires only one earnings per share figure.

C. A complex capital structure requires both primary and fully diluted EPS.

   1. Primary EPS only considers common stock and common stock equivalents.

   2. Fully diluted EPS considers, in addition, other potentially dilutive securities.

LEARNING OBJECTIVES CHART

Learning Objectives	Questions	Exercises	A & B Problems	Case
1. Define and explain the significance of retained earnings.	1, 2	1	7	
2. Account for cash dividends, stock dividends, and stock splits.	4, 5, 6	2, 3	2, 4, 7	1
3. Account for treasury stock transactions.	8	5	1, 2, 7	1
4. Define prior period adjustments and prepare a statement of retained earnings.	3, 9		2, 7	
5. Account for the appropriation of retained earnings.	7	4	2	
6. Define the basic terms of corporate tax liability, and calculate corporate tax liability.	10	6	3	
7. Describe the disclosure on the income statement of discontinued operations, extraordinary items, and accounting changes.	11, 13, 17	7, IAI	5	
8. Compute primary and fully diluted earnings per share.	12, 14, 15, 16	8	5, 6	

DIFFICULTY AND TIME CHART

A & B Problems	Difficulty	Time (in minutes)
1	easy	15
2	easy	20
3	medium	25
4	easy	25
5	medium	20
6	medium	20
7	difficult	40
Case 17-1	difficult	50

TEN-MINUTE QUIZ

T F   1. Issued shares of stock minus outstanding shares equals treasury stock.

T F   2. The corporate tax rate is a flat percentage of a corporation's taxable income.

T F   3. The purchase of treasury stock will decrease total stockholders' equity.

T F   4. When a large stock dividend is declared, the par or stated value of the stock should be transferred from Contributed Capital to Retained Earnings.

T F   5. An appropriation of retained earnings may be described as a cash fund established for a specific future purpose.

T F   6. A company with convertible bonds is considered to have a complex capital structure.

T F   7. Common stock equivalents should be included in the computation of primary earnings per share, but not in fully diluted earnings per share.

T F   8. A deficit is defined as negative retained earnings.

T F   9. Treasury stock should be listed as an asset in the balance sheet.

T F   10. A prior period adjustment always includes a debit or credit to Retained Earnings.

_____   11. Which of the following is not true about a 3 for 1 stock split?
         a. Par value will be reduced to one-third of what it was before the split.
         b. Total contributed capital increases.
         c. The market price will probably decrease.
         d. A stockholder with 10 shares before the split owns 30 shares after the split.
         e. Retained Earnings remains the same.

     284

_____ 12. A company purchases 200 shares of its $50 par value stock at $55
per share. It then reissues 30 shares at $58 per share. The entry
upon reissue of the stock would include a
a. credit to Cash for $174.
b. credit to Treasury Stock for $174.
c. credit to Retained Earnings for $240.
d. credit to Paid-in Capital, Treasury Stock for $90.
e. debit to Retained Earnings for $90.

_____ 13. A company has common stock outstanding for the following months:
18,000 shares from January to April, 30,000 shares from May to
October, and 50,000 shares from November to December. What is the
weighted average number of shares used in earnings per share calculations?
a. 98,000
b. 29,333
c. 27,833
d. 50,000
e. 32,667

_____ 14. Which of the following is included in the computation of fully diluted earnings per share, but is not included in primary earnings
per share?
a. Common stock equivalents
b. Net income applicable to common stock
c. Potentially dilutive securities
d. Weighted-average common shares
e. Weighted-average preferred shares

_____ 15. A prior period adjustment
a. may be recorded for a law suit that was initiated two years ago
but was settled this year.
b. is disclosed in the balance sheet.
c. may be recorded for a computational error of a prior period
that was discovered this period.
d. may be recorded for an additional tax assessment for a prior
year.
e. should not be disclosed in any financial statement, but must be
footnoted.

_____ 16. Which of the following would least likely be considered an extraordinary item?
a. Gain on property taken over by a foreign government
b. Loss resulting from new law prohibiting a company's product
c. Loss from meteorite destruction
d. Gain on sale of company vehicle
e. Loss from fire destruction

_____ 17. Which of the following is not true about a 10% stock dividend?
a. Retained Earnings decrease.
b. Contributed Capital increases.
c. Par value decreases.
d. The market value of the stock is needed to record the stock
dividend.
e. Total stockholders' equity remains the same.

_____ 18. All of the following assets would normally be considered capital assets under the federal tax laws, except
a. inventory.
b. equipment.
c. stocks.
d. bonds.
e. land.

_____ 19. Which of the following would not affect total retained earnings?
a. Appropriation of Retained Earnings
b. Net Income
c. Cash dividend
d. Prior period adjustment
e. Stock dividend

_____ 20. A company changes from the double-declining-balance method of depreciation to straight-line. Depreciation taken prior to the change was $8,000, but would have been $5,000 if straight-line had been used all along. Ignoring taxes, what should be done to account for the change?
a. The $3,000 should be amortized over the remaining life of the asset.
b. A prior period adjustment should be made for the $3,000.
c. The $3,000 should be included in the balance sheet as a deferred charge.
d. The $3,000 should be included in the income statement in the year of the change.
e. Nothing should be done about prior years nor the current year, but the undepreciated balance should be depreciated over the remaining life using the straight-line method.

ANSWERS TO TEN-MINUTE QUIZ

True-False			Multiple-Choice	
1.	T		11.	b
2.	F		12.	d
3.	T		13.	b
4.	F		14.	c
5.	F		15.	c
6.	T		16.	d
7.	F		17.	c
8.	T		18.	a
9.	F		19.	a
10.	T		20.	d

     287

LONG-TERM LIABILITIES

CHAPTER OUTLINE

Nature of Bonds
    Secured or Unsecured Bonds
    Term or Serial Bonds
    Registered or Coupon Bonds
Accounting for Bonds Payable
    Balance Sheet Disclosure of Bonds
    Bonds Issued at Face Value
    Sales of Bonds Between Interest Dates
    The Effect of the Market Rate of Interest on Bond Prices
    Using Present Value to Value a Bond
    Bonds Issued at a Discount
    Calculation of Total Interest Cost
    Amortizing the Bond Discount
    Bonds Issued at a Premium
    Amortizing Bond Premium
    Bond Issue Costs
    Year-End Accrual for Bond Interest Expense
Retirement of Bonds
Conversion of Bonds into Stock
Bond Sinking Fund
Other Long-Term Liabilities
    Mortgages Payable
    Long-Term Leases
    Pensions
Financial Reporting and Income Tax Allocation
Chapter Review
    Review of Learning Objectives
    Review Problem: Interest and Amortization of Bond Discount, Bond Retirement,
                    and Bond Conversion
    Answer to Review Problem
Chapter Assignments
    Questions
    Classroom Exercises
    Interpreting Accounting Information: J. C. Penney
    Problem Set A
    Problem Set B
    Financial Decision Case 18-1: Gianni Chemical Corporation

LEARNING OBJECTIVES:

RESOURCE MATERIALS AND LECTURE OUTLINES

OBJECTIVE 1:   Identify and contrast the major characteristics of bonds
               (pp. 653-655)

Summary Statement

Corporations frequently issue long-term bonds or notes to obtain funds. The
holders of these debt instruments are creditors of the corporation, and are entitled to periodic interest plus the principal of the debt on some specified
date. As is true for all creditors, their claims for interest and principal
take priority over stockholders' claims.

Bonds are normally due ten to fifty years after issue, and interest is usually
paid semi-annually. When bonds are issued, the corporation executes a contract
with the bondholders called a bond indenture. In addition, the company issues
bond certificates as evidence of its indebtedness. A bond issue is made up of
the total number of bonds available at the same time. Bonds are usually issued
in denominations of $1,000, and carry a variety of features.

a. Secured bonds give the bondholders a claim to certain assets of the company
   upon default, whereas unsecured bonds (called debenture bonds) do not.

b. When all the bonds of an issue mature on the same date, they are called term
   bonds. When the bonds mature over several maturity dates, they are called
   serial bonds.

c. When registered bonds are issued, the corporation maintains a record of all
   bondholders and pays interest by check to the bondholders of record. Coupon
   bonds, on the other hand, entitle the bearer to interest when the detachable
   coupons are deposited with the bank.

New Words and Terms

bond (p. 653)
bond certificate (p. 653)
bond issue (p. 654)
bond indenture (p. 654)
unsecured bonds (p. 654)
debenture bonds (p. 654)
secured bonds (p. 654)
term bonds (p. 654)

serial bonds (p. 654)
registered bonds (p. 654)
coupon bonds (p. 655)

Lecture Outline

A. Bonds represent long-term borrowing, with periodic interest payments.

B. A bond indenture is the bond contract.

C. Distinguish between secured bonds and unsecured (debenture) bonds.

D. Distinguish between registered and coupon bonds.

E. Distinguish between term and serial bonds.

OBJECTIVE 2: Record the issuance of bonds at face value, between interest
dates, and at a discount or premium (pp. 655-660)

Summary Statement

Bonds payable due in the current period can be classified as a current liability only if they will be paid with current assets. In addition, the characteristics of all bonds should be disclosed in the notes to the financial statements.

Bond prices are expressed as a percentage of face value. For example, when bonds with a face value of $100,000 are issued at 97, the company will receive $97,000.

When the bond interest rate equals the market rate for similar bonds on the issue date, the company will probably receive face value for the bonds.

Regardless of the issue price, bondholders are entitled to interest, which is based on the face amount. Interest for a period of time is computed by the formula

$$\text{interest} = \text{principal} \times \text{rate} \times \text{time}$$

A 360-day year is used.

When the bond interest rate is less than the market rate for similar bonds on the issue date, the bonds will probably sell at a discount (less than face value).

A discount on bonds payable is considered an interest charge that must be amortized (spread out) over the life of the bond. Amortization is generally recorded on the interest payment dates, using either the straight-line or effective interest method.

Unamortized Bond Discount is a contra account to Bonds Payable in the balance sheet. The difference between the two amounts is called the carrying value, an amount that increases as the discount is amortized, and that equals the face value of the bonds at maturity.

When the bond interest rate is greater than the market rate for similar bonds on the issue date, the bonds will probably sell at a <u>premium</u> (greater than face value).

Premium on Bonds Payable is added to Bonds Payable in the balance sheet to produce the carrying value.

When bonds are issued between interest dates, the interest that has accrued since the last interest date is collected from the investor upon issue and returned to the investor (along with the interest earned) on the next interest date.

<u>New Words and Terms</u>

discount (p. 658)
premium (p. 658)

<u>Lecture Outline</u>

A. Bond prices are expressed as a percentage of face value.

B. Journalize the issuance of bonds at face value.

C. Explain why bonds might be issued at a discount.

   1. Journalize a bond issue at a discount.

   2. Unamortized Bond Discount is a contra account to Bonds Payable.

D. Explain why bonds might be issued at a premium.

   1. Journalize a bond issue at a premium.

   2. Premium on Bonds Payable is added to Bonds Payable on the balance sheet.

E. Journalize the issuance of bonds between interest dates.

OBJECTIVE 3: Amortize bond discount and premium by using the effective interest
              method, and make year-end adjustments (pp. 660-666)

Summary Statement

Under the straight-line method of amortization, the amount to be amortized each
interest period equals the bond discount divided by the number of interest
periods during the life of the bond.

The _effective interest method_ of amortization is more difficult to apply than
the straight-line method, but should be used instead when the amounts differ
significantly.

To apply the effective interest method when a discount is involved, the market
rate of interest must first be determined for similar securities when the bonds
were issued (called the effective rate of interest). This interest rate
(halved for semiannual interest) is multiplied by the existing carrying value
of the bonds for each interest period to obtain Bond Interest Expense to be recorded. The actual interest paid is then subtracted from the bond interest expense recorded to obtain the discount amortization for the period. Because the
unamortized discount is now less, the carrying value is now greater. This new
carrying value is applied to the next period, and the same amortization procedure is applied.

Amortization of the premium functions as an offset against interest paid in
determining Interest Expense to be recorded. Under the straight-line method,
the premium to be amortized in each period equals the bond premium divided by
the number of interest periods during the life of the bond.

The effective interest method is applied to bond premiums in the same way that
it is applied to bond discounts. The only difference is that the amortization
for the period is computed by subtracting the Bond Interest Expense recorded
from the actual interest paid (the reverse is done for amortizing a discount).

When the accounting period ends between interest dates, the accrued interest as
well as the proportionate discount or premium amortization must be recorded.

New Words and Terms

effective interest method (p. 661)

Related Text Illustrations

*Table 18-1 Interest and Amortization of Bond Discount--Effective Interest
             Method (p. 662)

*Table 18-2   Interest and Amortization of Bond Premium--Effective Interest
              Method (p. 664)

<u>Lecture Outline</u>

A. Bond discount or premium may be amortized using the straight-line method.

B. The effective interest method is theoretically better than the straight-line
   method.

   1. Use this method to amortize a bond discount.

      a. First, determine the effective rate of interest.

      b. Refer to table 13-1 of the text for an excellent illustration.

      c. The amortized discount increases the interest expense that is recorded.

      d. Journalize the amortization.

      e. The carrying value at maturity equals the face value.

   2. Use this method to amortize a bond premium.

      a. It is the same as amortizing a discount, except that the amortized
         premium <u>decreases</u> interest expense that is recorded.

      b. Journalize the amortization.

C. Make year-end adjustments when the accounting period ends between interest
   dates, including premium or discount amortization.

OBJECTIVE 4:   Account for the retirement and conversion of bonds   (pp. 666-667)

<u>Summary Statement</u>

<u>Callable bonds</u> are bonds that may be retired by the corporation prior to
maturity date.

When the market rate for bond interest drops, a company may wish to call its bonds and substitute debt with a lower interest rate. When bonds are called (for whatever reason), an entry is needed to eliminate Bonds Payable and any unamortized premium or discount, and to record the payment of cash at the call price. In addition, a gain or loss on the retirement of the bonds would be recorded.

Convertible bonds are bonds that may be exchanged for other securities (usually common stock) at the option of the bondholder.

When a bondholder converts his or her bonds into common stock, the common stock is recorded by the company at the carrying value of the bonds. Specifically, the entry will eliminate Bonds Payable as well as any unamortized discount or premium, and will record common stock and paid-in capital in excess of par value; no gain or loss is recorded.

New Words and Terms

callable bonds   (p. 666)
convertible bonds   (p. 667)

Lecture Outline

A. Callable bonds may be retired prior to maturity by the corporation.

   1. Explain why a corporation might call its bonds.

   2. Journalize the retirement of bonds, illustrating a gain and a loss.

B. Convertible bonds may be exchanged for stock by the bondholder.

   1. The common stock is recorded at the carrying value of the bonds.

   2. Journalize the conversion of bonds (no gain or loss is recorded).

OBJECTIVE 5:   Compute sinking fund requirements, and prepare accounting entries
               associated with sinking bonds payable (pp. 668-669)

Summary Statement

A bond sinking fund is established by corporations to assure that the bondholders will be paid at maturity. Over the life of the bonds, the corporation will make fixed deposits to the sinking fund trustee, whose function is to invest the funds. At the maturity date, the sum of the fixed deposits plus sinking fund earnings should approximately equal the maturity value of the bonds. Bond sinking funds are classified in the balance sheet as long-term investments. In addition to, or instead of, the sinking fund, an appropriation of retained earnings may be established. A deposit into a bond sinking fund is recorded with a debit to Bond Sinking Fund and a credit to Cash. Sinking fund earnings are recorded with a debit to Bond Sinking Fund and a credit to Income from Bond Sinking Fund; a loss from the sale of sinking fund investments would be recorded with a debit to Loss on Sale of Sinking Fund Investment and a credit to Bond Sinking Fund. When the bonds are retired with the use of the sinking fund, Bonds Payable would be debited, Bond Sinking Fund credited, and Cash debited or credited, depending on whether there was an excess or a deficiency.

New Words and Terms

bond sinking fund (p. 668)

Related Text Illustrations

Table 18-3 Growth of Annual Investments in Sinking Fund (p. 668)

Lecture Outline

A. A bond sinking fund is established for the retirement of bonds.

   1. Annual contributions are made to a trustee.

   2. The amount is calculated by using table D-2 of the text.

B. Prepare journal entries for a bond sinking fund.

   1. Journalize a deposit into a sinking fund.

   2. Journalize sinking-fund earnings.

   3. Journalize a loss from sinking-fund investments.

   4. Journalize the retirement of bonds with the use of a sinking fund.

      a. Illustrate an excess.

      b. Illustrate a deficiency.

OBJECTIVE 6: Explain the basic features of mortgages payable, long-term leases, and pensions as long-term liabilities (pp. 670-674)

Summary Statement

A mortgage is a long-term debt payable in equal monthly installments, and secured by real property. Upon payment of the mortgage, both Mortgage Payable and Mortgage Interest Expense are debited, and Cash is credited. Each month, the interest portion of the payment decreases, while the principal portion of the payment increases.

A lease is a contract that allows a business or individual to use an asset for a specific length of time in return for periodic payments. A capital lease is in substance a sale (as determined by certain criteria), and should be recorded as an asset (to be depreciated) and a related liability by the lessee. An operating lease is a lease that does not meet the criteria for capital leases, and should be recorded only as Rent Expense for each period leased.

A pension plan is a program whereby a company agrees to pay benefits to its employees after they retire. Benefits to retirees are usually paid out of a pension fund. The two costs associated with pension plans are normal pension costs and past service costs. Normal pension costs measure service credit earned for the current year as translated into payments to the employee upon retirement. Past service costs, on the other hand, measure service credit earned during years *prior* to the initiation of the pension plan.

New Words and Terms

mortgage (p. 670)
operating lease (p. 670)
capital lease (p. 671)
pension plan (p. 672)
pension fund (p. 672)
normal pension costs (p. 673)
past service costs (p. 673)

Related Text Illustrations

*Table 18-4 Monthly Payment Schedule on $50,000, 15 Percent Mortgage (p. 670)
*Table 18-5 Payment Schedule on 16 Percent Capital Lease (p. 672)

Lecture Outline

A. A mortgage is a long-term debt secured by real property.

   1. Journalize the payment of a mortgage.

2. Explain the interest and principal portions of the fixed payments.

B. A lease is a contract for the use of an asset.

1. A capital lease is in substance a sale, and an asset and liability should be recorded by the lessee.

2. An operating lease is a true lease.

C. A pension plan is a retirement program for employees.

1. Benefits are paid out of a pension fund.

2. Distinguish between normal pension costs and past service costs.

OBJECTIVE 7: Explain why income tax allocation is necessary, and account for the differences between accounting and taxable income (pp. 674-676)

Summary Statement

Computing income taxes for financial reporting purposes differs from computing income taxes due the government for the same accounting period. This difference is caused by the fact that financial reporting income is governed by generally accepted accounting principles, whereas taxable income is governed by the internal revenue code. Accordingly, when income for financial reporting purposes differs materially from taxable income, the income tax allocation technique should be used. Under this method, the difference between the current tax liability and income tax expense is debited or credited to an account called Deferred Income Taxes.

New Words and Terms

income tax allocation (p. 675)
Deferred Income Taxes (p. 675)

Lecture Outline

A. Because accounting income usually differs from taxable income, income tax allocation is usually necessary.

1. Discuss the concept of timing difference.

2. Illustrate the journal entries for income tax allocation.

3. The account Deferred Income Taxes may have a debit balance (asset) or a credit balance (liability).

Chapter Eighteen Long-Term Liabilities

Learning Objectives	Questions	Exercises	A & B Problems	Case
1. Identify and contrast the major characteristics of bonds.	1, 2			
2. Record the issuance of bonds at face value, between interest dates, and at a discount or premium.	3, 4, 6	1, 2, 9, IAI	1, 2, 3	1
3. Amortize bond discount and premium by using the effective interest method, and make year-end adjustments.	5, 7	2, 5, 6	1, 2, 3	
4. Account for the retirement and conversion of bonds.	8, 9	3, 4	4	
5. Compute sinking fund requirements, and prepare accounting entries associated with sinking fund bonds payable.	10			
6. Explain the basic features of mortgages payable, long-term leases, and pensions as long-term liabilities.	11, 12, 13	7, 10	3, 5	1
7. Explain why income tax allocation is necessary, and account for the differences between accounting and taxable income.	14	8	5	

DIFFICULTY AND TIME CHART

A & B Problems	Difficulty	Time (in minutes)
1	medium	35
2	medium	30
3	medium	40
4	difficult	45
5	medium	20
6	difficult	45
Case 18-1	difficult	30

TEN-MINUTE QUIZ

T F 1. Bondholders are considered owners of a corporation.

T F 2. A bond that matures in installments is called a serial bond.

T F 3. Callable bonds are bonds that may be redeemed at any time at the option of the bondholder.

T F 4. Under the effective interest method, the amortization per year of a bond premium will increase over the life of the bond.

T F 5. When a bond issue is converted into common stock, total contributed capital is increased by the carrying value of the bonds converted.

T F 6. Normal pension costs measure service credit earned in the current year.

T F 7. Under an operating lease, Rent Expense should be recorded each period.

T F 8. Bonds with a higher interest rate than market (for similar bonds) will probably sell at a premium.

T F 9. Under the effective interest method, the amortization of a bond discount will result in decreasing interest expense that is recorded over the life of the bond.

T F 10. Premium on Bonds Payable is presented on the balance sheet as an asset.

_____ 11. A company has $900,000 in bonds payable with an unamortized discount of $21,000. If two-thirds of the bonds are converted to common stock, the carrying value of the bonds payable will decrease by
a. $614,000.
b. $293,000.
c. $586,000.
d. $614,000.
e. $307,000.

_____ 12. A corporation issues bonds that pay interest each March 1 and
September 1. The corporation's December 31 adjusting entry might
include a
a. debit to Cash.
b. debit to Unamortized Bond Premium.
c. credit to Bond Interest Earned.
d. debit to Accrued Interest Payable.
e. credit to Cash.

_____ 13. When there is a difference in the timing of revenues and expenses
for accounting and for income tax purposes, it is usually necessary
to
a. adjust taxable income.
b. perform income tax allocation procedures.
c. do nothing because such differences are a result of two different
sets of rules.
d. adjust accounting income.
e. debit or credit the difference to Retained Earnings.

_____ 14. A $100,000 bond issue with a carrying value of $97,000 is called at
101 and retired. Which of the following statements is true?
a. No gain or loss is recorded.
b. Total stockholders' equity increases.
c. A loss of $1,000 is recorded.
d. A gain of $3,000 is recorded.
e. A loss of $4,000 is recorded.

_____ 15. Which of the following is not true about a bond sinking fund?
a. It is classified as a long-term investment on the balance sheet.
b. Its function is to pay off bondholders on the bonds' maturity
date.
c. A fixed deposit will probably be made to the fund each period.
d. Sinking fund earnings will probably be about equal each year.
e. The account Bond Sinking Fund is credited on the maturity date.

_____ 16. Bond issue costs
a. should be expensed in the year incurred.
b. have the effect of decreasing a bond discount.
c. have the effect of increasing a bond premium.
d. have the effect of decreasing a bond premium.
e. have the effect of decreasing the effective interest rate.

_____ 17. The effective interest method of amortization of bond premiums and
discounts is superior to the straight-line method because
a. it results in an interest rate that is close to the market
interest rate.
b. it results in a uniform rate of interest.
c. it results in a more variable interest rate.
d. it results in an interest rate that increases or decreases
slightly over time.
e. it results in higher interest expense in the early years of the
bond.

_____ 18. A company issues $100,000 of 20-year, 8 percent bonds at 96. If interest is paid semiannually, what is the amount of Bond Interest Expense recorded (assuming straight-line amortization) on any interest date?
a. $8,100
b. $4,000
c. $4,100
d. $7,900
e. $3,900

_____ 19. A bond premium has the effect of
a. lowering the carrying value of the bond.
b. lowering the effective interest rate below the face interest rate.
c. increasing the amount of interest expense recorded on the interest date.
d. increasing the amount of cash paid for interest each six months.
e. increasing the amount of cash paid to the bondholders on the maturity date.

_____ 20. Which of the following best describes the behavior over time of the components of equal mortgage payments?
a. The proportion of interest expense to principal remains the same.
b. Interest expense increases and principal decreases.
c. Principal increases and interest expense decreases.
d. Both principal and interest increase.
e. Both principal and interest decrease.

ANSWERS TO TEN-MINUTE QUIZ

<u>True-False</u>

1. F
2. T
3. F
4. T
5. T
6. T
7. T
8. T
9. F
10. F

<u>Multiple-Choice</u>

11. c
12. b
13. b
14. e
15. d
16. d
17. b
18. c
19. b
20. c

CHAPTER NINETEEN

STATEMENT OF CHANGES IN FINANCIAL POSITION AND CASH FLOW STATEMENT

CHAPTER OUTLINE

LEARNING OBJECTIVES:

RESOURCE MATERIALS AND LECTURE OUTLINES

OBJECTIVE 1: Distinguish cash from working capital as a concept of funds
              (pp. 694-695)

Summary Statement

The _statement of changes in financial position_ is a major financial statement
that is presented with the balance sheet, income statement, and statement of retained earnings. Its major purpose is to summarize the significant financing
and investing activities of a company during a given period.

In accounting, _funds_ are usually defined as working capital (current assets
minus current liabilities), and not as cash. This is because working capital
is more relevant than cash to a company's operating cycle. Accordingly, the
statement of changes in financial position generally utilizes the working capital concept of funds rather than the cash concept.

New Words and Terms

statement of changes in financial position (p. 694)
funds (p. 695)

Lecture Outline

A. The statement of changes in financial position (SCFP) summarizes significant
   financing and investing activities.

B. Funds may be defined as cash or working capital.

   1. Working capital = current assets - current liabilities.

   2. Because working capital considers all short-term assets and liabilities,
      it is more meaningful than merely cash as a definition of funds.

OBJECTIVE 2: Identify the types of transactions that cause changes in working
              capital (pp. 695-697)

Summary Statement

The change in working capital is calculated by subtracting one year's ending
working capital from the subsequent year's. It may be expressed as an increase
or a decrease.

An increase in a current asset or a decrease in a current liability will result
in an increase in working capital. A decrease in a current asset or an increase in a current liability will result in a decrease in working capital.

If a transaction is to affect working capital, at least one current and one
noncurrent account must be involved. For example, the purchase of inventory
for cash would not affect working capital because both accounts are current in
nature. However, the purchase of land for cash would affect (decrease) working
capital because land is a noncurrent account and cash is a current account.

Related Text Illustrations

*Figure 19-1 Effect of Transactions on Working Capital (p. 696)
*Figure 19-2 Types of Transactions Affecting the Balance Sheet (p. 697)

Lecture Outline

A. A change in only current items will not affect working capital.

B. To affect working capital, at least one current and one noncurrent item must
   be involved.

C. Current assets and current liabilities affect working capital in opposite
   ways.

OBJECTIVE 3: Identify common sources and uses of working capital (pp. 697-703)

Summary Statement

Business transactions that increase working capital are called <u>sources of working capital</u>. These transactions are described as financing activities, and include (a) net income from operations, (b) the sale of noncurrent assets, (c)
long-term borrowing, and (d) the sale of capital stock.

a. Net income from operations increases working capital because cash receipts and receivables that arise from the sale of goods and services exceed cash payments and payables that arise when expenses are incurred. However, to obtain working capital provided from operations, certain items must be added to, or subtracted from, net income. For example, although depreciation was a deduction in arriving at net income, it must be added back because depreciation does not cause a change in working capital. On the other hand, the year's amortization of bond premium would be treated in the opposite manner (that is, deducted).

b. The sale of a noncurrent asset increases cash and decreases the noncurrent asset, resulting in an increase in working capital. Working capital increases by the amount of the proceeds, regardless of the existence of a gain or loss.

c. Long-term borrowing increases both cash and long-term liabilities, resulting in an increase in working capital.

d. The issuance of the company's stock increases both cash and stockholders' equity, resulting in an increase in working capital.

Business transactions that decrease working capital are called uses of working capital. These transactions are described as investing activities, and include (a) an operating loss, (b) the purchase of noncurrent assets, (c) the declaration of cash dividends, (d) the purchase or retirement of stock, and (e) the retirement or reclassification of a long-term debt. In preparing the uses of working capital section of the statement of changes in financial position, one should remember that nonworking capital expenses such as depreciation must still be added back to a net loss to obtain working capital applied to operations. In addition, the declaration of a cash dividend reduces working capital, but the eventual payment of the dividend does not affect working capital (since no non-current account is involved). Finally, when a long-term debt is reclassified as a current liability because it is currently due, it results in a decrease in working capital.

An exchange transaction is a transaction that involves only noncurrent accounts, and therefore has no effect on working capital. Such a transaction is viewed, however, as both a source and a use of working capital, according to the all financial resources concept of funds. Examples of exchange transactions are the purchase of land in exchange for a long-term note, and the conversion of bonds payable into common stock.

The following steps should be taken in preparing a statement of changes in financial position.

a. Compute the change in working capital from last year to this year.

b. Prepare a work sheet for the statement of changes in financial position.

c. Classify changes in noncurrent accounts as sources or uses of working capital.

d. Prepare the statement of changes in financial position, as well as the supporting schedule of changes in working capital.

New Words and Terms

source of working capital (p. 697)
use of working capital (p. 697)
exchange transaction (p. 702)
all financial resources (p. 703)

Related Text Illustrations

Figure 19-3   Common Sources and Uses of Working Capital (p. 698)
Figure 19-4   Sources of Capital and Uses Other than Operations Reported by 600
              Companies (p. 703)

Lecture Outline

A. Financing activities are represented on the SCFP as sources of working capital. Examples follow.

   1. Net income from operations

      a. Add back depreciation expense (a noncash expense).

   2. Sale of noncurrent assets

   3. Long-term borrowing

   4. Sale of capital stock

B. Investing activities are represented on the SCFP as uses of working capital.
   Examples follow.

   1. An operating loss

      a. Add back depreciation expense.

   2. Purchase of noncurrent assets

   3. Declaration (not payment) of a cash dividend

   4. Purchase or retirement of stock

5. Retirement or reclassification of a long-term debt

C. An exchange transaction should be disclosed as both a source and a use of
   working capital.

OBJECTIVE 4:   Prepare a statement of changes in financial position work sheet
               (pp. 703-712)

Summary Statement

The work sheet for the statement of changes in financial position is designed
to aid in the preparation of the statement by (a) providing a mechanism for
analyzing each transaction that affects working capital, and (b) classifying
the effect of those transactions as a source or use of working capital.

Related Text Illustrations

Figure 19-5 Comparative Balance Sheet (p. 705)
Figure 19-6 Computation of Change in Working Capital (p. 706)
*Figure 19-7 Sample Work Sheet (p. 707)

Lecture Outline

A. The SCFP work sheet should contain four columns (see fig. 19-7 of the text).

   1. A description column (A)

   2. Account balances at the end of the prior year (B)

   3. Analysis of transactions for the current year (C)

   4. Account balances at the end of the current year (D)

B. Enter working capital in columns B and D, and place the difference in column
   C.

C. Enter all noncurrent debits and amounts; total the debits for each year.

D. Enter all noncurrent credits and amounts; total the credits for each year.

E. Enter the titles "sources of working capital" and "uses of working capital."

F. Analyze the changes in the noncurrent accounts.

G. Add debits and credits of column C. The figure for working capital should be added to balance the columns.

OBJECTIVE 5:   Prepare a statement of changes in financial position including changes in components of working capital (pp. 712-714)

Summary Statement

On the formal statement of changes in financial position, total uses of working capital is subtracted from total sources of working capital to obtain an increase (or decrease) in working capital. An accompanying schedule of changes in working capital is required, showing how each working capital account has changed, and substantiating the working capital change previously obtained.

Related Text Illustrations

Figure 19-8   Statement of Changes in Financial Position (p. 713)
Figure 19-9   Schedule of Changes in Working Capital (p. 714)

Lecture Outline

A. The bottom portion of the work sheet is used to prepare the formal SCFP (see fig. 19-8 of the text).

B. The changes in the components of working capital must accompany the statement (see fig. 19-9 of the text).

OBJECTIVE 6:   Prepare a cash flow statement (pp. 714-718)

Summary Statement

The <u>cash flow statement</u> provides information about a company's debt-paying abil-ity by presenting the company's sources and uses of cash during the period, as well as the increase or decrease in cash during the period.

a. In preparing the cash flow statement, cash flow from operations is first determined by converting the income statement from an accrual basis to a cash basis statement or by the short-cut method.

b. Cash flow from operations is now listed with all other sources of cash, and totaled. All uses of cash are listed beneath, and totaled. The difference between the total sources and total uses of cash will signify the increase or decrease in cash for the period.

New Words and Terms

cash flow statement (p. 714)

Related Text Illustrations

Figure 19-10 Condensed Income Statement (p. 715)
Figure 19-11 Schedule of Cash Flow from Operations (p. 717)
Figure 19-12 Cash Flow Statement (p. 718)

Lecture Outline

A. A cash flow statement calculates the increase or decrease in cash during the period.

B. First, calculate cash flow from operations by converting the income state-ment to a cash basis statement.

C. Then, prepare a cash flow statement, subtracting uses of cash from sources of cash.

Chapter Nineteen   Statement of Changes in Financial Position and Cash Flow Statement

Learning Objectives	Questions	Exercises	A & B Problems	Case
1. Distinguish cash from working capital as a concept of funds.	1, 4			
2. Identify the types of transactions that cause changes in working capital.	4, 7, 8, 9, 10, 13	2, IAI	1	
3. Identify common sources and uses of working capital.	5, 6, 7	2, 5		
4. Prepare a statement of changes in financial position work sheet.			3, 4, 5	
5. Prepare a statement of changes in financial position including changes in components of working capital.	2, 3, 11, 12	1, 3, 4	2, 3, 4, 5	
6. Prepare a cash flow statement.	14	5, 6	2, 6	1

DIFFICULTY AND TIME CHART

A & B Problems	Difficulty	Time (in minutes)
1	easy	10
2	medium	25
3	medium	45
4	difficult	45
5	difficult	60
6	difficult	40
Case 19-1	difficult	40

TEN-MINUTE QUIZ

T F   1. The purchase of inventory for cash will decrease working capital.

T F   2. The declaration of a cash dividend is a use of working capital, but the payment of the same dividend is not a use of working capital.

T F   3. An increase in prepaid expenses will have a positive effect on cash flow.

T F   4. When a net loss has occurred, depreciation expense is not included in the statement of changes in financial position.

T F   5. Depreciation expense is treated differently in the preparation of a cash flow statement than in the preparation of a statement of changes in financial position.

T F   6. The amortization of an intangible asset is added back to net income to arrive at working capital provided from operations.

T F   7. The reclassification of a long-term debt as a short-term debt is treated as a source of working capital in the statement of changes in financial position.

T F   8. The all financial resources concept of funds deals with the treatment of exchange transactions on the statement of changes in financial position.

T F   9. In preparing the work sheet for the statement of changes in financial position, it is important to account for each change in noncurrent assets.

T F 10. Inventory would not appear in a schedule of changes in the components of working capital.

_____ 11. In a schedule of cash flow from operations, which of the following would be deducted?
  a. Increase in inventory
  b. Decrease in Accounts Receivable
  c. Depreciation
  d. Increase in Accounts Payable
  e. Decrease in Prepaid Rent

_____ 12. A company has credit sales of $50,000 and cash sales of $80,000 during the same year that the Accounts Receivable account decreased by $10,000. What was the total of cash receipts from sales?
   a. $120,000
   b. $140,000
   c. $130,000
   d. $90,000
   e. $60,000

_____ 13. An exchange transaction
   a. appears in the schedule of changes in the components of working capital.
   b. has no effect on working capital.
   c. appears as a source of working capital only.
   d. appears as a use of working capital only.
   e. should not appear on the statement of changes in financial position.

_____ 14. Which of the following is a source of working capital?
   a. Retirement of bonds
   b. Net loss from operations
   c. Purchase of treasury stock
   d. Receipt of cash on an account receivable
   e. Sale of equipment at less than book value

_____ 15. Which of the following would appear on the statement of changes in financial position but not on the cash flow statement?
   a. Sale of building for cash
   b. Issuance of common stock for cash
   c. Cash dividend declared
   d. Cash dividend paid
   e. Purchase of building for cash

_____ 16. The first step in the preparation of a work sheet for the statement of changes in financial position is to
   a. analyze the noncurrent accounts that were a use of working capital.
   b. analyze the noncurrent accounts that were a source of working capital.
   c. determine the change in working capital for the year.
   d. prepare the formal statement of changes in financial position.
   e. prepare the formal schedule of changes in the components of working capital.

_____ 17. Which of the following would not involve Retained Earnings in the statement of changes in financial position work sheet?
   a. Net income
   b. Dividends
   c. Gain on sale of equipment
   d. Purchase of land
   e. Net loss

_____ 18. A company estimates bad debts at year-end to be $3,000 and makes the appropriate adjusting entry. Earlier that year, specific accounts amounting to $2,300 were written off. As a result of the above facts, working capital
a. decreased by $3,000.
b. decreased by $700.
c. decreased by $2,300.
d. decreased by $5,300.
e. increased by $700.

_____ 19. Which of the following has a negative effect on cash flow from operations?
a. Depreciation expenses
b. Decrease in notes payable
c. Decrease in inventory
d. Increase in accounts payable
e. Bad debts expense

_____ 20. Which of the following transactions is considered an exchange transaction in the preparation of the statement of changes in financial position?
a. Exchange of an account receivable for a note receivable
b. Exchange of land for common stock
c. Exchange of inventory for notes payable
d. Purchase of a long-term investment for cash
e. Recording depreciation

ANSWERS TO TEN-MINUTE QUIZ

True-False			Multiple-Choice	
1.	F		11.	a
2.	T		12.	b
3.	F		13.	b
4.	F		14.	e
5.	F		15.	c
6.	T		16.	c
7.	F		17.	d
8.	T		18.	a
9.	T		19.	b
10.	F		20.	b

CHAPTER TWENTY

INTERCOMPANY INVESTMENTS AND INTERNATIONAL ACCOUNTING

CHAPTER OUTLINE

Classification of Long-Term Investments
    Noninfluential and Noncontrolling Investment
    Influential but Noncontrolling Investment
    Controlling Investment
Consolidated Financial Statements
    Methods of Accounting for Consolidations
    Consolidated Balance Sheet
        100 Percent Purchase at Book Value
        Less than 100 Percent Purchase at Book Value
        Purchase at More than or Less than Book Value
        Intercompany Receivables and Payables
    Consolidated Income Statement
    Other Consolidated Financial Statements
Accounting for Bond Investments
    Purchase of Bonds Between Interest Dates
    Amortization of Premium or Discount
    Sale of Bonds
International Accounting
    Accounting for Transactions in Foreign Currencies
        Foreign Sales
        Foreign Purchases
        Realized Versus Unrealized Exchange Gain or Loss
    Restatement of Foreign Subsidiary Financial Statements
        Restatement Rates
        Example of Restatement
    The Search for Uniformity of International Accounting Standards
Chapter Review
    Review of Learning Objectives
    Review Problem: Consolidated Balance Sheet Work Sheet
    Answer to Review Problem
Chapter Assignments
    Questions
    Classroom Exercises
    Interpreting Accounting Information: U.S. Steel and Marathon Oil
    Problem Set A
    Problem Set B
    Financial Decision Case 20-1: San Antonio Corporation

LEARNING OBJECTIVES:

RESOURCE MATERIALS AND LECTURE OUTLINES

OBJECTIVE 1:   Apply the lower-of-cost-or-market method and the equity method to the appropriate situations in accounting for long-term investments (pp. 739-745)

Summary Statement

Two ways a company may expand are by increasing its operations and by investing in other companies. Companies that have expanded operations throughout the world are called multinational or transnational corporations.

A closely held corporation is one whose stock is owned by a few individuals and not traded publicly. On the other hand, a publicly held corporation is one whose securities are registered with the SEC and are traded by the public at large.

All long-term investments in the stock of other companies are recorded at cost. Subsequent to purchase, the accounting treatment depends upon the extent of influence exercised by the investing company. If the investing company can affect the operating and financing policies of the investee, even though it owns less than 50 percent of its voting stock, it possesses significant influence over the investee. If the investing company can affect the operating and financing policies of the investee, but owns more than 50 percent of its voting stock, it possesses control over the investee.

The extent of influence exercised over another company is often difficult to measure accurately. Therefore, unless there is evidence to the contrary, long-term investments in stock are classified as (a) noninfluential and noncontrolling (generally less than 20 percent ownership), (b) influential but noncontrolling (generally 20 to 50 percent ownership), and (c) controlling (over 50 percent ownership).

The cost method should be used in accounting for noninfluential and noncontrolling investments, and the equity method should be used in accounting for all other (that is, influential or controlling) investments. In addition, consolidated financial statements should usually be prepared when a controlling relationship exists.

a. Under the cost method, the investor records investment income as dividends are received. In addition, the securities are recorded on the balance sheet at the lower of cost or market. This is accomplished by debiting Unrealized Loss on Long-Term Investments and crediting Allowance to Reduce Long-Term Investments to Market for the excess of cost in aggregate over market in aggregate.

b. Under the equity method, the investory records investment income as a debit to the investment account and a credit to an investment income account for the investee's periodic net income times the ownership percentage. When the investor receives a cash dividend, the Cash account is debited and the investment account is credited.

c. When a company has a controlling interest in another company, the investor is called the parent company and the investee is called the subsidiary. When such a relationship exists, consolidated financial statements (combined statements of the parent and its subsidiaries) should usually be prepared, using the purchase method (described in this chapter) or the pooling-of-interests method (described in a more advanced accounting course).

New Words and Terms

multinational or transnational corporations (p. 739)
closely held corporation (p. 739)
publicly held corporation (p. 739)
going public (p. 739)
significant influence (p. 741)
control (p. 741)
cost method (p. 741)
equity method (p. 744)
parent company (p. 745)
subsidiary (p. 745)
consolidated financial statements (p. 745)

Related Text Illustrations

Figure 20-1 A Possible Growth Pattern for a Successful Business (p. 740)
*Table 20-1   Accounting Treatments of Long-Term Investments (p. 745)

Lecture Outline

A. Define multinational, closely held, and publicly held corporations.

B. All long-term investments are initially recorded at cost.

C. There are three classifications for investments in stock:

1. Noninfluential and noncontrolling (less than 20%).

2. Influential, but noncontrolling (20-50%).

3. Controlling (over 50%).

D. The cost method should be used for noninfluential and noncontrolling investments.

1. Investment Income is recorded as dividends are received.

2. The balance sheet valuation is at the lower of cost or market (a year-end adjustment is made).

E. The equity method should be used for influential, but noncontrolling investments.

1. The investment account decreases upon the receipt of a dividend.

2. The investment account increases or decreases for a percentage of the periodic income or loss, respectively.

F. Consolidated financial statements should be prepared when a controlling relationships exists.

OBJECTIVE 2: Explain when to prepare consolidated financial statements and describe their uses (pp. 745-747)

<u>Summary Statement</u>

Consolidated financial statements should be prepared when an investing company has legal and effective control over another company (usually more than 50% ownership). There are some circumstances, however, which preclude the preparation of consolidated financial statements even though control exists.

The two methods of preparing consolidated financial statements are the <u>purchase method</u> and the pooling of interests method. Under both methods, intercompany receivables and payables, as well as the investment in the subsidiary company, must be <u>eliminated</u> when preparing a consolidated balance sheet. In addition, under the purchase method, the entire stockholders' equity section is eliminated.

CHAPTER TWENTY

Consolidated financial statements are useful because they present a financial
picture of the entire economic entity.

<u>New Words and Terms</u>

purchase method (p. 746)
eliminations (p. 746)

<u>Lecture Outline</u>

A. Though there are exceptions, consolidated financial statements should be
   prepared when a (parent) company has control over another (subsidiary)
   company.

B. The two methods of consolidation are the purchase method and the pooling-of-
   interests method.

C. Under both methods, certain elimination entries must be made in preparing
   the consolidated balance sheet.

   1. Intercompany receivables and payables

   2. The investment in the subsidiary company

   3. Elimination of all of stockholders' equity (purchase method)

D. Consolidated financial statements present a picture of an entire economic
   entity.

OBJECTIVE 3a: Prepare consolidated balance sheets at acquisition date for pur-
               chase at book value (pp. 747-749)

<u>Summary Statement</u>

Under the purchase method, when the carrying value of the net assets purchased
equals their cost, the assets and liabilities acquired should not be written
up or down in the consolidated balance sheet at the acquisition date, nor
should goodwill be recorded.

When less than 100 percent of the subsidiary has been purchased, the <u>minority
interest</u> (outside ownership) must be disclosed in the consolidated balance
sheet.

New Words and Terms
<u>New Words and Terms</u>

minority interest (p. 749)

<u>Related Text Illustrations</u>

Figure 20-2 Work Sheet for Preparation of Consolidated Balance Sheet (p. 748)
Figure 20-3 Work Sheet Showing Elimination of Less than 100 Percent Ownership
             (p. 749)

<u>Lecture Outline</u>

A. When a purchase is made at book value, assets and liabilities are not written up or down, nor is goodwill recorded.

B. Discuss how minority interest would arise on a consolidated balance sheet.

OBJECTIVE 3b: Prepare consolidated balance sheets at acquisition date for pur-
               chase at other than book value (pp. 750-751)

<u>Summary Statement</u>

Under the purchase method, if the cost exceeds the book value of the net assets
purchased, the excess should be allocated to the assets and liabilities acquired to the extent of their fair market values (at the date of acquisition)
when consolidated financial statements are being prepared. Any unassigned excess should be recorded as <u>goodwill</u> in the consolidated financial statements.

When the book value of the net assets purchased exceeds their cost, the assets
should be reduced proportionately until the excess is eliminated.

<u>New Words and Terms</u>

Goodwill (p. 750)
Goodwill from Consolidation (p. 750)

<u>Related Text Illustrations</u>

Figure 20-4 Worksheet Showing Elimination Where Purchase Cost Is Greater than
             Book Value (p. 751)

<u>Lecture Outline</u>

A. When a purchase is made at more than book value, the excess is first assigned to assets and liabilities.

B. Any unassigned excess is recorded as goodwill.

C. When a purchase is made at less than book value, assets should be reduced to eliminate the excess.

OBJECTIVE 4:   Prepare consolidated income statements for intercompany transactions (pp. 751-753)

<u>Summary Statement</u>

Under both the purchase and pooling of interests methods, intercompany items must be eliminated when preparing a consolidated income statement. Specifically, intercompany purchases and sales, and intercompany interest expense and interest income should be eliminated.

<u>Related Text Illustrations</u>

Figure 20-5 Work Sheet Showing Eliminations for Preparing a Consolidated Income Statement (p. 753)

<u>Lecture Outline</u>

A. Certain items must be eliminated when preparing a consolidated income statement.

1. Intercompany purchases and sales

2. Intercompany interest expense and interest income

OBJECTIVE 5:   Account for bond investment transactions (pp. 752-756)

<u>Summary Statement</u>

When bonds are purchased as long-term investments, the investment account is debited at cost (which includes broker's commission). Accrued Interest Receivable is debited for accrued interest since the last interest date, and Cash is credited for cash paid. When interest is received on the investment, Cash is debited for cash received, Bond Interest Earned is credited for cash received plus the amortization of a bond discount or minus the amortization of a bond premium, and the investment account is debited (when there is a discount) or credited (when there is a premium) to balance the entry. Prior entries to accrue interest may slightly alter the above entry. Under this method of amortization, a bond discount or bond premium account is not used. At the maturity date, the bond investment account should equal the maturity value. However, if the bonds are sold prior to maturity, a gain or loss should be recorded for the difference between cash received and the bonds' carrying value.

<u>Lecture Ouline</u>

A. Journalize the purchase of bonds as long-term investments.

B. Journalize the receipt of interest from the investment.

   1. Explain the relevance of amortized bond discount or premium.

   2. Explain, however, that a bond discount or premium account is not used.

C. At maturity, the bond investment account should equal the maturity value.

D. Journalize the sale of bonds prior to maturity.

OBJECTIVE 6: Show how changing exchange rates affect financial reporting
            (pp. 757-761)

<u>Summary Statement</u>

When businesses expand internationally, two accounting problems arise: (a) the financial statements of foreign subsidiaries involve different currencies and thus must be translated into domestic currency by means of an <u>exchange rate</u>, and (b) the foreign financial statements are not necessarily prepared in accordance with domestic generally accepted accounting principles.

When purchases and sales are made with foreign countries, there is no accounting problem for the domestic company when domestic currency is being used. However, when the transaction involves foreign currency, the domestic company should record an exchange gain or loss. The exchange gain or loss reflects the change in the exchange rate from the transaction date to the date of payment.

When financial statements are prepared between the transaction date and the date of payment, an unrealized gain or loss should be recorded if the exchange rate has changed.

New Words and Terms

exchange rate (p. 757)

Related Text Illustrations

Table 20-2 Extent of Foreign Business for Selected Companies (p. 757)
Table 20-3 Partial Listing of Foreign Exchange Rates (p. 758)

Lecture Outline

A. Foreign operations cause two accounting problems:

   1. Foreign currencies must be translated into domestic currency.

   2. Foreign financial statements may not follow the same accounting princi-
      ples as the domestic company.

B. When a transaction involves foreign currency, an exchange gain or loss may
   occur.

C. Discuss the accounting treatment when financial statements are prepared between the transaction date and the payment date.

OBJECTIVE 7: Restate a foreign subsidiary's financial statements in U.S.
              dollars (pp. 761-765)

Summary Statement

When the financial statements of a foreign subsidiary are being included in a
parent company's consolidated financial statements, the subsidiary's financial
statements must first be restated into the parent's reporting currency. The
method of restatement depends upon the foreign subsidiary's functional currency, or the currency with which they transact most of their business.

a. Financial statements of type I subsidiaries (those that are self-contained within a foreign country) must be translated from the functional currency (local currency in this case) to the reporting currency. However, financial statements of type II subsidiaries (those that are merely an extension of the parent's operations) must be remeasured from the local currency to the functional currency (which in this case is the same as the reporting currency).

b. Depending upon the type of subsidiary being restated, the alternative exchange rates used are the current rate, the historical rate, and the average rate. A parent's investment in its subsidiary will probably change from year to year, and a portion of that change may be due to exchange rate fluctuations called translation adjustments. For type I subsidiaries, these translation adjustments should be included in the stockholders' equity section of the balance sheet, and not as part of net income. For type II subsidiaries, however, translation gains and losses should be included in net income.

New Words and Terms

reporting currency (p. 761)
functional currency (p. 761)
translation adjustments (p. 762)
translation gains or losses (p. 763)

Related Text Illustrations

Table 20-4   Restatement Rates for Foreign Subsidiaries' Financial Statements
(p. 763)
*Table 20-5   Restatement of Types I and II Subsidiaries' Financial Statements
(p. 764)

Lecture Outline

A. A foreign subsidiary's financial statement must be restated into the parent's reporting currency.

1. Financial statements of type I subsidiaries must be translated from the functional currency to the reporting currency.

2. Financial statements of type II subsidiaries must be translated from the local currency to the functional currency.

B. Discuss the restatement of the balance sheet and income statement accounts for type I and type II subsidiaries.

1. Current rate

2. Historical rate

3. Average rate

4. No adjustment

C. For type I subsidiaries, translation adjustments should be included in stockholders' equity.

D. For type II subsidiaries, translation gains and losses should be included in net income.

OBJECTIVE 8:   Describe progress toward international accounting standards
               (pp. 765-766)

Summary Statement

At present, there are no recognized worldwide standards of accounting. However, much progress has been made by the International Accounting Standards Committee (IASC) and the International Federation of Accountants (IFAC) in setting up international accounting standards. Despite the efforts of these bodies, there are still serious inconsistencies in financial statements among countries, and comparison remains a difficult task.

Lecture Outline

A. Discuss the obstacles encountered when establishing international accounting standards.

B. The IASC and IFAC are trying to overcome these obstacles.

Chapter Twenty Intercompany Investments and International Accounting

Learning Objectives	Questions	Exercises	A & B Problems	Case
1. Apply the lower-of-cost-or-market method and the equity method to the appropriate situations in accounting for long-term investments.	1, 2, 3, 6, 7	1, 2, 3	1, 2	1
2. Explain when to prepare consolidated financial statements and describe their uses.	4, 5, 8			
3. Prepare consolidated balance sheets at acquisition date for purchase at (a) book value and (b) other than book value.	9, 10, 11	4, 5, 6, 7, IAI	3, 4, 5	
4. Prepare consolidated income statements for intercompany transactions.	12		4	
5. Account for bond investment transactions.	13	8	6	
6. Show how changing exchange rates affect financial reporting.	14, 15	9	7	
7. Restate a foreign subsidiary's financial statements in U.S. dollars.	16			
8. Describe progress toward international accounting standards.	17			

DIFFICULTY AND TIME CHART

A & B Problems	Difficulty	Time (in minutes)
1	easy	20
2	medium	30
3	medium	25
4	medium	25
5	difficult	40
6	difficult	45
7	difficult	40
Case 20-1	difficult	30

TEN-MINUTE QUIZ

T F 1. When a parent company and its 100 percent owned subsidiary are consolidated using the purchase method, only the stockholders' equity of the parent company remains.

T F 2. If a parent pays more than book value for a 100 percent owned subsidiary, minority interest appears on the consolidated financial statements.

T F 3. An exchange rate of .53 German marks in terms of U.S. dollars means that $100 could be exchanged for 53 marks.

T F 4. Minority interest is shown as a footnote to the consolidated balance sheet.

T F 5. When a parent company pays less than book value for its investment in the subsidiary, the difference should be recorded as negative goodwill.

T F 6. When a parent company pays more than book value for its investment in the subsidiary, the excess should be allocated to the assets and liabilities acquired (to the extent of their fair market values) when consolidated financial statements are prepared.

T F 7. A closely held corporation is one whose operations have not expanded to other nations.

T F 8. When accounting for bonds as an investment, an Unamortized Bond Discount or Unamortized Bond Premium account must be established, depending on whether a discount or premium resulted upon purchase.

T F 9. A type II subsidiary is one that is self-contained within a foreign country.

T F 10. A company's functional currency is the currency in which it transacts most of its business.

_____ 11. When bonds are purchased at a discount, the investor's journal entry upon the receipt of an interest check would include a
a. debit to Investment in Bonds.
b. debit to Interest Expense.
c. debit to Interest Earned.
d. credit to Investment in Bonds.
e. credit to Cash.

_____ 12. A U.S. corporation purchases goods from a French supplier. The U.S. corporation would record an exchange gain or loss when
a. the financial statements are prepared before payment is made.
b. payment is made in U.S. dollars.
c. the exchange rate changes after payment is made.
d. the exchange rate changes between the purchase and payment dates.
e. the financial statements are prepared after payment is made.

_____ 13. The cost method of accounting for investments is used when the investment is
a. noninfluential and noncontrolling.
b. influential and noncontrolling.
c. noninfluential and controlling.
d. controlling.
e. greater than 20% ownership.

_____ 14. Vanalden Corporation owns 30 percent of the voting stock of Northbrooke Corporation and accounts for the investment using the equity method. Northbrooke reports a net loss of $50,000. Vanalden Corporation's entry would include a
a. credit to Investment in Northbrooke Corporation for $50,000.
b. credit to Investment in Northbrooke Corporation for $15,000.
c. debit to Cash for $15,000.
d. credit to Loss, Northbrooke Corporation Investment for $15,000.
e. No journal entry is made.

_____ 15. Which of the following transactions would not require an eliminating entry when preparing consolidated financial statements?
a. Amount owed by parent to subsidiary.
b. Sale to customer
c. Parent's investment in the subsidiary
d. Amount owed by subsidiary to parent
e. Purchase of parent's merchandise by subsidiary

_____ 16. ABC Corporation purchases 75 percent of the stock of XYZ Corporation for $181,500. XYZ has contributed capital of $100,000 and retained earnings of $142,000. The consolidated financial statements would contain
a. neither minority interest nor goodwill.
b. minority interest and negative goodwill.
c. minority interest but not goodwill.
d. goodwill but not minority interest.
e. minority interest and goodwill.

_____ 17. A company uses the equity method of accounting for its investment. When it receives a cash dividend from its investee, its journal entry would include a
  a. credit to Cash.
  b. credit to the investment account.
  c. debit to Dividend Income
  d. credit to Dividend Income.
  e. debit to the investment account.

_____ 18. In translating an income statement prepared in a foreign currency to U.S. dollars, which of the following rates would be used to translate revenues?
  a. Current rate
  b. Average rate for the period
  c. Historical rate
  d. Rate at the beginning of the period
  e. Replacement rate

_____ 19. Valdez Enterprises has a credit balance of $40,000 in its Allowance to Reduce Long-Term Investments to Market account. Its investment portfolio has a total cost of $250,000 and a market value of $225,000. The year-end adjustment would include which of the following?
  a. A debit to Unrealized Loss on Long-Term Investments for $25,000
  b. A credit to Allowance to Reduce Long-Term Investments to Market for $65,000
  c. A credit to Long-Term Investments for $25,000
  d. A debit to Allowance to Reduce Long-Term Investments to Market for $15,000
  e. A credit to Unrealized Loss on Long-Term Investments for $25,000

_____ 20. Under the cost method of accounting for an investment,
  a. Investment Income is credited when dividends are received.
  b. the investment account is credited when the investee reports a net income.
  c. the investment account is credited when dividends are received.
  d. Investment Income is credited when the investee reports a net income.
  e. the investment is reported on the balance sheet at cost, even if the market value is lower on the balance sheet date.

ANSWERS TO TEN-MINUTE QUIZ

<u>True-False</u>

1. T
2. F
3. F
4. F
5. F
6. T
7. F
8. F
9. F
10. T

<u>Multiple-Choice</u>

11. a
12. d
13. a
14. b
15. b
16. c
17. b
18. b
19. d
20. a

FINANCIAL STATEMENT ANALYSIS

CHAPTER OUTLINE

Objectives of Financial Statement Analysis
- Assessment of Past Performance and Current Position
- Assessment of Future Potential and Related Risk

Standards for Financial Statement Analysis
- Rule-of-Thumb Measures
- Past Performance of the Company
- Industry Norms

Sources of Information
- Published Reports
- SEC Reports
- Business Periodicals and Credit and Investment Advisory Services

Tools and Techniques of Financial Analysis
- Horizontal Analysis
- Trend Analysis
- Vertical Analysis
- Ratio Analysis

Survey of Commonly Used Ratios
- Evaluating Liquidity
  - Current Ratio
  - Quick Ratio
  - Receivable Turnover
  - Inventory Turnover
- Evaluating Profitability
  - Profit Margin
  - Asset Turnover
  - Return on Assets
  - Return on Equity
  - Earnings per Share
- Evaluation of Long-Term Solvency
  - Debt to Equity Ratio
  - Interest Coverage Ratio
- Market Test Ratios
  - Price/Earnings Ratio
  - Dividends Yield
  - Market Risk

LEARNING OBJECTIVES:

RESOURCE MATERIALS AND LECTURE OUTLINES

OBJECTIVE 1: Describe and discuss the objectives of financial statement analysis (pp. 785-787)

Summary Statement

Decision makers obtain specific information from general-purpose financial statements by means of financial statement analysis.

The users of financial statements are classified as either internal or external. The main internal user is management, whereas the main external users are creditors and owners. Both creditors and owners will probably acquire a portfolio, or group of loans or investments, because the risk of loss is far less with several investments than with one investment.

Creditors and investors use financial statement analysis to (a) assess past performance and the current position, and (b) assess future potential and the risk associated with the potential. Obtaining information about the past and present is very helpful in making projections about the future. Moreover, the easier it is to predict future performance, the less risk involved, and therefore the lower the compensation required by the investor or creditor.

New Words and Terms

financial statement analysis (p. 785)
portfolio (p. 786)

Lecture Outline

A. Creditors and investors use financial statement analysis as follows:

  1. To assess past performance and current position

  2. To assess future potential and risk

B. To reduce risk, investors will probably purchase a portfolio of investments.

OBJECTIVE 2: Describe and discuss the standards for financial statement analysis (pp. 787-789)

Summary Statement

Decision makers assess performance by means of (a) rule-of-thumb measures, (b) analysis of past performance of the company, and (c) comparison with industry norms.

a. Rule-of-thumb measures for key financial ratios are helpful, but should not be the sole basis for making a decision. For example, a company may report high earnings per share, but may lack sufficient assets to pay current debts.

b. Past performance of a company is helpful in disclosing trends. The skill lies in the analyst's ability to predict whether a trend will continue or will reverse itself.

c. Comparing a company's performance with the performance of other companies in the same industry is helpful, but there are three limitations to using industry norms as standards. First, no two companies are exactly the same. Second, many companies, called <u>diversified companies</u> or <u>conglomerates</u>, operate in unrelated industries, so that comparison is difficult. (However, the recent requirement to report financial information by segments has been somewhat helpful.) Third, different companies often use different accounting procedures for recording similar items.

New Words and Terms

diversified companies (p. 788)
conglomerates (p. 788)

Related Text Illustrations

Figure 21-1 Segment Information (p. 789)

Lecture Outline

A. Decision-makers assess performance in (at least) three ways:

   1. Rule-of-thumb measures

2. Past performance

3. Comparison with industry norms (however, there are limitations)

OBJECTIVE 3: State the sources of information for financial statement analysis
              (pp. 790-791)

Summary Statement

The chief sources of information about publicly held corporations are published
reports, SEC reports, business periodicals, and credit and investment advisory
services.

a. A company's annual report provides useful financial information, and includes the following sections: (1) analysis of the past year's operations,
   (2) the financial statements, (3) footnotes, (4) accounting procedures, (5)
   the auditor's report, and (6) a five- or ten-year summary of operations.

b. <u>Interim financial statements</u> may indicate significant changes in a company's
   earnings trend. They consist of limited financial information for less than
   a year (usually quarterly).

c. Publicly held corporations are required to file with the SEC an annual report (form 10-K), a quarterly report (form 10-Q), and a current report of
   significant events (form 8-K). These reports are available to the public
   and are sources of valuable financial information.

d. Financial analysts obtain information from such sources as the *Wall Street
   Journal*, *Forbes*, *Barron's*, *Fortune*, the *Commercial and Financial Chronicle*,
   Moody's, Standard and Poor's, and Dun and Bradstreet.

New Words and Terms

interim financial statements (p. 790)

Lecture Outline

A. A company's annual report provides a significant amount of information.

B. Interim financial statements may indicate recent changes.

C. Forms 10-K, 10-Q, and 8-K are filed with the SEC.

D. Publications such as *Barron's*, *Moody's*, and the *Wall Street Journal*.

OBJECTIVE 4: Apply horizontal analysis, trend analysis, and vertical analysis
to financial statements (pp. 791-796)

Summary Statement

The most common tools and techniques of financial analysis are horizontal analysis, trend analysis, vertical analysis, and ratio analysis.

a. Comparative financial statements consist of the current and prior year's statements presented side by side to facilitate financial statement analysis. Horizontal analysis shows absolute and percentage changes in specific items from one year to the next. The first of the two years being considered is called the base year, and the percentage change is computed by dividing the amount of the change by the base-year amount.

b. Trend analysis is the same as horizontal analysis, except that percentage changes are calculated for several consecutive years. For percentage changes to be shown over several years, index numbers must be used.

c. Vertical analysis presents the percentage relationship of individual items on the statement to a total within the statement (as the percentage that cost of goods sold is to net sales), resulting in a common-size statement. On a common-size balance sheet, total assets and total equities would each be labeled 100 percent. On a common-size income statement, sales would be labeled 100 percent. Common-size statements may be presented in comparative form to disclose information both within the period and between periods.

New Words and Terms

horizontal analysis (p. 791)
base year (p. 791)
trend analysis (p. 793)
index number (p. 794)
vertical analysis (p. 794)
common-size statement (p. 795)

Related Text Illustrations

Figure 21-2 Comparative Balance Sheet with Horizontal Analysis (p. 792)
Figure 21-3 Comparative Income Statement with Horizontal Analysis (p. 793)
Figure 21-4 Trend Analysis (p. 794)
Figure 21-5 Common-Size Balance Sheet (p. 795)
Figure 21-6 Common-Size Income Statement (p. 796)

<u>Lecture Outline</u>

A. Horizontal analysis shows absolute and percentage changes from one year to the next.

B. Trend analysis is an application of horizontal analysis for several consecutive years.

C. Vertical analysis calculates percentage relationships within a statement.

   1. The result is a common-size statement.

   2. On a common-size balance sheet, total assets and total equities are labeled 100.

   3. On a common-size income statement, sales is labeled 100.

   4. Common-size statements may be presented in comparative form.

OBJECTIVE 5: Apply ratio analysis to financial statements in the study of an enterprise's liquidity, profitability, long-term solvency, and market tests (pp. 796-805)

<u>Summary Statement</u>

<u>Ratio analysis</u> consists of determining certain relationships (ratios) between financial statement items, and comparing the ratios with those of prior years or other companies. Ratios provide information about a company's liquidity, profitability, long-run solvency, and market strength. The most common ratios are as follows.

Ratio	Components	Use or Meaning
Liquidity Ratios		
Current ratio	$\dfrac{\text{current assets}}{\text{current liabilities}}$	Measure of short-term debt-paying ability

Ratio	Components	Use or Meaning
Liquidity Ratios (cont.)		
Quick ratio	$$\frac{\text{cash + short-term investments + receivables}}{\text{current liabilities}}$$	Measure of short-term liquidity
Receivable turnover	$$\frac{\text{sales}}{\text{average accounts receivable}}$$	Measure of relative size of accounts receivable balance and effectiveness of credit policies
Average days' sales uncollected	$$\frac{\text{days in year}}{\text{receivable turnover}}$$	Measure of time it takes to collect an average receivable
Inventory turnover	$$\frac{\text{cost of goods sold}}{\text{average inventory}}$$	Measure of relative size of inventory
Profitability Ratios		
Profit margin	$$\frac{\text{net income}}{\text{sales}}$$	Income produced by each dollar of sales
Asset turnover	$$\frac{\text{sales}}{\text{average total assets}}$$	Measure of how efficiently assets are used to produce sales
Return on assets	$$\frac{\text{net income}}{\text{average total assets}}$$	Overall measure of earning power or profitability of all assets employed in the business
Return on equity	$$\frac{\text{net income}}{\text{average owners' equity}}$$	Profitability of owners' investment
Earnings per share	$$\frac{\text{net income}}{\text{outstanding shares}}$$	Means of placing earnings on a common basis for comparisons

Ratio	Components	Use or Meaning
Long-Term Solvency Ratios		
<u>Debt to equity</u>	$\dfrac{\text{total liabilities}}{\text{owners' equity}}$	Measure of relationship of debt financing to equity financing. A company with debt is said to be <u>leveraged</u>.
<u>Interest coverage</u>	$\dfrac{\text{net income before taxes} + \text{interest expense}}{\text{interest expense}}$	Measure of protection of creditors from a default on interest payments
Market Test Ratios		
<u>Price/earnings (P/E)</u>	$\dfrac{\text{market price per share}}{\text{earnings per share}}$	Measure of amount the market will pay for a dollar of earnings
<u>Dividends yield</u>	$\dfrac{\text{dividends per share}}{\text{market price per share}}$	Measure of current return to investor
<u>Market risk</u>	$\dfrac{\text{specific change in market price}}{\text{average change in market price}}$	Measure of volatility (called <u>beta</u>) of the market price of a stock in relation to that of other stocks

<u>New Words and Terms</u>

ratio analysis (p. 796)
current ratio (p. 797)
quick ratio (p. 797)
receivable turnover (p. 798)
average days' sales uncollected (p. 798)
inventory turnover (p. 799)
profit margin (p. 799)
asset turnover (p. 800)
return on assets (p. 800)
return on equity (p. 801)

leverage (p. 801)
debt to equity ratio (p. 802)
interest coverage ratio (p. 802)
price/earnings (P/E) ratio (p. 803)
dividends yield (p. 803)
market risk (p. 804)
beta (p. 805)

<u>Lecture Outline</u>

A. Ratio analysis consists of comparing certain current financial relationships with those of prior years or of other companies

B. There are four major types of ratios, listed as follows:

   1. Liquidity ratios

      a. Current ratio

      b. Quick ratio

      c. Receivable turnover

      d. Average days' sales uncollected

      e. Inventory turnover

   2. Profitability ratios

      a. Profit margin

      b. Asset turnover

      c. Return on assets

      d. Return on equity

      e. Earnings per share

3. Long-term solvency ratios

   a. Debt to equity ratio

   b. Interest coverage

4. Market test ratios

   a. Price-earnings ratio

   b. Dividends yield

   c. Market risk

Chapter Twenty-One   Financial Statement Analysis

Learning Objectives	Questions	Exercises	A & B Problems	Case
1. Describe and discuss the objectives of financial statement analysis.	1, 2			
2. Describe and discuss the standards for financial statement analysis.	3			1
3. State the sources of information for financial statement analysis.	4			
4. Apply horizontal analysis, trend analysis, and vertical analysis to financial statements.	5, 6, 7	1, 2, 3	2, 3	1
5. Apply ratio analysis to financial statements in the study of an enterprise's liquidity, profitability, long-term solvency, and market tests.	8, 9, 10, 11, 12, 13, 14, 15, 16, 17	4, 5, 6, IAI	1, 4, 5, 6	

DIFFICULTY AND TIME CHART

A & B Problems	Difficulty	Time (in minutes)
1	easy	20
2	easy	25
3	medium	40
4	medium	45
5	medium	60
6	difficult	30
Case 21-1	difficult	40

TEN-MINUTE QUIZ

T   F   1.   A company with a beta of 1.5 is considered more risky than a company with a beta of 1.0.

T   F   2.   Most companies issue interim financial statements to the public on a monthly basis.

T   F   3.   When index numbers are used, the last number in a series is set to 100.

T   F   4.   A company with debt financing and a net income before taxes of $0 has an interest coverage ratio of 1.

T   F   5.   The profit margin indicates income produced by each dollar of sales.

T   F   6.   The analysis of diversified companies is aided by the disclosure of segment information.

T   F   7.   When a company's market price increases, its dividends yield decreases.

T   F   8.   A current ratio of .5 indicates that current liabilities are double current assets.

T   F   9.   A base year is determined when performing vertical analysis.

T   F   10.   Publicly held corporations are required to report certain significant events to the SEC within 15 days of the event's occurrence.

_____   11.   To find the most comprehensive information about a company's performance during the year, one would look to
         a.   the annual report sent to the SEC.
         b.   the interim financial statements.
         c.   the Wall Street Journal.
         d.   the annual report sent to stockholders.
         e.   the tax forms submitted to the Internal Revenue Service.

_____   12.   An example of horizontal analysis is
         a.   common-size statements.
         b.   trend analysis.
         c.   profitability analysis.
         d.   ratio analysis.
         e.   portfolio analysis.

_____ 13. A common measure of long-term solvency is
    a. the current ratio.
    b. asset turnover.
    c. debt to equity ratio.
    d. receivable turnover.
    e. earnings per share.

_____ 14. A company that is leveraged is one that
    a. contains equity financing.
    b. has minimized its risk of loss by acquiring a portfolio of investments.
    c. contains debt financing.
    d. has a high earnings per share.
    e. operates in several unrelated industries.

_____ 15. A common measure of liquidity is
    a. inventory turnover.
    b. asset turnover.
    c. dividends yield.
    d. interest coverage.
    e. earnings per share.

_____ 16. In a common-size balance sheet and income statement, which of the following would be given a label of 100 percent?
    a. Total liabilities and gross profit from sales
    b. Total assets and net income
    c. Total stockholders' equity and net income
    d. Total liabilities and stockholders' equity and total operating costs
    e. Total assets and sales

_____ 17. A high receivable turnover indicates that
    a. the company is having difficulty in collecting its accounts receivable quickly.
    b. a large proportion of the company's sales are credit sales.
    c. many customers are defaulting on their debt.
    d. the company is making collection from its customers very quickly.
    e. the company's inventory is moving very quickly.

_____ 18. Which of the following accounts is not included in the quick ratio computation?
    a. Accounts Receivable
    b. Accounts Payable
    c. Inventory
    d. Cash
    e. Short-term Investments

_____ 19. Which of the following is _not_ a measure of profitability?
    a. Return on assets
    b. Asset turnover
    c. Dividends yield
    d. Earnings per share
    e. Return on equity

20. The best way to study the composition of financial statements is to
    a. prepare common-size statements.
    b. perform ratio analysis.
    c. perform horizontal analysis.
    d. prepare interim statements.
    e. perform trend analysis.

ANSWERS TO TEN-MINUTE QUIZ

<u>True-False</u>

1.   T
2.   F
3.   F
4.   T
5.   T
6.   T
7.   T
8.   T
9.   F
10.   T

<u>Multiple-Choice</u>

11.   a
12.   b
13.   c
14.   c
15.   a
16.   e
17.   d
18.   c
19.   c
20.   a

CHAPTER TWENTY-TWO

MANUFACTURING ACCOUNTING: COST ELEMENTS AND REPORTING

CHAPTER OUTLINE

Management Accounting
Merchandising Versus Manufacturing Operations
Manufacturing Cost Elements
    Direct Materials Costs
        Direct Materials Purchases
        Direct Materials Usage
    Direct Labor Costs
        Labor Documentation
        Gross Versus Net Payroll
        Labor-related Costs
    Factory Overhead
        Overhead Cost Behavior
        Overhead Cost Allocation
    Unit Cost Determination
    Product and Period Costs
Periodic Versus Perpetual Inventory Methods in Manufacturing Accounting
Manufacturing Inventory Accounts
    Materials Inventory
    Work in Process Inventory
    Finished Goods Inventory
Manufacturing Cost Flow
The Manufacturing Statements
    Statement of Cost of Goods Manufactured
    Cost of Goods Sold
Chapter Review
    Review of Learning Objectives
    Review Problem: Cost of Goods Manufactured--Three Fundamental Steps
    Answer to Review Problem
Chapter Assignments
    Questions
    Classroom Exercises
    Interpreting Accounting Information: Rusty Manufacturing Company
    Problem Set A
    Problem Set B
    Management Decision Case 22-1: Noreen Municipal Hospital

LEARNING OBJECTIVES:

RESOURCE MATERIALS AND LECTURE OUTLINES

OBJECTIVE 1: Describe the field of management accounting (pp. 832-834)

Summary Statement

Management accounting assists in the decision-making process by providing management with pertinent financial information. The types of information that management seeks are (a) product costing information, (b) planning and control information, and (c) special reports and analyses to support management's decisions.

New Words and Terms

cost accounting system (p. 832)

Lecture Outline

A. Management accounting provides management with pertinent financial information, listed as follows:

1. Product costing information

2. Planning and control information

3. Special reports and analyses

OBJECTIVE 2: Identify the differences in accounting for manufacturing and merchandising companies (pp. 834-836)

<u>Summary Statement</u>

Merchandising companies purchase goods in finished form and resell them. Manufacturing companies, on the other hand, produce the goods that they sell. To obtain product costs and inventory valuation, the merchandiser merely utilizes the purchase cost figures. The manufacturer, however, must accumulate the costs of production for those results.

Manufacturers use cost accounting systems to determine the costs of their manufactured products. Obtaining accurate cost data is necessary for producing reliable financial statements. Accordingly, the manufacturing company must accumulate the cost of materials, labor, and overhead for its products. The cost of goods that are sold appears in the income statement as cost of goods sold. The ending inventory accounts in the balance sheet contain period-end costs of materials, work in process, and finished goods.

The manufacturing firm has three types of inventory: materials, work in process, and finished goods. Materials are the substances used in manufacturing a product. Work in process consists of the costs attached to all goods that have been begun but are unfinished. Finished goods are goods that are ready for sale.

<u>Related Text Illustrations</u>

*Figure 22-1 Cost of Goods Sold: A Merchandising Company (p. 835)
*Figure 22-2 Cost of Goods Sold: A Manufacturing Company (p. 836)

<u>Lecture Outline</u>

A. Merchandisers purchase and sell goods in finished form.

B. Manufacturers produce the goods that they sell.

C. Manufacturers must accumulate the costs of materials, labor, and overhead.

D. The manufacturer has three types of inventory:

   1. Materials

   2. Work-in-Process

   3. Finished goods

OBJECTIVE 3: State the differences among the three manufacturing cost elements:
              direct materials costs, direct labor costs, and factory (manufac-
              turing) overhead costs (p. 836)

Summary Statement

Manufacturing costs are classified as direct materials, direct labor, or factory (manufacturing) overhead (indirect manufacturing costs).

A <u>direct cost</u> is any cost that can be conveniently and economically traced to a specific product or cost objective, whereas an <u>indirect cost</u> is one that cannot.

<u>Direct materials</u> are materials that are conveniently and economically traceable to specific products. Direct materials used in producing a desk consist of legs, drawers, and a desk top; however, the costs of nails, glue, and screws used to construct the desk are too insignificant to assign as part of its direct materials cost. These costs are termed <u>indirect materials</u> and are classified with other indirect costs as factory overhead.

New Words and Terms

direct costs (p. 836)
indirect costs (p. 837)
direct materials (p. 837)
indirect materials (p. 837)

Lecture Outline

A. There are three manufacturing costs:

1. Direct materials can be conveniently and economically traced to products.

2. Direct labor can be conveniently and economically traced to products.

3. Factory overhead includes all factory costs that are not direct materials or direct labor.

   a. Indirect materials

   b. Indirect labor

   c. Factory depreciation

   d. Factory rent

   e. Factory insurance

   f. etc.

OBJECTIVE 4:   Identify the source documents used to collect data on manufacturing cost accumulation (pp. 837-843)

Summary Statement

To ensure an efficient system of materials purchases, certain documents should be used. A <u>purchase requisition (purchase request)</u> is a request by a production department for the company to purchase certain materials. The materials are purchased when the purchasing department sends the supplier a <u>purchase order</u>. Upon receipt of the ordered goods, a <u>receiving report</u> is prepared, indicating the quantity and condition of the goods received. When materials are needed for production, a <u>materials requisition</u> form is prepared and presented to the storeroom clerk.

<u>Direct labor</u> consists of all labor costs that are conveniently and economically traceable to specific products. Wages for machine operators are an example of a direct labor cost. On the other hand, wages for maintenance workers are termed <u>indirect labor</u>, and are classified as factory overhead.

The number of hours worked by employees can be accurately determined by means of <u>time cards</u>. <u>Job cards</u>, on the other hand, contain a record of labor hours per job and help verify the time recorded on the time cards.

<u>Gross payroll</u> equals all wages and salaries earned by the employees, and is used in computing manufacturing costs. <u>Net payroll</u> is the amount paid to the employees after all payroll deductions have been subtracted from the gross payroll. Labor-related costs that are a function of direct labor costs and that can be conveniently traced to such costs should be accounted for as direct labor. Otherwise, they are considered part of factory overhead. Examples of labor-related costs are employee fringe benefits such as vacations, sick pay, and pension plans, and employer payroll taxes such as unemployment taxes and the employer's share of social security.

<u>Factory (manufacturing) overhead</u> consists of all manufacturing costs that are not classified as direct materials or direct labor. Examples of manufacturing overhead are depreciation, insurance, utilities, and all indirect labor and materials associated with the manufacturing operation.

Manufacturing costs may be classified as variable, fixed, or semivariable depending upon the way the cost changes with changes in production. <u>Variable manufacturing costs</u> increase or decrease in direct proportion to the number of units produced. Examples are direct materials and direct labor. Costs such as insurance, rent, and supervisory salaries that do not vary with units produced are called <u>fixed manufacturing costs</u>. Semivariable costs, such as those for telephone use, are part fixed and part variable.

<u>Product costs</u> (also called inventoriable costs) are costs such as direct materials, direct labor, and applied overhead that are included in the cost of a product. A product cost becomes an expense in the year in which the associated product is sold. Because <u>period costs</u> do not benefit future periods, they are classified as expenses in the period incurred. Selling and administrative costs are considered period costs or expenses.

Under the <u>periodic inventory method</u>, manufacturing costs are recorded in the general ledger but are not assigned to specific inventory items. It is not until the end of the accounting period that the beginning inventory balances are updated, and then only by taking a physical inventory. Accordingly, interim inventory balances are not determinable without a physical count.

Under the <u>perpetual inventory method</u>, manufacturing costs are recorded in the general ledger and are assigned to inventory accounts as production takes place. Therefore, inventory account balances can be determined at any point in time without a physical count because they are continuously being updated. However, a physical count should be taken periodically to verify the account balances.

The manufacturer's inventories consist of <u>materials, work in process</u>, and <u>finished goods</u>. The Materials Inventory balance represents costs attached to all purchased but unused materials. The Work in Process Inventory balance contains an accumulation of costs attached to partially completed products. The Finished Goods Inventory balance represents the cost of goods completed but not yet sold.

<u>New Words and Terms</u>

purchase requisitions (p. 837)
purchase request (p. 837)
purchase order (p. 837)
receiving report (p. 837)
materials requisition (p. 838)
direct labor (p. 839)
indirect labor (p. 839)
time card (p. 839)
job cards (p. 839)
net payroll (p. 839)
gross payroll (p. 839)
factory overhead (p. 841)
variable manufacturing costs (p. 841)
fixed manufacturing costs (p. 841)
product costs (p. 842)
period costs (expenses) (p. 842)

<u>Related Text Illustrations</u>

Figure 22-3 The Materials Requisition Form (p. 838)

<u>Lecture Outline</u>

A. Several documents are needed to collect manufacturing cost data.

   1. A purchase requisition is issued by a production department.

   2. A purchase order is sent to the supplier by the purchasing department.

3. A receiving report is prepared upon receipt of ordered goods.

4. A materials requisition form is prepared to obtain materials from the storeroom.

B. Hours worked by employees are recorded on time cards.

C. Hours worked per job are recorded on job cards.

D. Net payroll equals gross payroll less payroll deductions.

E. Labor-related costs should be classified as direct or indirect.

F. Manufacturing costs may also be classified as fixed, variable, or semi-variable.

1. Define and provide examples of fixed costs.

2. Define and provide examples of variable costs.

3. Define and provide examples of semivariable costs.

G. Distinguish between product costs and period costs.

H. Distinguish between periodic and perpetual inventory systems.

OBJECTIVE 5: Describe the nature, contents, and flow of costs through the Materials, Work in Process, and Finished Goods inventory accounts (pp. 844-850)

Summary Statement

Product costing and inventory valuation rely on a structured flow of manufacturing costs. Manufacturing cost flow begins when materials are purchased and other manufacturing costs are incurred. Once incurred, these costs are classified as direct materials, direct labor, or factory (manufacturing) overhead, and are transferred into the Work in Process Inventory account. When the goods are complete, their cost is assigned to a Finished Goods Inventory account. Finally, costs attached to goods sold are transferred to the Cost of Goods Sold account.

The manufacturer's income statement is the same as the merchandiser's, except that the manufacturer uses the caption Cost of Goods Manufactured instead of Merchandise Purchases, and Finished Goods Inventory instead of Merchandise Inventory.

New Words and Terms

Materials Inventory (p. 844)
Work in Process Inventory (p. 844)
Finished Goods Inventory (p. 846)
manufacturing cost flow (p. 847)

Related Text Illustrations

Figure 22-4   Materials Inventory Versus Merchandise Inventory Accounting
              (Perpetual) (p. 845)
*Figure 22-5 The Work in Process Inventory Account (Perpetual) (p. 846)
*Figure 22-6 Accounting for Finished Goods Inventory (Perpetual) (p. 847)
*Figure 22-7 Manufacturing Cost Flow: An Example (p. 848)
*Figure 22-8 Manufacturing Cost Flow: Basic Concepts (p. 850)

Lecture Outline

A. Manufacturing cost flow begins as materials, labor, and overhead are accumulated in Work In Process Inventory.

B. When the goods are completed, the costs are transferred to Finished Goods Inventory.

C. When the goods are sold, the costs are transferred to Cost of Goods Sold.

OBJECTIVE 6: Prepare a statement of cost of goods manufactured (pp. 850-854)

Summary Statement

The manufacturer prepares a __statement of cost of goods manufactured__ so that cost of goods sold can be computed in the income statement. Three steps are involved in preparing this statement, as follows:

a. First, the cost of materials used must be computed. Arbitrary numbers will be used to facilitate understanding.

Materials Inventory, beginning of period	$100
Add materials purchased	350
Cost of materials available for use	$450
Less Materials Inventory, end of period	200
Cost of materials used	$250

b. Second, <u>total manufacturing costs</u> must be computed.

Cost of materials used (computed in section a)	$ 250
Add direct labor costs	900
Add factory overhead costs	750
Total manufacturing costs	$1,900

c. Third, <u>cost of goods manufactured</u> must be computed.

Total manufacturing costs (computed in section b)	$1,900
Add Work in Process Inventory, beginning of period	400
Total cost of work in process during the period	$2,300
Less Work in Process Inventory, end of period	700
Cost of goods manufactured	$1,600

When the figure for cost of goods manufactured has been computed, it can be transferred to the cost of goods sold section of the income statement, as follows:

Finished Goods Inventory, beginning of period	$1,250
Add cost of goods manufactured (computed in section c)	1,600
Total cost of finished goods available for sale	$2,850
Less Finished Goods Inventory, end of period	300
Cost of goods sold	$2,550

The objective of the statement of cost of goods manufactured is to translate manufacturing cost data into usable information for inventory valuation, profit measurement, and external reporting. However, a cost accumulation system is first needed for day-to-day activities.

<u>New Words and Terms</u>

statement of cost of goods manufactured (p. 851)
total manufacturing costs (p. 853)
cost of goods manufactured (p. 853)

<u>Related Text Illustrations</u>

*Figure 22-9 Income Statement for a Manufacturing Company (p. 851)
*Figure 22-10 Statement of Cost of Goods Manufactured (p. 852)

Lecture Outline

A. A manufacturer must prepare a statement of cost of goods manufactured to determine cost of goods sold.

B. The cost of materials used must first be calculated.

C. Direct labor and factory overhead must be added to arrive at total manufacturing costs.

D. An adjustment for beginning and ending work in process is needed to determine cost of goods manufactured.

OBJECTIVE 7: Prepare the year-end work sheets, closing journal entries, and financial statements for a manufacturing company, using a periodic inventory approach (See Work Sheet Analysis in the Working Papers)

Summary Statement

The year-end work sheets for a manufacturer are the same as those for a merchandiser, except that two columns are included for the statement of cost of goods manufactured. These two columns contain amounts for all items appearing in that statement. When a periodic inventory system is used, Materials and Work in Process must be debited for their beginning balances (amounts in Adjusted Trial Balance column) and credited for their ending balances as determined by a physical inventory. When the columns are totaled, a credit entitled Cost of Goods Manufactured to Income Statement must be added to balance the columns; the corresponding debit goes to the Income Statement column.

A manufacturer using the periodic inventory system prepares closing entries that (a) close all manufacturing accounts to Manufacturing Summary, (b) close the beginning balances in Materials Inventory and Work in Process Inventory to Manufacturing Summary and establish ending balances in these inventory accounts, (c) close Manufacturing Summary and all revenue and nonmanufacturing expenses to Income Summary, (d) close beginning Finished Goods Inventory to Income Summary and establish ending Finished Goods Inventory, and (e) close Income Summary to Retained Earnings.

Lecture Outline

A. Direct the students to the Work Sheet Analysis in the Working Papers.

B. Explain the work sheet of a manufacturer, line by line, assuming a periodic inventory system.

1. Columns are included for statement of cost of goods manufactured accounts.

2. Adjustments must be made for beginning and ending materials and work in process.

3. "Cost of goods manufactured to income statement" balances the columns.

C. A manufacturer's closing entries serve five purposes:

1. Close manufacturing accounts to Manufacturing Summary.

2. Close beginning and establish ending materials and work in process.

3. Close Manufacturing Summary and all revenues and nonmanufacturing expenses to Income Summary.

4. Close beginning finished goods and establish ending finished goods.

5. Close Income Summary to Retained Earnings.

D. Review the financial statements of a manufacturer.

Chapter Twenty-Two   Manufacturing Accounting: Cost Elements and Reporting

Learning Objectives	Questions	Exercises	A & B Problems	Case
1. Describe the field of management accounting.	1, 3	9		
2. Identify differences in accounting for manufacturing and merchandising companies.	2, 19			1
3. State the differences among the three manufacturing cost elements: direct materials costs, direct labor costs, and factory (manufacturing) overhead costs.	4, 5, 6, 7, 9, 10, 11	1, 4	1, 2	1
4. Identify the source documents used to collect data on manufacturing cost accumulation.	8			
5. Describe the nature, contents, and flow of costs through the Materials, Work in Process, and Finished Goods inventory accounts.	14, 15	5, 6, 8	2	
6. Prepare a statement of cost of goods manufactured.	16, 17, 18, 19	2, 3, 7 IAI	3, 4	
7. Prepare the year-end work sheets, closing journal entries, and financial statements for a manufacturing company, using a periodic inventory approach. (See Work Sheet Analysis in the Working Papers.)		IAI	5	

DIFFICULTY AND TIME CHART

A & B Problems	Difficulty	Time (in minutes)
1	medium	30
2	easy	25
3	medium	25
4	medium	25
5	difficult	90
Case 22-1	difficult	75

TEN-MINUTE QUIZ

T F   1. Direct materials, direct labor, and factory overhead are all consid-
           ered elements of manufacturing costs.

T F   2. Indirect material and indirect labor are both considered factory
           overhead.

T F   3. The cost of goods manufactured is added to the beginning balance of
           Finished Goods Inventory to obtain the total cost of goods available
           for sale during the period.

T F   4. Direct materials are considered a variable manufacturing cost.

T F   5. Cost of goods manufactured and total manufacturing costs are synony-
           mous expressions.

T F   6. Depreciation on the sales office is considered factory overhead.

T F   7. Factory overhead costs do not flow through the Work in Process Inven-
           tory account.

T F   8. The cost of an item of material is transferred to the Work in Process
           Inventory account when the item has been requisitioned into produc-
           tion.

T F   9. A manufacturing company maintains three different types of inventory
           accounts, whereas a merchandising company utilizes only one inventory
           account.

T F 10. Net payroll is a measure of the total wages and salaries earned by
           employees and is used to determine total manufacturing costs.

_____ 11. A manufacturer has beginning Finished Goods Inventory of $40,000,
           ending Finished Goods Inventory of $17,000, beginning Work in Process
           Inventory of $10,000, ending Work in Process Inventory of $22,000,
           and Cost of Goods Manufactured of $30,000. Given the above informa-
           tion, what is the cost of goods sold?
           a. $41,000   b. $18,000   c. $53,000   d. $7,000   e. $42,000

_____ 12. Given the information in question 11, what are the total manufactur-
           ing costs?
           a. $41,000   b. $18,000   c. $53,000   d. $7,000   e. $42,000

13. Which of the following costs is considered a product cost and not a period expense?
    a. Advertising
    b. The company president's salary
    c. Allocated overhead
    d. Salaries of the sales force
    e. Freight-Out

14. Which of the following is considered a fixed manufacturing cost?
    a. Factory rent
    b. Direct labor
    c. Factory utilities
    d. Direct materials
    e. Depreciation based on units produced

15. The last document involved in the purchasing function is the
    a. purchase requisition.
    b. materials requisition.
    c. purchase order.
    d. receiving report.
    e. invoice.

16. Which of the following costs is most likely to be semivariable?
    a. Rent
    b. Direct labor
    c. Telephone
    d. Indirect materials
    e. Insurance

17. Which of the following costs is considered a direct cost?
    a. Depreciation on machinery
    b. Glue used in the manufacturing process
    c. The superintendent's salary
    d. Factory insurance
    e. Assembly-line labor costs

18. The cost of materials purchased flows through all of the following manufacturing accounts except
    a. Finished Goods Inventory
    b. Factory Payroll
    c. Cost of Goods Sold
    d. Work in Process Inventory
    e. Materials Inventory

19. Which of the following costs exists for a merchandiser, but not for a manufacturer?
    a. Cost of goods sold
    b. Purchases of merchandise
    c. Selling expenses
    d. Income tax expense
    e. Administrative expenses

_____ 20. Which of the following employee costs is borne by the employer?
           a. Union dues
           b. Federal income taxes
           c. All FICA taxes
           d. State income taxes
           e. Federal unemployment taxes

ANSWERS TO TEN-MINUTE QUIZ

<u>True-False</u>

1. T
2. T
3. T
4. T
5. F
6. F
7. F
8. T
9. T
10. F

<u>Multiple-Choice</u>

11. c
12. e
13. c
14. a
15. e
16. c
17. e
18. b
19. b
20. e

CHAPTER TWENTY-THREE

PRODUCT COSTING: THE JOB ORDER SYSTEM

CHAPTER OUTLINE

LEARNING OBJECTIVES:

RESOURCE MATERIALS AND LECTURE OUTLINES

OBJECTIVE 1:   Describe the difference between job order costing and process
               costing (pp. 869-870)

Summary Statement

The primary reason for installing a cost accounting system is to compute the
unit cost of manufacturing a company's products. Unit cost information aids a
business in (a) determining a proper selling price, (b) forecasting and controlling operations and costs, (c) determining ending inventory balances, and (d)
determining Cost of Goods Sold.

The two basic approaches to cost accounting systems are job order costing and
process costing. The production circumstances will dictate which of the two
approaches should be incorporated into the system.

A job order cost accounting system is used in companies that manufacture goods
according to unique or special orders, as for ships, wedding invitations, or
bridges. When a job order cost system is used, (a) all manufacturing costs are
assigned to and accumulated for specific jobs, (b) emphasis is placed on job
completion periods rather than on weekly or monthly time periods, and (c) one
Work in Process Inventory account is used, whose balance is supported by the
job order cost sheets of jobs still in production.

A process cost accounting system is used when a large number of similar products
are being manufactured. Companies producing paint, automobiles, or breakfast
cereal would probably use some form of a process costing system. When a process
cost system is used, (a) manufacturing costs are accumulated by department with
little concern for specific job orders, (b) emphasis is placed on a weekly or
monthly time period rather than on the completion period of a specific order,
and (c) a Work in Process Inventory account is used for each department in the
manufacturing process.

New Words and Terms

job order (p. 869)
job order cost accounting system (p. 870)
process cost accounting system (p. 870)

CHAPTER TWENTY-THREE

<u>Lecture Outline</u>

A. Unit cost information serves four purposes:

   1. Determining a selling price

   2. Forecasting and controlling operations and costs

   3. Determining ending inventory

   4. Determining cost of goods sold

B. Explain when a job order cost system is used.

   1. Costs are accumulated for specific jobs.

   2. Emphasis is on job completion.

   3. One Work In Process Inventory account is used.

C. Explain when a process cost system is used.

   1. Costs are accumulated by department.

   2. Emphasis is on weekly or monthly cost data.

   3. A Work In Process Inventory account is used for each department.

OBJECTIVE 2: Describe the concept of absorption costing (p. 871)

<u>Summary Statement</u>

Product costing may be accomplished only when the costing method being used
specifies the types of manufacturing costs to be included in the analysis. The
most common product costing methods are based on <u>absorption costing</u>, in which
direct materials, direct labor, variable factory overhead, and fixed factory
overhead are assigned to their products. Job order costing generally utilizes
absorption costing.

          372

New Words and Terms

absorption costing (p. 871)

Lecture Outline

A. Absorption costing includes direct materials, direct labor, and all factory overhead (variable _and_ fixed) in unit cost.

B. Job order costing uses absorption costing.

OBJECTIVE 3: Compute a predetermined overhead rate, and use this rate to apply overhead costs to production (pp. 871-873)

Summary Statement

Predetermined overhead rates are useful for product costing, price determination, and inventory valuation. The rate is determined at the beginning of the accounting period by dividing total estimated overhead for the period by some logical allocation activity basis. The most common activity bases are (a) estimated direct labor hours, (b) estimated direct labor dollars, (c) estimated machine hours, and (d) estimated units produced. After the rate has been determined, it is multiplied by the actual activity (hours, dollars, etc.) for each job or product to obtain the overhead that should be applied.

Related Text Illustrations

Figure 23-1 Overhead Cost Allocation (p. 873)

Lecture Outline

A. Factory overhead is applied (allocated) to production by means of a predetermined overhead rate.

B. First, the predetermined overhead rate is determined at the beginning of the period.

C. Then, the rate is multiplied by actual activity for a job.

D. The predetermined overhead rate equals estimated overhead divided by an allocation basis.

E. Explain when the following allocation bases would be appropriate.

1. Estimated direct labor hours

2. Estimated direct labor dollars

3. Estimated machine hours

4. Estimated units produced

OBJECTIVE 4: Dispose of underapplied or overapplied overhead (pp. 873-876)

Summary Statement

If estimated figures for overhead costs and activity basis equal the actual
amounts for the period, then total overhead applied to jobs will equal actual
overhead incurred during that period. Because equality of estimates and actual
amounts will seldom occur, there will usually be an under- or overapplication of
overhead. When actual overhead exceeds applied overhead, overhead has been <u>underapplied</u>. When the reverse is true, overhead has been <u>overapplied</u>. The only
way to assure that actual overhead will equal applied overhead is to wait until
the end of the year to apply the year's actual overhead to the jobs worked on
during the year. However, this is not done because interim cost figures are
usually necessary, and a small under- or overapplication of overhead must therefore be tolerated.

At the end of the period, an adjustment must be made for the difference between
actual and applied overhead.

a. If the difference is immaterial or if all items worked on during the period
   have been sold, the entire amount can be added to or subtracted from Cost of
   Goods Sold. When overhead has been underapplied, Cost of Goods Sold and Factory Overhead Applied are debited and Factory Overhead Control is credited;
   the entry is the same when overhead has been overapplied, except that Cost of
   Goods Sold is credited.

b. When the difference is material and when the costs of the items worked on
   during the period are included in Work in Process, Finished Goods, and Cost
   of Goods Sold at the end of the period, the difference should be prorated
   among these three accounts in a logical manner.

New Words and Terms

underapplied (p. 873)
overapplied (p. 873)

<u>Lecture Outline</u>

A. Explain the concept of underapplied overhead.

B. Explain the concept of overapplied overhead.

C. Misapplied overhead is disposed of in two ways:

1. An immaterial amount is closed into Cost of Goods Sold.

2. A material amount is prorated among Work in Process, Finished Goods, and
   Cost of Goods Sold.

OBJECTIVE 5: Explain the relationship between product costing and inventory
              valuation (pp. 876-878)

<u>Summary Statement</u>

Product costing is very important for income statement and balance sheet purposes. Only those manufacturing costs assigned to units sold should be reported
in the income statement (as cost of goods sold). The manufacturing costs assigned to goods in ending inventory should appear on the balance sheet, and
should be transferred to the income statement only in the period in which the
goods are sold.

<u>Lecture Outline</u>

A. Manufacturing costs assigned to units sold appear in the income statement as
   Cost of Goods Sold.

B. Manufacturing costs assigned to unsold units appear in the balance sheet as
   ending inventory.

OBJECTIVE 6: Describe the cost flow in a job order cost accounting system
              (pp. 878-882)

<u>Summary Statement</u>

Under a job order cost system, there is a specific procedure for recording materials, labor, and factory overhead. Basically, a perpetual inventory system is used, with costs flowing through the Work in Process and Finished Goods Inventory accounts to Cost of Goods Sold. The costs are associated with specific jobs by means of <u>job order cost cards</u>. One job card is maintained for each job to accumulate its costs, and the cost cards for all uncompleted jobs comprise the Work in Process <u>subsidiary ledger</u> (detailed records to support the <u>control account</u>).

<u>New Words and Terms</u>

job order cost cards (p. 878)

<u>Related Text Illustrations</u>

*Figure 23-2 Job Order Cost Flow (p. 879)
Figure 23-3 Job Order Cost Card (p. 880)

<u>Lecture Outline</u>

A. Under a job order cost system, a perpetual inventory system is used.

B. Costs flow through Work In Process, Finished Goods, and Cost of Goods Sold (in that order).

C. Job cards for uncompleted jobs comprise the work in process subsidiary ledger.

OBJECTIVE 7: Journalize transactions in a job order cost accounting system (pp. 881-888)

<u>Summary Statement</u>

The journal entries in a job order cost system reflect the actual flow of costs during production. Note from the following analysis that costs are transferred into an account with a debit, and out of an account with a credit.

a. The purchase of materials is recorded by debiting Materials Inventory Control and crediting Cash or Accounts Payable.

b. When materials or supplies are issued into production, Work in Process Inventory Control is debited for the direct materials portion, Factory Overhead Control is debited for the indirect materials portion, and Materials Inventory Control is credited.

c. The factory payroll and actual overhead costs are recorded by debiting Factory Payroll and Factory Overhead Control, respectively, and crediting Cash or some other appropriate account.

d. To distribute the payroll to the production accounts, Work in Process Inventory Control is debited for the direct labor portion, Factory Overhead Control is debited for the indirect labor portion, and Factory Payroll is credited for the gross payroll.

e. Factory overhead is applied to specific jobs by debiting Work in Process Inventory Control and crediting Factory Overhead Applied.

f. Upon the completion of a specific job, Finished Goods Inventory Control is debited, and Work in Process Inventory Control is credited.

g. When the finished goods are sold, two entries must be made. First, the sale is recorded by debiting Cash or Accounts Receivable and crediting Sales for the total sales price. Second, Cost of Goods Sold is debited and Finished Goods Inventory Control is credited for the cost attached to the goods sold.

h. At the end of the period, an adjustment must be made for under- or overapplied overhead.

New Words and Terms

control or controlling account (p. 881)

Related Text Illustrations

*Figure 23-4 The Job Order Cost System (p. 882)

Lecture Outline

A. The flow of costs are journalized in a job order cost system:

1. Journalize the purchase of materials.

2. Journalize the issuance of materials into production.

3. Journalize the factory payroll.

4. Journalize actual overhead costs.

5. Journalize the distribution of the factory payroll to production.

6. Journalize the application of factory overhead.

7. Journalize the completion of a job.

8. Journalize the sale of goods (two entries).

9. Journalize the adjustment for misapplied overhead.

OBJECTIVE 8: Compute product unit cost for a specific job order (pp. 888-889)

Summary Statement

The first step in computing unit costs in a job order cost system is to total
all manufacturing costs accumulated on a particular job order cost card. Then,
this amount is divided by the number of units produced for that job to obtain
the unit cost. Finally, the unit cost is entered on the job order cost card and
used for inventory valuation purposes.

New Words and Terms

unit cost (p. 886)

Lecture Outline

A. Unit cost equals total manufacturing costs divided by units produced.

OBJECTIVE 9: Prepare the year-end work sheets, closing journal entries, and
              financial statements for a manufacturing company, using a per-
              petual inventory approach. (See Work Sheet Analysis in the
              Working Papers)

Summary Statement

When a perpetual inventory system is used, the work sheet of a manufacturer
will differ from the work sheet prepared when a periodic inventory system is
used. First of all, Cost of Goods Manufactured columns are not provided.
Second, adjustments are not made to eliminate beginning inventories and to establish ending inventories because the inventory accounts are always current
under a perpetual system. Third, a balancing figure labeled Cost of Goods Manufactured to Income Statement is not used.

A manufacturer's closing entries are much simpler under a perpetual inventory system than under a periodic system. The only accounts that need closing are Sales, Cost of Goods Sold, operating expenses, and miscellaneous nonoperating items.

<u>Lecture Outline</u>

A. Direct the students to the Work Sheet Analysis in the Working Papers.

B. Explain the work sheet of a manufacturer, line by line, assuming a perpetual inventory system (compare with periodic inventory system).

1. Cost of goods manufactured columns are <u>not</u> provided.

2. Adjustments are <u>not</u> made for beginning and ending materials and work in process.

3. A balancing figure labeled "Cost of goods manufactured to income statement" is <u>not</u> used.

C. Discuss the closing entries under a perpetual inventory system.

1. Closing entries are <u>not</u> made for inventory.

Chapter Twenty-Three   Product Costing: The Job Order System

Learning Objectives	Questions	Exercises	A & B Problems	Case
1. Describe the difference between job order costing and process costing.	9	6		
2. Describe the concept of absorption costing.	2	2		
3. Compute a predetermined overhead rate, and use this rate to apply overhead costs to production.	4, 5	1, 3, 10 IAI	1	
4. Dispose of underapplied or overapplied overhead.	6, 7	4, 5	1	
5. Explain the relationship between product costing and inventory valuation.	8			1
6. Describe the cost flow in a job order cost accounting system.	3, 10, 12, 13, 14	7	2, 3	1
7. Journalize transactions in a job order cost accounting system.		8, 9	4, 5	
8. Compute product unit cost for a specific job order.				1
9. Prepare the year-end work sheets, closing journal entries, and financial statements for a manufacturing company, using a perpetual inventory approach. (See Work Sheet Analysis in the Working Papers.)				

DIFFICULTY AND TIME CHART

A & B Problems	Difficulty	Time (in minutes)
1	medium	35
2	easy	25
3	difficult	35
4	medium	55
5	medium	50
Case 23-1	difficult	60

TEN-MINUTE QUIZ

T F   1. When a job order cost system is used, a Work in Process Inventory account is used for each department in the manufacturing process.

T F   2. The proper procedure for recording the cost of goods shipped is to debit Cost of Goods Sold and credit Work in Process Inventory.

T F   3. Predetermined overhead rates are computed at the end of the period when actual overhead is known.

T F   4. Absorption costing is generally used in job order costing.

T F   5. When actual overhead equals estimated overhead, then overhead will not have been underapplied or overapplied during the period.

T F   6. All inventory balances in a job order cost system are maintained on a perpetual basis.

T F   7. Unit cost information can be found on job order cost cards.

T F   8. The journal entry to record the incurrence and payment of factory rent is a debit to Factory Overhead Control and a credit to Cash.

T F   9. All manufacturing costs incurred during the period must be accounted for in the year-end financial statements. However, not all of these costs will appear in the income statement.

T F 10. The journal entry to record the factory payroll liability for the period will include a credit to Factory Payroll.

_____ 11. Which of the following is an example of a predetermined overhead rate?
    a. Actual units produced divided by estimated overhead
    b. Estimated direct labor dollars divided by estimated overhead
    c. Estimated overhead divided by actual direct labor hours
    d. Estimated overhead divided by estimated units produced
    e. Actual machine hours divided by actual overhead

_____ 12. Job order cost cards make up the subsidiary ledger of the
    a. Work in Process Inventory Control account.
    b. Finished Goods Inventory Control account.
    c. Factory Overhead Control account.
    d. Materials Inventory Control account.
    e. Cost of Goods Sold Control account.

_____ 13. For a calendar year, a manufacturer estimates that overhead will total $64,000 and that direct labor hours will total 16,000. Actual overhead for the year totaled $100,000; actual direct labor hours totaled 20,000. If 1,500 direct labor hours were worked in January of that year, and $8,000 direct labor dollars were paid, how much overhead was applied to production in January?
a. $6,000　b. $7,500　c. $8,000　d. $32,000　e. $40,000

_____ 14. When goods are completed by a manufacturer, the journal entry is
a. a debit to Cost of Goods Sold and a credit to Work in Process.
b. a debit to Finished Goods and a credit to Cost of Goods Sold.
c. a debit to Work in Process and a credit to Cost of Goods Sold.
d. a debit to Finished Goods and a credit to Work in Process.
e. a debit to Work in Process and a credit to Finished Goods.

_____ 15. Which cost, if any, is not included when using absorption costing in costing a product?
a. Direct material
b. Direct labor
c. Variable factory overhead
d. Fixed factory overhead
e. All of the above are included.

_____ 16. Overhead is said to be overapplied when
a. estimated overhead exceeds actual overhead.
b. actual overhead exceeds applied overhead.
c. applied overhead exceeds estimated overhead.
d. applied overhead exceeds actual overhead.
e. estimated overhead exceeds applied overhead.

_____ 17. Two journal entries are generally made when
a. goods are transferred out of work in process and into finished goods.
b. finished goods are sold.
c. overhead is applied to production.
d. materials are requisitioned for production.
e. an adjustment is made for misapplied overhead.

_____ 18. When factory overhead is applied to production, the proper journal entry is
a. a debit to Work in Process Inventory Control and a credit to Factory Overhead Applied.
b. a debit to Factory Overhead Applied and a credit to Factory Overhead Control.
c. a debit to Factory Overhead Control and a credit to Factory Overhead Applied.
d. a debit to Factory Overhead Applied and a credit to Work in Process Inventory Control.
e. a debit to Work in Process Inventory Control and a credit to Factory Overhead Control.

_____ 19. Manufacturing costs assigned to inventory should appear in the income
statement in the period in which
a. the goods are completed.
b. the sale of the goods is recorded.
c. cash is collected for the goods sold.
d. the purchase order is received to manufacture the goods.
e. the manufacturing process is begun.

_____ 20. In accounting for an immaterial amount of under- or overapplied overhead, which of the following could <u>not</u> be part of the adjusting
journal entry?
a. Credit to Factory Overhead Control
b. Debit to Cost of Goods Sold
c. Debit to Factory Overhead Applied
d. Credit to Cost of Goods Sold
e. Debit to Factory Overhead Control

ANSWERS TO TEN-MINUTE QUIZ

<table>
<tr><td colspan="2"><u>True-False</u></td><td colspan="2"><u>Multiple-Choice</u></td></tr>
<tr><td>1.</td><td>F</td><td>11.</td><td>d</td></tr>
<tr><td>2.</td><td>F</td><td>12.</td><td>a</td></tr>
<tr><td>3.</td><td>F</td><td>13.</td><td>a</td></tr>
<tr><td>4.</td><td>T</td><td>14.</td><td>d</td></tr>
<tr><td>5.</td><td>F</td><td>15.</td><td>e</td></tr>
<tr><td>6.</td><td>T</td><td>16.</td><td>d</td></tr>
<tr><td>7.</td><td>T</td><td>17.</td><td>b</td></tr>
<tr><td>8.</td><td>T</td><td>18.</td><td>a</td></tr>
<tr><td>9.</td><td>T</td><td>19.</td><td>b</td></tr>
<tr><td>10.</td><td>F</td><td>20.</td><td>e</td></tr>
</table>

CHAPTER TWENTY-FOUR

PRODUCT COSTING: THE PROCESS COST ACCOUNTING SYSTEM

CHAPTER OUTLINE

Cost Flow Through Work in Process Inventory Accounts
    Work in Process Inventory Accounts
    Production Flow Combinations
The Concept of Equivalent Production
    No Beginning Work in Process Inventory
    With Beginning Work in Process Inventory
    The "Average" Cost Flow Assumption
Cost Analysis Schedules
    Unit Cost Analysis Schedule
    Cost Summary Schedule
    Illustrative Analysis
        January
        February
Journal Entry Analysis
Illustrative Problem: Two Production Departments
Cost-based Pricing of Products
Chapter Review
    Review of Learning Objectives
    Special Problem: Costs Transferred In
    Answer to Special Problem
Chapter Assignments
    Questions
    Classroom Exercises
    Interpreting Accounting Information: Tennessee Tire
    Problem Set A
    Problem Set B
    Management Decision Case 24-1: Opry Cola, Inc.

LEARNING OBJECTIVES:

RESOURCE MATERIALS AND LECTURE OUTLINES

OBJECTIVE 1:   Explain the role of the Work in Process Inventory account(s) in a
process cost accounting system (pp. 907-908)

Summary Statement

A process cost system is used primarily by companies that produce large quantities of identical products and have a continuous product flow. The objectives
of such a system are to determine (a) product unit costs and (b) ending balances
for Work in Process and Finished Goods Inventories. Whereas job order costing
is concerned with the cost of a particular batch or job, process costing deals
with production cost over a specific period of time.

Related Text Illustrations

*Figure 24-1 Cost Elements and Process Cost Accounts (p. 908)

Lecture Outline

A. A process cost system uses one work in process account for each department.

B. A unit cost is computed for a given period of time.

C. The work in process account accumulates materials, labor, and overhead for
that period of time.

D. The finished goods of Department 1 becomes the direct materials input of
Department 2.

   1. The unit cost of Department 1 transfers to Department 2.

E. The process costing analysis revolves around:

1. The schedule of equivalent production

2. The unit cost analysis schedule

3. The cost summary schedule

OBJECTIVE 2: Describe product flow and cost flow through a process cost accounting system (pp. 908-909)

Summary Statement

Before a product is in finished form, it usually must go through several departments. For example, a bookcase might go through cutting, assembling, and staining departments. In a process cost system, a separate Work in Process Inventory account is maintained for each department. Each Work in Process Inventory account contains costs of materials, (if any), direct labor, and manufacturing overhead for that department plus any costs that have been transferred in from the previous department.

Related Text Illustrations

Figure 24-2 Cost Flow for Process Costing (p. 909)

Lecture Outline

A. There are hundreds of possible combinations of production process configurations.

B. With a series configuration, one department at a time works on the goods.

C. Discuss other possible production configurations.

OBJECTIVE 3: Compute equivalent production for situations with and without units in the beginning work in process inventory (pp. 909-915)

Summary Statement

Equivalent units (also called equivalent production) produced equals the sum of (a) the number of units started and completed during the period, (b) the number

of units in ending Work in Process Inventory times their percentage of completion as of the end of the period, and (c) the number of units in beginning Work
in Process Inventory times (100 percent minus their percentage of completion as
of the beginning of the period). Equivalent unit figures for both materials
and conversion costs must be computed in the schedule of equivalent production.
Because production flows in a first-in, first-out manner in operations utilizing
a process cost system, a FIFO product and cost flow is frequently assumed for
product costing.

New Words and Terms

equivalent production (p. 910)
equivalent units (p. 910)
conversion costs (p. 910)
schedule of equivalent production (p. 911)

Related Text Illustrations

*Figure 24-3 Equivalent Unit Computation (p. 911)
Figure 24-4 Equivalent Units--No Beginning Inventory (p. 912)
Figure 24-5 Equivalent Units--With Beginning Inventory (FIFO) (p. 914)
Figure 24-6 Equivalent Units--With Beginning Inventory (Average Costing
             Approach) (p. 915)

Lecture Outline

A. Discuss the concept of equivalent units.

B. Equivalent units are the sum of:

   1. Units started and completed during the period

   2. Units in ending work in process times their percentage of completion

   3. Units in beginning work in process times one minus their percentage of
      completion.

C. The schedule of equivalent production includes unit figures for:

1. Materials

2. Conversion costs

D. FIFO cost flow is frequently assumed under process costing.

E. The average cost technique is easier to apply than FIFO.

F. Refer to fig. 24-5 and 24-6 of the text to illustrate detailed computation.

OBJECTIVE 4:   Compute product unit cost for a specific time period (unit cost
               analysis schedule) (pp. 915-916)

<u>Summary Statement</u>

The product unit cost for a department consists of the unit cost for materials,
direct labor, and factory overhead.

a. The unit cost for materials is computed by dividing total material costs by
   the equivalent units for materials.

b. The unit cost for direct labor and overhead equals direct labor and overhead
   costs (also called conversion costs) divided by equivalent units for direct
   labor and factory overhead.

The process costing analysis revolves around (a) the schedule of equivalent production, (b) the unit cost analysis schedule, and (c) the cost summary schedule.

The purposes of a <u>unit cost analysis schedule</u> are to (a) accumulate all costs
charged to the Work in Process Inventory account of each department, and (b)
compute the cost per equivalent unit for both materials and conversion costs.
The schedule is divided into a "total cost analysis" part and a "computation of
equivalent unit costs" part.

a. The total cost analysis consists of beginning inventory costs plus current
   period costs for both materials and conversion costs. The result is total
   costs to be accounted for.

b. The computation of equivalent unit costs equals the two *current period* costs
   divided by equivalent units for materials and conversion costs as computed
   in the schedule of equivalent production.

<u>New Words and Terms</u>

unit cost analysis schedule (p. 915)

Lecture Outline
===============

A. Compute the unit cost for materials, direct labor, and overhead.

   1. Divide cost of materials by equivalent units for materials.

   2. Divide conversion costs by equivalent units for direct labor and overhead.

B. The unit cost analysis schedule serves two purposes:

   1. It accumulates costs charged to work in process for each department.

   2. It computes the cost per equivalent unit (materials and conversion costs).

C. Refer to Fig. 24-7 and 24-9 of text to illustrate detailed computation.

OBJECTIVE 5:   Prepare a cost summary schedule that assigns costs to units com-
               pleted and transferred out of the department during the period,
               and find the ending Work in Process Inventory balance
               (pp. 916-920)

Summary Statement
=================

The cost summary schedule distributes total costs accumulated during the period
to units in ending Work in Process Inventory and to units completed and transferred out of the department. Data for the cost summary schedule are taken from
the schedule of equivalent production and the unit cost analysis schedule. When
figures for ending Work in Process Inventory and cost of goods transferred out
of the department have been computed, they are totaled and compared with "total
costs to be accounted for" in the unit cost analysis schedule. If the figures
do not agree, then a computational error has occurred.

a. Ending Work in Process Inventory is computed by (1) multiplying equivalent
   units for materials in ending Work in Process Inventory by the unit cost as
   computed in the unit cost analysis schedule, (2) multiplying equivalent units
   for conversion costs in ending Work in Process Inventory by the unit cost as
   computed in the unit cost analysis schedule, and (3) adding the two amounts
   together.

b. The cost of goods transferred out of the department is computed by (1) multiplying units started and completed by the total unit cost as computed in the
   unit cost analysis schedule, (2) determining the costs attached to units in
   beginning inventory (same as ending inventory of preceding period), (3) determining the costs necessary to complete the units in beginning inventory by

using unit cost and equivalent unit figures, and (4) adding the amounts together.

New Words and Terms

cost summary schedule (p. 916)

Related Text Illustrations

Figure 24-7   Unit Cost Determination--No Beginning Inventories (p. 917)
Figure 24-8   Ending Inventory Computation--No Beginning Inventories (p. 918)
Figure 24-9   Unit Cost Determination--With Beginning Inventories (p. 919)
Figure 24-10 Ending Inventory Computation--With Beginning Inventories (p. 919)

Lecture Outline

A. The cost summary schedule assigns costs to:

   1. Units completed and transferred out of the department.

   2. Units in ending work in process.

B. Information is needed from the following:

   1. Schedule of equivalent production

   2. Unit cost analysis schedule

C. A computational check should be performed.

   1. "Total costs to be accounted for" should agree with the amount calculated
      in the cost summary schedule.

D. Refer to fig. 24-8 and 24-10 of text to illustrate detailed computation.

OBJECTIVE 6: Make the journal entry(ies) needed to transfer costs of completed
              units out of the Work in Process Inventory account (pp. 920-923)

Summary Statement

Once the figure for cost of goods transferred out of the department has been computed, it can be journalized to record the transfer of goods to a subsequent department; then Work in Process Inventory (next department) is debited and Work in Process Inventory (this department) is credited. When goods are completed, the debit is instead to Finished Goods Inventory.

Lecture Outline

A. Costs flow through the ledger by means of journal entries.

1. Work in Process Inventory (old department) is credited when goods are transferred out.

2. Work in Process Inventory (new department) is debited when goods are transferred in.

3. Finished Goods Inventory is debited when goods are completed.

Chapter Twenty-Four   Product Costing: The Process Cost Accounting System

Learning Objectives	Questions	Exercises	A & B Problems	Case
1. Explain the role of the Work in Process Inventory account(s) in a process cost accounting system.	2			
2. Describe product flow and cost flow through a process cost accounting system.	14	1		
3. Compute equivalent production for situations with and without units in the beginning work in process inventory.	3, 4, 5, 6, 7, 8, 9	2, 3, 6	1, 2, 3, 4	1
4. Compute product unit cost for a specific time period (unit cost analysis schedule).	6, 10	4, IAI	1, 2, 3, 4	1
5. Prepare a cost summary schedule that assigns costs to units completed and transferred out of the department during the period, and find the ending Work in Process Inventory balance.	6, 11, 12	5	1, 2, 3, 4	
6. Make the journal entry(ies) needed to transfer costs of completed units out of the Work in Process Inventory account.	13	6	1, 2, 3, 4	

DIFFICULTY AND TIME CHART

A & B Problems	Difficulty	Time (in minutes)
1	medium	30
2	medium	30
3	difficult	60
4	difficult	70
Case 24-1	difficult	60

TEN-MINUTE QUIZ

T F 1. If 6,000 units of beginning work in process inventory are 80 percent complete as to conversion costs, 4,800 equivalent units of conversion costs must be incurred to complete these units during the current period.

T F 2. The unit cost analysis schedule is a process costing statement used to (a) accumulate all costs charged to the Work in Process Inventory account of each department or production process, and to (b) compute the cost per equivalent unit for the period.

T F 3. In a process cost system, the amount of total costs to be accounted for is made up of costs of materials and conversion costs incurred during the current period plus those costs included in the beginning balance of Work in Process Inventory.

T F 4. A product costing system used by companies that produce a large number of similar products or have a continuous production flow is a process cost system.

T F 5. Under a process costing system, a Work in Process Inventory account may include costs that have been transferred in from the previous department.

T F 6. A process cost system places emphasis on weekly or monthly cost information, rather than on cost information for a particular order.

T F 7. The computational check for total costs to be accounted for is made in the schedule of equivalent production.

T F 8. In a process cost system, based on a FIFO cost and product flow assumption, costs attached to units in beginning inventory are included in the process of computing costs per equivalent unit.

T F 9. The process costing analysis revolves around the following three schedules: unit cost analysis schedule, schedule of work in process inventory, and schedule of good units produced.

T F 10. One reason for preparing a process cost analysis of a particular department is to determine the amount of costs to transfer to the next department or to Finished Goods Inventory at period end.

For questions 11 through 15, assume the following information for a corporation that uses a process costing system:

> **Beginning Work in Process Inventory**
> 10,000 units – 100% complete as to materials
> 70% complete as to conversion costs

> **Units Started During the Month:**
> 30,000 units

> **Ending Work in Process Inventory:**
> 16,000 units – 100% complete as to materials
> 40% complete as to conversion costs

In addition, no units were lost or spoiled during the month, and a FIFO cost and product flow is assumed.

_____ 11. Units started and completed during the month totaled
a. 14,000.   b. 17,000.   c. 24,000.   d. 26,600.   e. 30,000.

_____ 12. Units completed and transferred out of the department during the month totaled
a. 14,000.   b. 17,000.   c. 24,000.   d. 26,600.   e. 30,000.

_____ 13. Units to be accounted for during the month totaled
a. 24,000.   b. 26,000.   c. 30,000.   d. 40,000.   e. 46,000.

_____ 14. Equivalent units for raw materials during the month totaled
a. 24,000.   b. 26,000.   c. 30,000.   d. 46,000.   e. 56,000.

_____ 15. Equivalent units for conversion costs during the month totaled
a. 23,400.   b. 26,600.   c. 27,400.   d. 39,400.   e. 46,600.

_____ 16. Which of the following companies would be most likely to use a process cost system?
a. Ship builder
b. Special-order cake buyer
c. Brewery
d. Printer
e. Custom-made drapery shop

_____ 17. Which of the following would be a columnar heading in the unit cost analysis schedule?
a. Cost of ending work in process inventory
b. Total costs to be accounted for
c. Units to be accounted for
d. Cost of goods transferred to next department
e. Units started and completed

_____ 18. The purpose of the cost summary schedule is to
   a. compute equivalent units of production.
   b. distribute accumulated costs to ending work in process and to completed units.
   c. compute the cost per equivalent unit for materials and conversion costs.
   d. accumulate costs charged to the work in process account of each department.
   e. reconcile any differences between the unit cost analysis schedule and the schedule of equivalent production.

_____ 19. In which order should the following process costing schedules be prepared?
   a. Cost summary schedule, unit cost analysis schedule, schedule of equivalent production
   b. Schedule of equivalent production, cost summary schedule, unit cost analysis schedule
   c. Unit cost analysis schedule, schedule of equivalent production, cost summary schedule
   d. Schedule of equivalent production, unit cost analysis schedule, cost summary schedule
   e. Unit cost analysis schedule, cost summary schedule, schedule of equivalent production

_____ 20. Conversion costs are defined as
   a. direct material and direct labor only.
   b. factory overhead only.
   c. direct labor and factory overhead only.
   d. direct labor, direct materials, and factory overhead.
   e. direct materials and factory overhead only.

ANSWERS TO TEN-MINUTE QUIZ

<u>True-False</u>		<u>Multiple-Choice</u>	
1.	F	11.	a
2.	T	12.	c
3.	T	13.	d
4.	T	14.	c
5.	T	15.	a
6.	T	16.	c
7.	F	17.	b
8.	F	18.	b
9.	F	19.	d
10.	T	20.	c

CHAPTER TWENTY-FIVE

BASIC COST PLANNING AND CONTROL TOOLS

CHAPTER OUTLINE

Cost Behavior
    Variable and Fixed Costs
    Semivariable and Mixed Costs
    Operating Capacity: Definition and Cost Influence
Cost-Volume-Profit Relationships
    C-V-P Analysis: Break-even Point and Profit Planning
        Break-even Point
        Profit Planning
    Contribution Margin Concept
    Assumptions Underlying C-V-P Analysis
    Illustrative Problem: Profit Planning--Contribution Margin Approach
Cost Allocation
    Allocation of Manufacturing Costs
    The Role of Cost Assignment in Corporate Reporting
    Assigning Costs of Supporting Service Functions
    Illustrative Problem: Assigning Service Department Costs
Accounting for Joint Production Costs
    Physical Volume Method
    Relative Sales Value Method
Responsibility Accounting
    Organizational Structure and Reporting
    Cost and Revenue Controllability
Chapter Review
    Review of Learning Objectives
    Review Problem: Break-even/Profit Planning Analysis
    Answer to Review Problem
Chapter Assignments
    Questions
    Classroom Exercises
    Interpreting Accounting Information: Godeke Food Products
    Problem Set A
    Problem Set B
    Management Decision Case 25-1: American State Bank

LEARNING OBJECTIVES:

RESOURCE MATERIALS AND LECTURE OUTLINES

OBJECTIVE 1: Define and classify variable costs, semivariable costs, and fixed costs (pp. 940-944)

Summary Statement

Cost behavior refers to the movement of costs in relation to volume (units of output), and is useful in predicting future costs and in analyzing past cost performance. Normally, a cost can be classified as either variable or fixed.

a. Variable costs are costs that vary in direct proportion to volume. On a per-unit basis, variable costs remain constant as volume changes.

b. Fixed costs are costs that remain constant within the relevant range (the volume range within which actual operations are likely to occur) of activity. On a per-unit basis, fixed costs decrease as volume increases.

A semivariable cost possesses both variable and fixed cost elements. Telephone expense, for example, consists of a fixed monthly service charge plus charges for long-distance calls.

Mixed costs are a combination of fixed and variable costs charged to the same general ledger account.

Theoretical (ideal) capacity is the maximum productive output possible over a given period of time. Practical capacity is theoretical capacity reduced by normal and anticipated work stoppages. Normal capacity is the operating capacity that is required to satisfy anticipated sales demand. It realistically measures what *will* be produced rather than what *can* be produced. Excess capacity refers to extra machinery and equipment available when regular facilities are being repaired or when volume exceeds anticipated needs.

New Words and Terms

cost behavior (p. 940)
variable costs (p. 941)
fixed costs (p. 941)
relevant range (p. 941)
semivariable cost (p. 942)
mixed costs (p. 942)

theoretical or ideal capacity (p. 943)
practical capacity (p. 943)
excess capacity (p. 943)
normal capacity (p. 944)

Related Text Illustrations
 *Figure 25-1 A Common Cost Behavior Pattern: Variable Cost (p. 941)
**Figure 25-2 A Common Cost Behavior Pattern: Fixed Cost (p. 943)

Lecture Outline

A. Cost behavior is the movement of costs in relation to volume.

B. Discuss the importance of cost behavior analysis.

C. Distinguish between fixed costs and variable costs.

D. Define relevant range and relate to fixed costs.

E. Define semivariable and mixed costs.

F. Define theoretical (ideal) capacity.

G. Define practical capacity.

H. Define normal capacity.

I. Define excess capacity.

OBJECTIVE 2: Compute the break-even point in units of output and in sales
              dollars (pp. 944-946)

Summary Statement

Cost-volume-profit (C-V-P) analysis is used to determine net income at different
activity levels and to measure the performance of a department within a company.
In the formula used, sales revenues equal

    variable costs + fixed costs + net income

a. The <u>break-even point</u> is the point at which sales revenues equal the sum of all variable and fixed costs. The break-even point in *units* is computed as follows:

$$\frac{\text{fixed costs}}{\text{contribution margin per unit}}$$

The break-even point in <u>*dollars*</u> is computed as follows:

$$\text{break-even units x selling price per unit}$$

b. Graphically, the break-even point is at the intersection of the total revenue line and the total cost line. The area below the break-even point represents a loss, whereas the area above represents a profit.

<u>New Words and Terms</u>

cost-volume-profit analysis (C-V-P analysis) (p. 944)
break-even point (p. 944)

<u>Related Text Illustrations</u>
*Figure 25-3 Graphic Break-Even Analysis: Sterling Products, Inc. (p. 946)

<u>Lecture Outline</u>

A. Discuss the importance of cost-volume-profit analysis.

B. The C-V-P formula is Sales = variable costs + fixed costs + net income.

C. The break-even point is the point of zero profit.

   1. Break-even units = fixed costs divided by contribution margin per unit.

   2. Break-even dollars = break-even units times selling price per unit.

D. Illustrate the break-even point graphically.

OBJECTIVE 3: Use contribution margin analysis to estimate levels of sales that will produce planned profits (pp. 946-949)

Summary Statement

The <u>contribution margin</u> equals sales minus total variable cost; the contribution margin per unit equals selling price minus variable cost per unit. The break-even point in units equals fixed cost divided by contribution margin per unit. To determine units that must be sold for a certain net income, fixed cost plus the target net income are divided by the contribution margin per unit.

New Words and Terms

contribution margin (p. 946)

Lecture Outline

A. Illustrate units that must be sold for a certain net income.

   1. Divide fixed costs plus target net income by contribution margin per unit.

OBJECTIVE 4: State the role of cost objectives in the cost allocation process
(pp. 949-953)

Summary Statement

Many manufacturing costs apply to more than one segment of a corporation. A system of <u>cost allocation</u> (<u>cost assignment</u>) must be used to assign the costs to the segments in a logical manner.

a. A <u>cost center</u> is any segment of a business for which costs are accumulated.

b. A <u>cost objective</u> is anything (such as a department or a product) that receives an assigned cost. A direct cost is therefore any cost that can be traced to a specific cost objective; an indirect cost is one that cannot.

A <u>direct cost</u> is any cost that can be conveniently and economically traced to a specific product or cost objective, whereas an <u>indirect cost</u> is one that cannot.

New Words and Terms

cost allocation (p. 950)
cost center (p. 950)
cost objective (p. 950)

<u>Related Text Illustrations</u>

Figure 25-4   Cabinet Making: Assigning Manufacturing Costs to the Product
              (p. 951)
Table 25-1   Cost Classification and Traceability (p. 953)

<u>Lecture Outline</u>

A. Manufacturing costs must be allocated to the segments of a corporation.

   1. A cost center is a segment for which costs are accumulated.

   2. A cost objective is anything that receives an assigned cost.

B. Distinguish between direct and indirect costs, and discuss their relation
   to cost objectives.

OBJECTIVE 5:   Assign costs of supporting service functions to production
               departments   (pp. 953-956)

<u>Summary Statement</u>

Examples of <u>supporting service departments</u> are a repair and maintenance department, a production scheduling department, and an inspection department. These
departments assist the production departments, and their costs must be allocated
to the production departments in a logical manner.

<u>New Words and Terms</u>

supporting service function (p. 953)

<u>Related Text Illustrations</u>

Table 25-2 Cost Allocation Bases for Assigning Costs of Supporting Service
            Functions (p. 954)

<u>Lecture Outline</u>

A. Define and list examples of supporting service departments.

B. Illustrate the allocation of supporting service department costs to production departments.

OBJECTIVE 6: Allocate common manufacturing costs to joint products
              (pp. 956-959)

Summary Statement

A joint product is a combination of products (such as petroleum or beef) that are not identifiable as specific items throughout much of the production process. It is not until the split-off point that separate products emerge. A joint cost is a cost that relates to a joint product. Joint costs are allocated to the specific products by either the physical volume method or the relative sales value method.

New Words and Terms

joint cost (p. 956)
split-off point (p. 956)
physical volume method (p. 957)
relative sales value method (p. 958)

Related Text Illustrations

Figure 25-5 Joint Production Cost Allocation (p. 957)

Lecture Outline

A. Define and list examples of joint products.

B. Separate products do not emerge until the split-off point.

C. Joint costs must be allocated to joint products.

   1. Illustrate the physical volume method of allocation.

   2. Illustrate the relative sales value method of allocation.

OBJECTIVE 7: Describe a responsibility accounting system (pp. 959-962)

Summary Statement

A responsibility accounting system (also called activity accounting or profitability accounting) reports accounting information according to specific areas of managerial responsiblity within a company. The system consists of a report from each area of responsibility, listing only cost and revenue items that are controllable (can be influenced) by the area's management. Emphasis is on reports that communicate operating results throughout the company's organizational hierarchy.

In order to minimize costs and maximize profits, the origin of all controllable cost and revenue items must be determined, and the manager responsible for each item must be identified. This way, at least one manager is held accountable for each item in the company's performance reports, resulting in more efficient operations and in faster location of troublesome areas.

New Words and Terms

activity accounting (p. 959)
profitability accounting (p. 959)
responsibility accounting system (p. 959)
controllable costs (p. 961)

Related Text Illustrations

Figure 25-6 Organization Chart Emphasizing the Manufacturing Area (p. 960)
Figure 25-7 Reporting Within a Responsibility Reporting System (p. 962)

Lecture Outline

A. Define a responsibility accounting system.

B. Discuss the relevance of controllable costs.

   1. Their origin (manager responsible) must be determined.

   2. Operating results are communicated through performance reports.

   3. The result is location of troublesome areas and more efficient operations.

Chapter Twenty-Five   Basic Cost Planning and Control Tools

Learning Objectives	Questions	Exercises	A & B Problems	Case
1. Define and classify variable costs, semivariable costs, and fixed costs.	1, 2, 3, 4, 5, 6	1		
2. Compute the break-even point in units of output and in sales dollars.	7, 8, 13	2, 3	1	
3. Use contribution margin analysis to estimate levels of sales that will produce planned profits.	11, 12	4	3	
4. State the role of cost objectives in the cost allocation process.	14, 15	5, 6	2	
5. Assign costs of supporting service functions to production departments.	16	7	4	1
6. Allocate common manufacturing costs to joint products.	17, 18, 19	8, 9	5	
7. Describe a responsibility accounting system.	9, 10	IAI		1

DIFFICULTY AND TIME CHART

A & B Problems	Difficulty	Time (in minutes)
1	easy	20
2	easy	20
3	medium	30
4	medium	25
5	medium	35
Case 25-1	difficult	50

TEN-MINUTE QUIZ

T F 1. Under a responsibility accounting system, each manager is responsible for all costs of the company.

T F 2. Control of overhead costs is more difficult than control of materials and direct labor because the responsibility for incurring overhead costs is hard to identify.

T F 3. The cost to maintain supporting service departments should not be allocated to the production departments.

T F 4. Contribution margin is the excess of revenues over variable costs.

T F 5. At a particular point in the manufacturing process, called the split-off point, a common or joint product emerges from several separate raw materials.

T F 6. With less than normal capacity, all fixed overhead will be applied to units produced.

T F 7. Costs that are fixed within the relevant range may not be fixed outside the relevant range.

T F 8. A cost center is any segment of a business for which costs are accumulated.

T F 9. Under a responsibility accounting system, accounting information becomes less detailed as it travels upward in a company.

T F 10. On a per-unit basis, fixed costs remain constant with changes in volume.

Use the following information to answer questions 11 through 14:

Reliable Racket Company manufactures tennis rackets. During a given year, fixed costs are expected to be $150,000. Each racket requires $10 of variable cost to produce and will be sold to retail outlets for $15.

_____ 11. What is the break-even point in units?
            a. 10,000   b. 15,000   c. 6,000   d. 30,000   e. 45,000

_____ 12. What is the break-even point in dollars?
a. $300,000 b. $450,000 c. $150,000 d. $90,000 e. $675,000

_____ 13. How many rackets must be sold to earn an annual profit of $20,000?
a. 4,000   b. 14,000   c. 24,000   d. 34,000   e. 44,000

_____ 14. If 25,000 rackets are sold in a given year, and fixed costs are increased to $160,000, the overall profit or loss will be
a. $25,000 profit.
b. $25,000 loss.
c. $35,000 loss.
d. $45,000 loss.
e. $45,000 profit.

_____ 15. Why are the estimated overhead costs of service departments allocated to production departments?
a. So that financial statements may be prepared
b. To control service department costs
c. So that predetermined overhead rates may be computed and applied to production
d. To reduce the number of transactions to be recorded
e. To centralize all cost information into the production departments

The following information relates to questions 16 and 17:

A company spends $20,000 prior to the split-off point, after which it manufactures products A, B, and C. 4,000 units of Product A are produced, which will sell for $1 each; 8,000 units of Product B are produced, which will sell for $5 each; and 12,000 units of Product C are produced, which will sell for 50¢ each.

_____ 16. Under the physical volume method, what is the portion of the $20,000 joint costs that should be allocated to Product C?
a. $6,000   b. $6,667   c. $10,000   d. $2,400   e. $12,000

_____ 17. Under the relative sales value method, what is the portion of the $20,000 joint cost that should be allocated to Product B?
a. $16,000   b. $6,667   c. $8,000   d. $10,000   e. $4,000

_____ 18. When a company reaches the break-even point in sales, fixed costs equal
a. the contribution margin.
b. total costs.
c. variable costs.
d. sales.
e. zero.

_____ 19. The operating capacity that allows for normal work stoppages is
called
a. ideal capacity.
b. excess capacity.
c. normal capacity.
d. theoretical capacity.
e. practical capacity.

_____ 20. Which of the following is not an assumption underlying C-V-P analysis?
a. Productivity is constant within the relevant range.
b. Product sales mix will not change during the period.
c. Cost behavior can be determined accurately.
d. Production and sales volume will be approximately equal during
the planning period.
e. The break-even point will be reached and surpassed during the
period.

ANSWERS TO TEN-MINUTE QUIZ

<u>True-False</u>

1. F
2. T
3. F
4. T
5. F
6. F
7. T
8. T
9. T
10. F

<u>Multiple-Choice</u>

11. d
12. b
13. d
14. c
15. c
16. c
17. a
18. a
19. e
20. e

CHAPTER TWENTY-SIX

BUDGETARY CONTROL: THE PLANNING FUNCTION

CHAPTER OUTLINE

LEARNING OBJECTIVES:

RESOURCE MATERIALS AND LECTURE OUTLINES

OBJECTIVE 1: Identify the five groups of budgeting principles, and explain the principles in each group (pp. 976-980)

Summary Statement

The principles of effective budgeting are grouped as (a) long-range objectives and goal principles, (b) short-range goals and strategies principles, (c) human responsibilities and interaction principles, (d) budget housekeeping principles, and (e) follow-up principles.

a. Before annual operating budgets can be developed, top management must communicate to budget preparers their long-range goals for (among other things) product/service quality, company growth, and profit expectations.

b. The annual operating budget is a transformation of the long-range goals into detailed plans for the coming year. The budget director is the person responsible for developing the annual budget and its timetable.

c. When the budget director has effectively involved all levels of management in the budgeting process, participative budgeting has been achieved. Budget implementation tends to be less effective, however, when top management merely dictates its goals to lower-level management, or displays little support for their input.

d. Budgets should be based on realistic, not inflated, goals. In addition, they should be designed to facilitate changes in revenues and expenses during the period (should be flexible), and their deadlines should always be met.

e. Finally, the budget should be monitored at all times (called budgetary control) to assure that operations are adhering to it. Performance reports should be prepared for each operating segment, identifying and analyzing problem areas for inclusion into the next period's budget.

New Words and Terms

participative budgeting (p. 979)

<u>Related Text Illustrations</u>

Figure 26-1 Principles of Effective Budgeting (p. 977)

<u>Lecture Outline</u>

A. The principles of effective budgeting are grouped as:

   1. Long-range objectives and goal principles

   2. Short-range goals and strategies principles

   3. Human responsibilities and interaction principles

      a. Define participative budgeting

   4. Budget housekeeping principles

   5. Follow-up principles

OBJECTIVE 2: Define the concept of budgetary control (pp. 980-981)

<u>Summary Statement</u>

<u>Budgetary control</u> is the planning of future company activities and the control over operations to help achieve those plans. The planning function should consist of projecting a long-term plan covering five to ten years, and a short-term plan covering one year at a time. Long-term plans are general in nature, and must be translated by management into specific annual goals. Short-term plans, which are expressed in a <u>period budget</u>, consist of a forecast of operations as well as specific planned activities for segments of the company.

<u>New Words and Terms</u>

budgetary control (p. 980)
period budget (p. 981)

<u>Lecture Outline</u>

A. Budgetary control is the planning of, and control over operations.

B. Planning consists of a long-term and a short-term budget.

   1. Long-term budgets are general in nature.

   2. Short-term plans are expressed in a period budget.

OBJECTIVE 3: Identify the components of a master budget, and describe how they
              are related to each other (pp. 981-984)

<u>Summary Statement</u>

The <u>master budget</u> is an integrated set of departmental or functional period
budgets that have been consolidated into forecasted financial statements for the
whole company. Preparation of the master budget consists of preparing (a) detailed operating or period budgets, (b) the forecasted income statement, (c) the
cash budget, and (d) the forecasted balance sheet.

The detailed period budgets mentioned above normally include the (a) sales budget, (b) production budget, (c) selling expense budget, (d) materials purchase
budget, (e) materials usage budget, (f) labor hour requirement budget, (g) labor
dollar budget, (h) factory overhead budget, (i) general and administrative expense budget, and (j) capital expenditure budget. These budgets are interre-
lated, and must be prepared in a certain order (for instance, the sales budget
must always be prepared first).

Budget implementation will be successful if there is (a) proper communication of
budget targets to all key operating personnel, and (b) support and encouragement
from top management.

<u>New Words and Terms</u>

master budget (p. 981)

<u>Related Text Illustrations</u>

*Figure 26-2 Preparation of Master Budget (p. 983)

<u>Lecture Outline</u>

A. A master budget consists of the following:

1. Detailed period budgets

2. Forecasted income statement

3. Cash budget

4. Forecasted balance sheet

B. Detailed period budgets consist of the following:

1. Sales budget

2. Production budget

3. Selling expense budget

4. Materials purchases budget

5. Materials usage budget

6. Labor hour requirement budget

7. Labor dollar budget

8. Factory overhead budget

9. Factory overhead budget

10. Capital expenditure budget

C. A review of figure 26-2 of the text is recommended.

D. Budget implementation should include:

   1. Proper communication of budget targets

   2. Support and encouragement from top management

OBJECTIVE 4: Prepare a period budget (pp. 984-985)

Summary Statement

Responsibility accounting and cost-volume-profit analysis are cost accounting tools that are very helpful in preparing the period budget (one-year budget).

a. When a responsibility accounting system is used, budget preparation begins with the communication of annual sales and production plans of top management to the various managerial levels. This information then enables the segment managers to develop detailed operating budgets for their area of responsibility. Finally, these managers submit the detailed budgets to the budget director, who constructs the operating budget for the entire company.

b. When unit sales have been forecast, cost-volume-profit analysis can be used to determine associated costs and to predict net income for the period.

Lecture Outline

A. A period budget is an annual forecast for a segment of a company.

B. Describe the value of a responsibility accounting system in developing a period budget.

C. Describe the value of cost-volume-profit analysis in developing a period budget.

OBJECTIVE 5: Describe the purpose and make-up of a cash budget (pp. 986-989)

Summary Statement

A cash budget essentially is a summary of all planned cash transactions found in the detailed period budgets and in the forecasted income statement. For example, cash receipts may be derived primarily from reference to the sales budget. The main objectives of a cash budget are to (a) compute the projected ending cash balance, and (b) enable management to anticipate periods of high or low cash availability. A period of low anticipated cash availability, for example, would alert management that additional funds may be necessary for the company to remain liquid. Care must be exercised in including only items of cash inflow and outflow expected to be experienced during the period.

New Words and Terms

cash flow forecast (p. 986)
cash budget (p. 986)

Related Text Illustrations

Figure 26-3 Typical Cash Budget (p. 987)
Figure 26-4 Master Budget and Cash Budget Interrelationships (p. 988)

Lecture Outline

A. The cash budget requires cash information from the detailed period budgets and the forecasted income statement.

   1. Discuss the main source of cash receipts (sales budget).

   2. Discuss some sources of cash disbursements.

B. There are two purposes of a cash budget:

   1. To compute the projected ending cash balance

   2. To help anticipate periods of high or low cash availability

OBJECTIVE 6: Prepare a cash budget (pp. 989-991)

Summary Statement

A cash flow forecast (cash budget) is a period projection of beginning cash, cash receipts, cash disbursements, and ending cash.

<u>Related Text Illustrations</u>

Figure 26-5   Example of a Period Budget   (p. 991)

<u>Lecture Outline</u>

A. A cash budget is a projection of beginning cash, cash receipts, cash disbursements, and ending cash.

OBJECTIVE 7:   Describe the unique aspects of the budgeting process in not-for-profit and public-sector organizations   (pp. 991-995)

<u>Summary Statement</u>

The budgeting principles previously discussed for profit-oriented businesses also apply, for the most part, to not-for-profit and public-sector organizations. However, the budgeting process for such organizations results in anticipated changes in fund balances instead of in profits or losses. Generally, expenditures are restricted to funds available from appropriations, dues, or donations, and significant cost overruns must usually receive legislative or board approval.

<u>Related Text Illustrations</u>

Figure 26-6   Congressional Budget Process Timetable (p. 993)
Figure 26-7   Typical Not-for-Profit Budget (p. 994)

<u>Lecture Outline</u>

A. Not-for-profit and public-sector budgets result in anticipated changes in fund balances.

B. Expenditures are generally restricted to cash available from dues, etc.

C. Refer to Fig. 26-7 of text for illustration.

Chapter Twenty-Six   Budgetary Control: The Planning Function

Learning Objectives	Questions	Exercises	A & B Problems	Case
1. Identify the five groups of budgeting principles, and explain the principles in each group.	10, 11, 12, 13, 14	1, IAI		1
2. Define the concept of budgetary control.	1, 2			
3. Identify the components of a master budget, and describe how they are related to each other.	5, 6, 8, 9, 16	IAI	5	
4. Prepare a period budget.	3, 4, 15	2, 3, 5, 8	1, 2, 3	1
5. Describe the purpose and make-up of a cash budget.	7, 17			
6. Prepare a cash budget.		4, 7	4	
7. Describe the unique aspects of the budgeting process in not-for-profit and public-sector organizations.	18, 19	6		

DIFFICULTY AND TIME CHART

A & B Problems	Difficulty	Time (in minutes)
1	easy	35
2	medium	35
3	medium	40
4	medium	60
5	difficult	60
Case 26-1	difficult	60

TEN-MINUTE QUIZ

T F   1. A period budget is an integrated set of departmental or functional budgets that have been consolidated into forecasted financial statements for the entire company.

T F   2. The period budget process converts unit sales and production forecasts into revenue and cost estimates for each of the many operating segments of the company.

T F   3. The budgetary control process is comprised of the cost planning function and the cost control function.

T F   4. Long-term projections provide both broad goals and specific instructions on how to attain the anticipated results through annual production and sales efforts.

T F   5. Projected financial statements are the initial step in the budgeting process.

T F   6. One of the basic tenets of successful budgetary control is that any person who is held responsible for an operating area must have direct input into the planning or goal-setting process.

T F   7. Budgeting does not exist for not-for-profit organizations because their funds are usually restricted to dues and contributions.

T F   8. Participative budgeting relates most closely to human responsibilities and interaction principles.

T F   9. The most successful budgets are those handled entirely by top management.

T F 10. The labor requirement budget should be prepared before the production budget.

_____ 11. What provides the catalyst for all period budgets?
    a. Unit sales forecast
    b. Ten-year plan
    c. Capital expenditure budget
    d. Production budget (units)
    e. Cash budget

_____ 12. Which of the following budgets or forecasts should be prepared before
the others?
a. Factory overhead budget
b. Cost of goods sold budget
c. Cash budget
d. Production budget
e. Materials purchase budget

_____ 13. An example of a recurring short-term plan is
a. a change in the marketing strategy.
b. a product line change.
c. expansion of plant and facilities.
d. a unit sales forecast.
e. a change in management.

_____ 14. The preparation of performance reports most closely relates to
a. long-range objectives and goal principles.
b. short-range goals and strategies principles.
c. human responsibilities and interaction principles.
d. budget housekeeping principles.
e. follow-up principles.

_____ 15. Which of the following would not be a source of information for the
cash disbursements section of the cash budget?
a. Sales budget
b. Labor dollar budget
c. Capital expenditure budget
d. Forecasted income statement
e. Selling expense budget

_____ 16. Doherty Company forecasts sales of $20,000, $10,000, and $35,000 for
May, June, and July, respectively. If 70% of sales are collected in
the month of the sale, 20% in the month following the sale, and 8%
in the second month following the sale, (2% are uncollectible), what
are budgeted cash receipts for July?
a. $18,800 b. $24,500 c. $28,100 d. $34,300 e. More information
is needed

_____ 17. The budget director
a. is solely responsible for formulating the budget.
b. develops and communicates the budget timetable.
c. supplied budget targets to top management.
d. maintains little communication with lower-level management.

_____ 18. Which of the following is not a useful tool for budget preparation?
a. Cost/volume/profit analysis
b. Responsibility accounting
c. Cost behavior
d. All of the above are useful for budget preparation.

_____ 19. Which of the following is prepared directly after the cash budget?
    a. Capital expenditure budget
    b. Forecasted balance sheet
    c. Factory overhead budget
    d. Production budget
    e. Forecasted income statement

_____ 20. Which of the following is not a budget housekeeping principle?
    a. Use flexible application procedures.
    b. Practice realism in budget preparation.
    c. Require that budget deadlines be met.
    d. Identify all budget development participants.

ANSWERS TO TEN-MINUTE QUIZ

<u>True-False</u>   <u>Multiple-Choice</u>

1.   F   11.   a
2.   T   12.   d
3.   T   13.   d
4.   F   14.   e
5.   T   15.   a
6.   T   16.   c
7.   F   17.   b
8.   T   18.   d
9.   F   19.   b
10.   F   20.   d

CHAPTER TWENTY-SEVEN

COST CONTROL USING STANDARD COSTING

CHAPTER OUTLINE

Standard Cost Accounting
    Nature and Purpose of Standard Costs
    Development of Standard Costs
        Standard Direct Materials Cost
        Standard Direct Labor Cost
        Standard Factory Overhead Cost
    Using Standards for Product Costing
    Illustrative Problem: Use of Standard Costs
    Journal Entry Analysis
Cost Control Through Variance Analysis
    Evaluating Performance
    Flexible Budgets
    Variance Determination
        Direct Materials Variances
        Direct Labor Variances
        Factory Overhead Variances
    Variances in the Accounting Records
        Journal Entries for Direct Materials Transactions
        Journal Entry for Direct Labor Transactions
        Journal Entries for Application of Factory Overhead
        Journal Entry for Transfer of Completed Units to Finished Goods Inventory
        Journal Entry to Transfer Cost of Units Sold to Cost of Goods Sold Account
        Journal Entry to Dispose of End-of-Period Variance Account Balances
    Performance Reports Using Standard Costs
Cost Control--Public-Sector and Not-for-Profit Organizations
    Public-Sector Organizations
    Not-for-Profit Organizations
Chapter Review
    Review of Learning Objectives
    Review Problem: Variance Analysis
    Answer to Review Problem
Chapter Assignments
    Questions
    Classroom Exercises
    Interpreting Accounting Information: The National Association of Accountants
    Problem Set A
    Problem Set B
    Management Decision Case 27-1: Scandinavian Atlantic Corporation

LEARNING OBJECTIVES:

RESOURCE MATERIALS AND LECTURE OUTLINES

OBJECTIVE 1: Describe the nature and purpose of standard costs (pp. 1016-1018)

Summary Statement

Standard costs are predetermined costs that are expressed as a cost per unit of finished product. They are used in preparing operating budgets, in identifying production areas that need better cost control, and in simplifying cost accounting procedures for inventories and product costing. In general, standard cost figures are maintained for all manufacturing accounts and are compared with the actual cost figures at the end of the period. Any large variances, whether favorable or unfavorable, should then be analyzed.

New Words and Terms

standard costs (p. 1017)

Lecture Outline

A. Standard costs are predetermined costs per unit of finished product.

B. Standard costs are useful internally for:

1. Evaluating the performance of employees.

2. Preparing budgets and forecasts

3. Helping to develop selling prices

4. Simplifying inventory and product costing procedures.

OBJECTIVE 2:   Identify the six elements of a standard unit cost, and describe
               the factors to consider in developing each element   (pp. 1015-1017)

Summary Statement

The standard cost per unit of output is the result of the following standard
amounts:

a. <u>Standard direct materials cost</u> = <u>direct materials price standard</u> x <u>direct
   materials quantity standard</u>.

b. <u>Standard direct labor cost</u> = <u>direct labor time standard</u> x <u>direct labor rate
   standard</u>.

c. <u>Standard factory overhead cost</u> = (<u>standard variable overhead rate</u> + <u>standard
   fixed overhead rate</u>) x application basis.

New Words and Terms

standard direct materials cost (p. 1018)
direct materials price standard (p. 1018)
direct materials quantity standard (p. 1018)
standard direct labor cost (p. 1018)
direct labor time standard (p. 1018)
direct labor rate standards (p. 1019)
standard factory overhead cost (p. 1019)
standard variable overhead rate (p. 1019)
standard fixed overhead rate (p. 1019)
normal operating capacity (p. 1019)

Lecture Outline

A. There are six standards used in determining the standard cost per unit:

   1. Direct materials price standard

   2. Direct materials quantity standard

   3. Direct labor time standard

   4. Direct labor rate standard

   5. Standard variable overhead rate

   6. Standard fixed overhead rate

B. Standard direct materials cost is the product of "A1" and "A2" above.

C. Standard direct labor cost is the product of "A3" and "A4" above.

D. Standard factory overhead cost is the sum of "A5" and "A6" above, times the application basis.

OBJECTIVE 3: Compute a standard unit cost (pp. 1020-1022)

Summary Statement

A product's standard unit cost is determined by adding the standard direct materials cost, the standard direct labor cost, and the standard factory overhead cost. Under a standard cost system, the journal entries are similar to those discussed in prior chapters for a manufacturer's inventory system. However, direct materials, direct labor, and factory overhead are entered into Work in Process Inventory at standard (not actual) cost.

Lecture Outline

A. A product's standard unit cost is the sum of the following:

1. Standard direct materials cost

2. Standard direct labor cost

3. Standard factory overhead cost

B. Costs are entered into work in process at standard (not actual) cost.

OBJECTIVE 4: Prepare a flexible budget (pp. 1022-1026)

Summary Statement

A flexible budget is a cost control tool consisting of cost data for various levels of anticipated production. For each level of production, budgeted fixed and variable costs and their totals are presented. Also presented is the budgeted variable cost per unit, which of course is the same for all levels of output. Once prepared, the flexible budget is used to determine the flexible budget formula. This fomula can then be applied to any level of output to compute its budgeted total cost. The budgeted total cost can be compared with actual costs to measure the performance of individuals and departments.

New Words and Terms

flexible budget (p. 1023)

Related Text Illustrations

Figure 27-1   Performance Analysis: Comparison of Actual and Budgeted Data
(p. 1023)
Figure 27-2   Flexible Budget Preparation (p. 1024)
Figure 27-3   Performance Analysis Using Flexible Budget Data (p. 1025)

Lecture Outline

A. A flexible budget contains cost data for various levels of production.

1. Budgeted fixed and variable costs are presented.

2. Budgeted variable cost per unit is presented.

3. The flexible budget formula helps determine total cost at any level of output.

B. Budgeted costs are compared with actual costs to measure performance.

C. Refer to fig. 27-2 of text for illustration.

OBJECTIVE 5: Describe management by exception (p. 1026)

Summary Statement

Variances are differences between actual operating results and budgeted (standard) results. Once variances have been measured, corrective measures can be prescribed for those areas that are operating efficiently.

Management by exception involves locating and analyzing only those areas of unusual performance. It utilizes variance analysis to a great degree.

Variances between standard and actual costs are usually determined for direct materials, direct labor, and factory overhead. When standard costs exceed actual costs, the variance is favorable (F). When the reverse is true, the variance is unfavorable (U).

New Words and Terms

management by exception (p. 1026)

Related Text Illustrations

Figure 27-4 The Management by Exception Technique (p. 1026)

Lecture Outline

A. Variances measure the difference between standard and actual costs.

B. Variances are labeled favorable or unfavorable.

C. Management by exception involves investigating only those areas of unusual performance.

OBJECTIVE 6: Compute and evaluate direct materials, direct labor, and factory overhead variances (pp. 1027-1032)

Summary Statement

The total direct materials cost variance consists of the direct materials price variance plus the direct materials quantity variance.

a. The _direct materials price variance_ equals the difference between actual price and standard price, times actual quantity of material purchased.

b. The _direct materials quantity variance_ equals the difference between quantity of material used and standard quantity, times standard price.

The total direct labor cost variance consists of the direct labor rate variance plus the direct labor efficiency variance.

a. The _direct labor rate variance_ equals the difference between the actual labor rate and the standard labor rate, times actual hours worked.

b. The _direct labor efficiency variance_ equals the difference between actual hours worked and standard hours allowed, times the standard labor rate.

The total factory overhead variance consists of controllable overhead variance plus overhead volume variance.

a. The <u>controllable overhead variance</u> equals actual overhead costs minus budgeted factory overhead for the level of production achieved.

b. The <u>overhead volume variance</u> equals budgeted factory overhead for the level of production achieved minus factory overhead applied using the standard overhead rate.

<u>New Words and Terms</u>

direct materials price variance (p. 1027)
direct materials quantity variance (p. 1027)
direct labor rate variance (p. 1028)
direct labor efficiency variance (p. 1028)
controllable overhead variance (p. 1030)
overhead volume variance (p. 1030)

<u>Related Text Illustrations</u>

*Figure 27-5 Overhead Variance Analysis (p. 1031)

<u>Lecture Outline</u>

A. Six variances are computed for manufacturing operations:

1. Direct materials price variance

2. Direct materials quantity variance

3. Direct labor rate variance

4. Direct labor efficiency variance

5. Controllable overhead variance

6. Overhead volume variance

B. State possible causes for the above variances.

OBJECTIVE 7: Prepare journal entries involving variances from standard costs
              (pp. 1032-1036)

Summary Statement

As was already stated, cost data are journalized at standard cost under a standard cost system. However, when variances exist, they should also be recorded
in the accounts--as a debit when unfavorable and a credit when favorable. A
separate account should be maintained for each of the six variances already
described.

At the end of the accounting period, the variances are closed into Cost of
Goods Sold if their balances are small or if most or all of the goods produced
during the period were sold; otherwise, the net variance balance is prorated
among Work In Process Inventory, Finished Goods Inventory, and Cost of Goods
Sold based upon their relative ending balances.

Performance reports should contain only those cost items controllable by the
manager receiving the report. It would consist of actual costs, budgeted costs,
and variances.

Related Text Illustrations

Figure 27-6 Performance Report Using Variance Analysis (p. 1035)

Lecture Outline

A. Cost data are journalized at standard cost.

B. Variances are recorded as a debit when unfavorable.

C. Variances are recorded as a credit when favorable.

D. A separate account is maintained for each of the six variances.

E. Variances are closed at the end of the period.

   1. A small amount is closed into cost of goods sold.

   2. A large amount is prorated among work in process, finished goods, and
      cost of goods sold.

OBJECTIVE 8:   Describe the basic techniques used by public sector and not-for-profit organizations to control costs of operations (pp. 1033-1035)

<u>Summary Statement</u>

Public sector organizations (such as the federal government or a state university) and not-for-profit organizations (such as a charitable group or professional organization) must maintain effective cost control because their available funds are limited to appropriations, dues, or contributions. In general, the basis for cost control is the budget, approved by the legislature or governing body. Accordingly, any significant increase in cost (over budget) must be formally requested and approved.

<u>Lecture Outline</u>

A. Not-for-profit and public sector organizations must maintain cost control over operations.

   1. Funds are limited to donations, etc.

   2. The basis for cost control is the budget, approved by the governing body.

   3. Usually, increases in cost over budget must be formally requested and approved.

Chapter Twenty-Seven   Cost Control Using Standard Costing

Learning Objectives	Questions	Exercises	A & B Problems	Case
1. Describe the nature and purpose of standard costs.	1, 2			
2. Identify the six elements of a standard unit cost, and describe the factors to consider in developing each element.	3, 4, 5, 6		1, 3	
3. Compute a standard unit cost.		1, 3	3	
4. Prepare a flexible budget.	15, 16	2		
5. Describe management by exception.	8, 9, 10			
6. Compute and evaluate direct materials, direct labor, and factory overhead variances.	9, 11, 12, 13, 14, 17, 18, 19	4, 5, 6, 7	2, 4, 5	1
7. Prepare journal entries involving variances from standard costs.	7, 20, 21	8	3, 5	
8. Describe the basic techniques used by public sector and not-for-profit organizations to control costs of operations.	22, 23	IAI		

DIFFICULTY AND TIME CHART

A & B Problems	Difficulty	Time (in minutes)
1	difficult	25
2	medium	50
3	difficult	30
4	difficult	50
5	difficult	60
Case 27-1	difficult	60

TEN-MINUTE QUIZ

T F 1. When a company employs standard costs, all costs affecting the three inventory accounts and the Cost of Goods Sold account are stated in terms of standard or predetermined costs rather than actual costs incurred.

T F 2. The direct materials quantity standard is a carefully derived estimate or projected amount of what a particular type of material will cost when purchased during the next accounting period.

T F 3. Comparing what did happen with what should have happened is the basis for the control function of a company.

T F 4. Standard factory overhead = (standard variable overhead rate + standard fixed overhead rate) x application basis.

T F 5. Effective use of existing facilities and capacity is measured by the overhead volume variance.

T F 6. Labor efficiency variances are traceable to departmental supervisors.

T F 7. Direct labor time standards express the hourly labor cost per function or job classification that is expected to exist during the next accounting period.

T F 8. The more refined and detailed the variance analysis, the better its effectiveness for cost control purposes.

T F 9. The direct labor rate variance is the difference between actual hours worked and standard hours allowed for good units produced, times the standard labor rate.

T F 10. Before computing the overhead variances, we must calculate the total overhead rate, which is the variable rate and budgeted fixed factory overhead divided by normal capacity.

Use the following information to answer questions 11 through 16:

Aqueduct Manufacturing Company uses a standard cost system to manufacture baseball bats. The following standard costs were used for the month of May:

Materials (2 lbs. at $.75 per pound)	$1.50
Direct Labor (.1 hr. at $10 per hour)	1.00
Factory Overhead (.1 hr. at $5 per hour)	.50
	$3.00

From the company's flexible budget, the following annual factory overhead information was available:

$.30 per direct labor hour plus $19,000 fixed overhead

During May, the company produced and sold 40,000 bats, and actual costs incurred were:

Materials purchased and used:	
(84,000 lbs. at $.70)	$ 58,800
Direct labor:	
(3,900 hrs. at $10.20 per hr.)	39,780
Factory overhead	20,500
	$119,080

____ 11. How many standard direct labor hours were allowed for production in May?

    a. 2,000   b. 3,900   c. 4,000   d. 8,000   e. 40,000

____ 12. What was the direct materials price variance for May?

    a. $2,800 U   b. $3,000 U   c. $4,000 F   d. $4,000 U   e. $4,200 F

____ 13. What was the direct materials quantity variance for May?

    a. $2,800 U   b. $3,000 U   c. $4,000 F   d. $4,000 U   e. $4,200 F

____ 14. What was the direct labor rate variance for May?

    a. $780 F   b. $780 U   c. $800 U   d. $1,000 F   e. $1,000 U

____ 15. What was the direct labor efficiency variance for May?

    a. $780 F   b. $780 U   c. $800 U   d. $1,000 F   e. $1,000 U

____ 16. What was the controllable overhead variance for May?

    a. $270 F   b. $270 U   c. $300 U   d. $330 U   3. $330 U

____ 17. The formula used to compute budgeted total cost at any level of activity is presented in the

    a. performance report
    b. flexible budget.
    c. cash flow forecast.
    d. static budget.
    e. sales budget.

_____ 18. When more factory overhead is budgeted for the level of production
           achieved than overhead applied to production using the standard over-
           head rate, there exists a(n)
           a. favorable controllable overhead variance.
           b. unfavorable controllable overhead variance.
           c. favorable overhead volume variance.
           d. unfavorable overhead volume variance.
           e. favorable total overhead variance.

_____ 19. A favorable direct materials quantity variance would probably occur
           when
           a. the production department has cut its overhead costs.
           b. the purchasing agent has purchased materials at below the stan-
               dard price.
           c. the production department has used a smaller quantity of mate-
               rials than is standard.
           d. the purchasing agent has purchased less material than is needed.
           e. the production workers are paid less than standard wages.

_____ 20. Focusing on only those areas of unusually good or bad performance is
           the definition of
           a. management by exception.
           b. budgeting.
           c. standard costing.
           d. variance management.
           e. C-V-P analysis.

ANSWERS TO TEN-MINUTE QUIZ

<u>True-False</u>

1. T
2. F
3. T
4. T
5. T
6. T
7. F
8. T
9. F
10. T

<u>Multiple-Choice</u>

11. c
12. e
13. b
14. b
15. d
16. c
17. b
18. d
19. c
20. a

CHAPTER TWENTY-EIGHT

CAPITAL BUDGETING AND OTHER MANAGEMENT DECISIONS

CHAPTER OUTLINE

Relevant Information for Management
Management Decision Cycle
Accounting Tools and Reports for Decision Analysis
    Variable Costing
        Product Costing
        Performance Analysis: The Income Statement
        Contribution Reporting and Decisions
    Incremental Analysis
    Special Reports
The Capital Expenditure Decision
    Capital Budgeting: A Cooperative Venture
    Desired Rate of Return on Investment
        Cost of Capital Measures
        Other Cutoff Measures
    Accounting Rate of Return Method
    Cash Flow and the Payback Method
    Present Value Method
Other Operating Decisions of Management
    Make or Buy Decisions
    Special Product Orders
    Sales Mix Analysis
Income Taxes and Business Decisions
    Tax Effects on Capital Expenditure Decisions
    Minimizing Taxes Through Planning
Chapter Review
    Review of Learning Objectives
    Review Problem: Tax Effects on a Capital Expenditure Decision
    Answer to Review Problem
Chapter Assignments
    Questions
    Classroom Exercises
Interpreting Accounting Information: Altamonte Springs Federal Bank
    Problem Set A
    Problem Set B
    Management Decision Case 28-1: Van Trease Hotel Syndicate

LEARNING OBJECTIVES:

RESOURCE MATERIALS AND LECTURE OUTLINES

OBJECTIVE 1: Define and identify relevant decision information (pp. 1054-1055)

Summary Statement

One important function of the management accountant is to provide management
with relevant decision-making information. Relevant decision information refers
to future cost, revenue, or resource usage data that differ among alternative
courses of action.

New Words and Terms

relevant decision information (p. 1054)

Lecture Outline

A. Relevant decision information consists of costs or revenues that differ among
   alternative courses of action.

   1. For example, a difference in the cost of two proposed machines is relevant
      decision information.

   2. For example, a sunk cost is not relevant decision information.

OBJECTIVE 2: Describe the steps in the management decision cycle (p. 1055)

Summary Statement

The management decision cycle consists of (a) discovering the problem or need,
(b) identifying the alternative courses of action, (c) analyzing the effects of

each alternative on operations, (d) selecting the superior alternative, and (e) appraising the success of the decision.

Related Text Illustrations

Figure 28-1 The Management Decision Cycle (p. 1055)

Lecture Outline

A. The management decision cycle consists of five steps:

1. Discovering the problem or need

2. Identifying the alternative courses of action

3. Analyzing the effects of each alternative on operations

4. Selecting the superior alternative

5. Appraising the success of the decision

OBJECTIVE 3: Calculate product costs, using variable costing procedures
              (pp. 1056-1058)

Summary Statement

Variable costing and incremental analysis are the two most common decision tools used by the accountant. Variable costing (also called direct costing) includes only direct materials, direct labor, and variable factory overhead in product costing. Fixed factory overhead is considered a period cost (expense). Variable costing is very useful for internal management decision purposes, but is not acceptable for tax or financial reporting purposes. Under variable costing the income statement discloses the contribution margin, a very useful figure for decision analysis. Absorption costing includes one additional product cost over variable costing--fixed factory overhead. Therefore, unit cost will vary with volume under absorption costing, whereas it will remain the same under variable costing.

New Words and Terms

variable costing (p. 1056)

<u>Related Text Illustrations</u>

Figure 28-2 Variable Costing Versus Absorption Costing (p. 1057)

<u>Lecture Outline</u>

A. Direct costing (variable costing) includes the following costs in product
   costing:

   1. Direct materials

   2. Direct labor

   3. Variable factory overhead

B. Under direct costing, fixed factory overhead is considered a period expense.

C. Direct costing is very useful for managerial decision-making.

D. Direct costing is not acceptable for tax or financial reporting purposes.

E. The contribution margin equals sales minus variable costs.

F. Absorption costing includes fixed factory overhead in product cost.

OBJECTIVE 4: Prepare an income statement, using the contribution reporting form
              (pp. 1058-1059)

<u>Summary Statement</u>

Unlike the conventional "absorption costing" form of income statement, the contribution format focuses on the difference between fixed costs and variable
costs. First, variable cost of goods sold and variable operating expenses are
deducted from sales to arrive at a figure called the contribution margin. Then,
all fixed expenses (operating <u>and</u> manufacturing) are deducted from the contribution margin to arrive at pre-tax income. In general, the contribution format is
more useful for managerial decision-making than the conventional format.

<u>Related Text Illustrations</u>

Figure 28-3 The Income Statement--Contribution Versus Conventional Formats
            (p. 1059)

<u>Lecture Outline</u>

A. The contribution format focuses on the difference between fixed and variable
   costs.

B. Refer to fig. 28-3 of text, and explain the contribution income statement,
   line by line.

C. Contrast the contribution format with the conventional (absorption) format.

OBJECTIVE 5: Develop decision data, using the incremental analysis technique
            (pp. 1058-1060)

<u>Summary Statement</u>

<u>Incremental analysis</u> is a decision-making tool that compares only cost and rev-
enue data that differ among alternatives. According to this method, the alternative that results in the highest increase in net income or cost savings is the
best alternative.

When management needs quantitative information, the accountant can usually present the data in a contribution reporting or incremental analysis format. However, when special qualitative information is desired, the accountant must
prepare a special report that is structured to facilitate specific decision-
making needs.

<u>New Words and Terms</u>

incremental analysis   (p. 1058)

<u>Lecture Outline</u>

A. Incremental analysis compares costs and revenues that differ among alternatives.

B. The best alternative is the one that results in the highest income or cost
   savings.

OBJECTIVE 6:   Describe the purpose of a minimum desired rate of return, and
               explain the methods used to arrive at this rate (pp. 1061-1063)

Summary Statement

Determining when and how much to spend on capital facilities, such as buildings
or equipment, is referred to as the capital expenditure decision. Capital budgeting is the process of (a) identifying a facility need, (b) evaluating alternative courses of action, (c) preparing the reports for management, (d) selecting the best alternative, and (e) rationing available capital expenditure funds
among competing resource needs. Because it is probably the largest and most
complicated decision analysis facing management, it requires the aid of all
functional areas of the business.

Most companies have established a minimum rate of return, below which an expenditure request is automatically refused. The minimum rate of return often used
is the cost of capital, the corporate return on investment, the industry average
return on investment, or the bank interest rate. The cost of capital is the
cost of financing the company's activities. In many cases, a company will use
an average cost of capital measure based on (a) cost of debt, (b) cost of preferred stock, (c) cost of equity capital, and (d) cost of retained earnings.

New Words and Terms

capital expenditure decisions (p. 1061)
capital budgeting (p. 1061)
average cost of capital (p. 1062)
cost of debt (p. 1062)
cost of preferred stock (p. 1062)
cost of equity capital (p. 1062)
cost of retained earnings (p. 1062)

Lecture Outline

A. A minimum desired rate of return refers to capital budgeting.

B. Capital budgeting is the process of:

   1. Identifying a facility need (buildings and equipment)

   2. Evaluating alternative courses of action

   3. Preparing reports for management

   4. Selecting the best alternative

5. Rationing the available capital expenditure funds

C. Capital expenditure proposals must meet the minimum desired rate of return.

D. The average cost of capital is frequently used as the minimum desired rate of return, which is based on the following:

1. Cost of debt

2. Cost of preferred stock

3. Cost of equity capital

4. Cost of retained earnings

OBJECTIVE 7a: Evaluate capital expenditure proposals, using the accounting rate of return method (pp. 1063-1064)

<u>Summary Statement</u>

The evaluation part of capital budgeting may be accomplished by using the accounting rate of return method, the payback method, or the present value method.

The <u>accounting rate of return</u> equals

$$\frac{\text{project's average annual after-tax net income}}{\text{average investment cost}}$$

The average investment cost equals

$$\frac{\text{total investment + salvage value}}{2}$$

If this method is used, management should consider the investment if the computed rate of return is higher than the minimum desired rate.

<u>New Words and Terms</u>

accounting rate of return method (p. 1063)

Lecture Outline

A. State the formula, and illustrate the accounting rate of return method.

B. The answer will be expressed as a percentage.

OBJECTIVE 7b: Evaluate capital expenditure proposals, using the payback method
(pp. 1064-1065)

Summary Statement

The objective of the payback method is to determine the minimum length of time
it would take to recover the initial investment. When a choice must be made between investment alternatives, the one with the shortest payback period is best
under this method. The payback period is determined by dividing cost of capital
investment by annual net cash inflow.

New Words and Terms

payback method   (p. 1065)

Lecture Outline

A. State the formula, and illustrate the payback method.

B. The answer will be expressed as a number of years.

OBJECTIVE 7c: Evaluate capital expenditure proposals, using the present value
method   (pp. 1066-1068)

Summary Statement

The basis for the present value method is that cash flows from different time
periods have differing values measured in current dollars. For example, a dollar that will be received one year from now is worth somewhat less than a dollar
received today. The method is applied by first discounting all cash flows to
the present. (The discount multiplier is based on the minimum desired rate of
return and the discount period.) Then, if the discounted cash flow exceeds the
cost of the asset, the expenditure is justified.

New Words and Terms

discounted cash flow   (p. 1066)
present value method   (p. 1066)

Related Text Illustrations

Figure 28-4   Present Value Analysis: Equal Versus Unequal Cash Flows   (p. 1067)

Lecture Outline

A.   Illustrate the concept of discounted cash flow.

B.   Distinguish between the present value of an amount and of an annuity.

   1.   Discuss Table B-3 in Appendix B.

   2.   Discuss Table B-4 in Appendix B.

C.   Explain the significance of a positive net present value.

D.   Explain the significance of a negative net present value.

E.   Solve a present value method problem.

OBJECTIVE 8a: Prepare decision alternative evaluations for make or buy deci-
             sions (pp. 1068-1069)

Summary Statement

Management is continually faced with the _decision to make or buy_ component parts
for a product assembly. Probably the best method to employ is incremental analysis, whereby only the relevant costs are compared. All other things being
equal, the alternative resulting in the lowest incremental cost is the one that
should be adopted.

New Words and Terms

make or buy decision (p. 1068)

<u>Related Text Illustrations</u>

Figure 28-5 Incremental Analysis: Make or Buy Decision (p. 1069)

<u>Lecture Outline</u>

A. Discuss the decision to make or buy.

B. Incremental analysis is probably the best method to employ.

OBJECTIVE 8b: Prepare decision alternative evaluations for special order deci-
               sions (pp. 1070-1071)

<u>Summary Statement</u>

Management often must decide whether to accept or reject <u>special product orders</u>.
In these situations, both incremental analysis and contribution reporting can be
used. In either case, the objective is to compare data assuming acceptance
with data assuming rejection.

<u>New Words and Terms</u>

special order decisions (pp. 1069-1071)

<u>Related Text Illustrations</u>

Figure 28-6 Contribution Reporting: Special Product Order (p. 1071)

<u>Lecture Outline</u>

A. Discuss the decision to accept or reject special product orders.

   1. Apply incremental analysis

   2. Apply contribution reporting

OBJECTIVE 8c: Prepare decision alternative evaluations for sales mix analyses
            (pp. 1071-1073)

Summary Statement

<u>Sales mix analysis</u> is determining the most profitable combination of product
sales when the company is producing more than one product. Generally, the
strategy is first to compute the contribution margin for each product. Then,
a ratio of contribution margin to capital equipment should be obtained for each,
to see if some products are more profitable than others. If extra demand exists for the more profitable ones, then production should be shifted to those
products.

New Words and Terms

sales mix analysis (p. 1072)

Related Text Illustrations

Figure 28-7 Contribution Reporting: Sales Mix Analysis (p. 1073)

Lecture Outline

A. Explain what sales mix analysis attempts to accomplish.

   1. First, calculate the contribution margin for each product.

   2. Then, calculate contribution margin to capital equipment or to other
       scarce resources (such as hours).

   3. Shift production to the more profitable products if the demand exists.

OBJECTIVE 9: Analyze capital expenditure decision alternatives that incorporate
           the effects of income taxes (pp. 1073-1076)

Summary Statement

All capital expenditure analysis should include the effect of income taxes.
For example, a company's tax liability will increase (tax-related outflow) as
a result of revenues and gains on the sale of assets; the tax liability will
decrease (tax-related inflow) as a result of cash and noncash expenses and
losses on the sale of assets. One must be careful to apply the tax rate to the

gain or loss on the sale of assets, and not to the proceeds. In addition, even though noncash expenses such as depreciation decrease the tax liability, they must be added back to income (or loss) after taxes to arrive at the net cash inflow (or outflow).

There are many ways a business may plan to minimize its tax liability. For example, it may postpone or accelerate certain income and expense transactions near year-end to lower its taxable income. Similarly, it may take advantage of capital gains rates by timing the sale of capital assets very carefully. In addition, a business is allowed tax credits for certain expenditures that promote national goals (as for pollution control and energy conservation).

<u>Lecture Outline</u>

A. Explain the relevance of income taxes in capital expenditure analysis.

1. The tax liability will increase from revenues and gains on the sale of assets.

2. The tax liability will decrease from expenses and losses on the sale of assets.

Chapter Twenty-Eight   Capital Budgeting and Other Management Decisions

Learning Objectives	Questions	Exercises	A & B Problems	Case
1. Define and identify relevant decision information.	1	1		
2. Describe the steps in the management decision cycle.	2			
3. Calculate product costs, using variable costing procedures.	3, 4	3	1	
4. Prepare an income statement, using the contribution reporting form.	5	2	1	
5. Develop decision data, using the incremental analysis technique.	6, 7	1		
6. Describe the purpose of a minimum desired rate of return, and explain methods for arriving at this rate.		8	3	
7. Evaluate capital expenditure proposals, using (a) accounting rate of return method, (b) payback method, and (c) present value method.	8, 9, 10, 11, 12	4, 5, 6, 7, IAI	2, 6	1
8. Prepare decision alternative evaluations for (a) make or buy decisions, (b) special order decisions, and (c) sales mix analyses.	15, 16, 17	9, 10, 11	3, 4, 5	
9. Analyze capital expenditure decision alternatives that incorporate the effects of income taxes.	13, 14		6	

DIFFICULTY AND TIME CHART

A & B Problems	Difficulty	Time (in minutes)
1	medium	45
2	difficult	60
3	medium	30
4	medium	45
5	difficult	55
6	difficult	75
Case 28-1	easy	35

TEN-MINUTE QUIZ

T F   1. Incremental analysis is a good approach to the make or buy type of decision.

T F   2. Direct costing is used commonly in reports prepared for stockholders and other users of financial statements.

T F   3. Inventories resulting from direct costing are lower in value than those computed using the absorption costing technique.

T F   4. When two or more capital expenditure proposals are being evaluated using the accounting rate of return method, the alternative is selected that yields the highest ratio of net income after taxes to average cost of investment.

T F   5. The managerial accountant plays the role of data supplier in the managerial decision process.

T F   6. In determining the cost of capital, the goal is to find the cost of financing the company's activities.

T F   7. When members of top management want to evaluate the various alternatives available for solving a particular problem, they should be supplied with all details of the alternatives, no matter how small.

T F   8. Under all circumstances, the absorption costing approach to product costing will generate a different net income figure than the direct costing approach.

T F   9. Sales mix analysis is used to determine the most profitable combination of product sales when a company produces more than one product.

T F 10. The payback method of evaluating proposed capital expenditures does not take into account the time value of money.

T F 11. When using the direct costing approach to product costing, all manufacturing overhead costs are treated as costs of the period and are not inventoriable.

T F 12. When using the cost of preferred stock as a minimum desired rate of return, the amount must be adjusted to show the tax impact, because dividends are a deductible expense for tax purposes.

_____ 13. Decisions to install new equipment, replace old equipment, and purchase or construct a new building are examples of
a. sales mix analysis.
b. incremental analysis.
c. a direct costing decision.
d. a special order decision.
e. a capital expenditure decision.

_____ 14. Which of the following is not used to compute the average cost of capital?
a. Cost of debt
b. Cost of preferred stock
c. Cost of retained earnings
d. Cost of working capital
e. Cost of equity capital

Use the following information for questions 15 and 16:

Maynard Manufacturing Company incurred the following costs during 19xx: Direct materials of $40,000, direct labor of $50,000, variable factor overhead of $53,100 and fixed factory overhead of $28,000. During the period, 7,155 units were produced and 7,000 units were sold. There were no beginning or ending work-in-process inventories.

_____ 15. What would the actual product unit cost for Maynard be (if necessary, round to nearest cent) if direct costing procedures were being employed?
a. $12.58   b. $20   c. $20.44   d. $23.91   e. $24.44

_____ 16. What would the actual product unit cost for Maynard be (if necessary, round to nearest cent) if absorption costing procedures were being employed?
a. $12.58   b. $20   c. $20.44   d. $23.91   e. $24.44

_____ 17. The payback method of evaluating expenditures measures
a. the economic life of an investment.
b. the cash flow from an investment.
c. how quickly investment dollars may be recovered.
d. the rate of return on the capital investment.
e. the net present value of the capital investment.

_____ 18. Estimated future costs that differ between decision alternatives are called
a. fixed costs.
b. sunk costs.
c. relevant costs.
d. variable overhead costs.
e. historical costs.

_____ 19. A project is accepted under the present value method when
  a. total net cash inflows exceed the purchase price of the asset.
  b. the percentage return is greater than a predetermined minimum percentage.
  c. the present value of net cash inflows exceeds a predetermined minimum amount.
  d. the investment will be recouped within a predetermined minimum number of years.
  e. the purchase price of the asset is less than the present value of net cash inflows.

_____ 20. Products, A, B, C, and D have contribution margins of $2, $3, $4, and $5, respectively, and require 1-1/2, 2, 2-1/2, and 3 machine hours per unit, respectively. Assuming that all units produced could be sold, and that total machine hours per month are limited, on which product should the company concentrate its efforts?
  a. A
  b. B
  c. C
  d. D
  e. The sales price per unit product is needed to answer the question.

ANSWERS TO TEN-MINUTE QUIZ

True-False			Multiple-Choice	
1.	T		13.	e
2.	F		14.	d
3.	T		15.	b
4.	T		16.	d
5.	T		17.	c
6.	T		18.	c
7.	F		19.	e
8.	F		20.	d
9.	T			
10.	T			
11.	F			
12.	F			